THE RACIAL LOGIC
OF POLITICS:

Asian Americans and Party Competition

IN THE SERIES

ASIAN AMERICAN HISTORY AND CULTURE

edited by

Sucheng Chan, David Palumbo-Liu, Michael Omi,
K. Scott Wong, and Linda Trinh Võ

(A list of additional titles in this series appears at the back of this book)

THOMAS P. KIM

THE RACIAL LOGIC
OF POLITICS

Asian Americans and Party Competition

TEMPLE UNIVERSITY PRESS
Philadelphia

Temple University, Philadelphia 19122
Copyright © 2007 by Temple University Press
All rights reserved
Published 2007
Printed in the United States of America

Library of Congress Cataloging-in-Publication Data

Kim, Thomas P., 1969-
The racial logic of politics : Asian Americans and party competition / Thomas P. Kim.
p. cm. — (Asian American history and culture)
Includes bibliographical references and index.

ISBN 13: 978-1-59213-548-6 (cloth: alk. paper)   ISBN 10: 1-59213-548-X (cloth: alk. paper)
ISBN 13: 978-1-59213-549-3 (pbk. : alk. paper)   ISBN 10: 1-59213-549-8 (pbk. : alk. paper)

1. Asian Americans—Politics and government. 2. Asian Americans—Civil rights.
3. Political participation—United States. 4. Political parties—United States.
5. Racism—Political aspects—United States. 6. United States—Race relations—Political
aspects. I. Title. II. Series.
E184.A75K56 2007
324.089'95073—dc22   2 0 0 6 0 1 5 2 5 1

2 4 6 8 9 7 5 3 1

CONTENTS

ACKNOWLEDGMENTS

Writing this book has been a collective exercise, and I am deeply grateful to my parents, and to the many friends, colleagues, and teachers who were critical in moving this project forward to completion. Looking back, I can see how much I relied on so many people in so many different ways. My debt is to them is enormous, and I look forward to paying it off.

The arguments in this book would not have been possible had I not had the good fortune of conversing with some of the finest minds from multiple disciplines and studies. I thank Gary Jacobson for first enlightening me about what politics really looks like from the vantage point of actual politicians. The clarity of Elizabeth Gerber"s critiques— —always coupled with her support— —was instrumental in helping me understand the strengths and weaknesses of different methodological approaches. Through both his remarkable scholarship and his advice, Steven Erie reminded me that the political relevance of my writing was not something to be sacrificed for my career. I count myself extraordinarily lucky that Yen Le Espiritu didn"t politely toss me out of her office when I first came to talk to her. Knowing now what I didn"t know then about the academy, I would not have blamed her. For both her foresight and her intellectual guidance, my debt to her is profound— —her influence permeates the book. Moreover, I am sure that without her introduction, Michael Omi would have remained a faceless name on a famous book rather than the living role model that he actually became. Don Nakanishi played the role that he always does, and I happily join the growing ranks of scholars in Asian American politics whose paths were first mapped out by his life"s work. I thank Ling-chi Wang for his tireless work documenting the media coverage of the campaign finance controversy following the November 1996 election— —Chapter 3 would have been impossible without his efforts. Finally, Paul Frymer deserves special mention for his intellectual contributions and encouragement. Without him this book would not have seen the light of day.

Scripps College, and in particular the Department of Politics & International Relations, provided a wonderfully supportive environment for carrying out this project. I am particularly grateful to Nancy Neiman-Auerbach for her generous support and friendship. Her everyday presence allowed me to relax and, for better or worse, be myself. Becky Ballinger saw me being myself and still seems to like me, which is fortunate since without her administrative support I would never have gotten anything done. Early on, Rita Roberts provided me with the steadying hand and infinite wisdom borne of experience that every new faculty member— —especially one of color— — should have as they navigate higher education. A shout out goes to my colleagues in the Intercollegiate Department of Asian American Studies at the Claremont Colleges. They are shockingly normal and together must be the most functional community of diverse scholars that I have ever had the privilege to join. I was lucky enough to have no shortage of research assistants, and I thank Lee Ann Wang, Shiyuan Deng, Min Yoo, Yining Wan, and Lisa Hahn for their work on various aspects of the book. A special thank you goes out to Kirstine Taylor who provided unfailing assistance with putting the manuscript together— —everyone who writes a book should have an assistant like her, and perhaps one day she"ll deign to let me proofread for her.

Of course, my greatest debt is owed to my partner in life, whose influence on the book pales in comparison to her influence on me. It is to her and to the glorious study break that is our son that this book is dedicated.

1

INTRODUCTION

THE NOVEMBER ELECTION of 1996 marks the watershed that never was for Asian American politics. The reelection of Democratic president Bill Clinton to a second term, along with favorable political trends in Asian America, had Asian American political elites all but convinced that they were ascending as respected players on the national political scene. Asian American politicians and organized interest groups, aware of demographic trends, repeatedly pointed out that the Asian American population was the fastest-growing minority group in the 1990s.[1] Better still, Asian American communities had grown predominantly in Electoral College "vote-rich" states such as California, New York, Texas, and New Jersey.[2] A nationwide voter registration drive had enfranchised roughly seventy-five thousand new Asian American voters—the most ever in a single year. Drawing a contrast with heavily Democratic black communities and largely Democratic Latina/o communities, Asian American political elites were busy casting Asian American voters as largely nonpartisan blocs of swing voters that could be integrated into either party coalition, and attractive Asian American candidates drawing money and votes from Asian Americans were running in local, state, and national races.[3] Asian American political leaders were secure in the knowledge that they had contributed several million dollars to both of the national parties—as much as $10 million by some estimates—most of it going to support the winning presidential ticket.[4]

Politically experienced Asian American appointees, eager to take advantage of a president who openly courted Asian American votes and campaign donations and counted Asian Americans among his circle of longtime friends, were ready to facilitate greater integration of Asian Americans into the second Clinton administration. Expressing the pervasive optimism of the time, Ray Tsuneyoshi, then chair of the Asian American Government Executives Network (AAGEN), commented that Asian Americans were "fortunate to have a receptive White House and the experience of the current Asian Pacific American political appointees to help us position ourselves to be part of President Clinton's second term."[5] In the full expectation that their political demands would not go unheeded, Asian American elites were ambitiously discussing the possibility of not just one but two Asian American appointees to the second Clinton cabinet—even one would have been a historic first.[6]

Nineteen ninety-seven was a historic year for Asian Americans, but hardly in the way that they expected or hoped. Instead of reaping the benefits of their efforts, Asian American political aspirations took a huge step backward, as politically active Asian Americans were publicly attacked as disloyal to the United States. Despite the lack of cause, almost every single Asian American national elected official was investigated for possible fund-raising activities linked to foreign nations or corporations based in Asia, and some Asian American interest groups similarly fell under suspicion. Democrats and Republicans, both the recipients of Asian and Asian American campaign contributions, took turns accusing each other of putting electoral victory over the security and sovereignty of the United States by allowing "foreign" agents of Asian countries and corporations to insinuate themselves into U.S. elections. In return for their largest political investment to date to curry influence and gain access to mainstream political power, Asian American political interests found themselves on the very public receiving end of bipartisan hostility.[7]

As their political nightmare unfolded, presumptions of innocence were abandoned, as Asians in the United States were once again portrayed as perpetual, unassimilable foreigners.[8] Aware of the homogenizing, racist application of this cultural discourse to a diverse and complex formation of Asians in the United States, many individual Asian Americans sought, to no avail, to insulate themselves from the controversy by actively, explicitly, and publicly distancing themselves from the allegedly illegal actions of individuals with Asian surnames, and by pointing out that the vast majority of presumptively illegal activity had come from only a handful of individuals.[9] In positioning themselves as "innocent," "good," "law-abiding," and "loyal," some Asian Americans paradoxically reinforced the very allegations they were seeking to deny—namely, that major campaign finance laws had been broken by "guilty," "bad," "law-breaking," and "disloyal" Asian Americans.[10]

The campaign finance controversy dominated news coverage for weeks on end, until, in January 1998, the president's peccadillo with a certain intern overwhelmed coverage of all other issues and ended the public misery of Asian American political elites. A little more than a year after the election, Asian American political leader and University of California—Berkeley professor Ling-chi Wang bluntly summed up his opinion of the controversy when he testified before the U.S. Commission on Civil Rights that he could not "think of one issue in the 150-year annals of Asian American history that has been more of a setback to civil rights for this community."[11] Rather than marking a new zenith of national political power, the 1996 election began a political winter that continues to chill the development of Asian American political power today. Burned by both major parties, Asian Americans reassessed their political prospects, and many found themselves back at square one. Some angrily, some quietly, many individual Asian Americans decided to withdraw from the political game, seeing in the bipartisan hostility and the media rush to judgment the lesson that participation in conventional politics did not pay. Others, such as Washington State governor Gary Locke, argued that it was critically important that Asian Americans play the campaign finance game better and "cleaner" than other groups, since they were clearly going to be held to higher standards than others and consequently had to dot every "i" and cross every "t" of a Byzantine campaign finance system.[12]

TWO-PARTY COMPETITION, TWO-PARTY HOSTILITY

Why did Asian Americans find themselves an isolated minority facing a decidedly hostile bipartisan majority, when they had expected a place at the political table? Conventional wisdom clearly suggests that with the rapid population growth of Asian Americans in key states and their increasing levels of organized political activity, not to mention their availability for integration into a party coalition, this racial group, composed largely of immigrants, should have become further integrated into American political life via their party-based efforts. Instead, not only did both major parties pointedly and publicly leave Asian American political interests out in the cold, both parties actually mounted a calculated effort to explicitly repudiate Asian American efforts to use the two-party system as a means of gaining political power. The major parties' reaction is all the more puzzling once we recognize that bipartisan hostility toward this racial group became most pronounced immediately after Asian American interests had mounted their largest and most extensive campaign to date to influence electoral politics in the United States—precisely at the moment when the two-party system should have been most hospitable to Asian American political interests.

The political logic of two-party competition normally compels party elites to be receptive to organized interest groups. I argue that this logic, when applied specifically to Asian Americans, will systemically lead party elites into conscious and strategic attacks against Asian American political interests. Party elites recognize that racial and ethnic individuals and interest groups move through and within mainstream political institutions with "racial markers," and that Asian Americans can be racially represented as immutably "foreign" and "illiberal," thus standing outside America's ideological and cultural boundaries. Because these racial markers can be deployed to communicate important political information, especially to uncertain voters, party elites are compelled to incorporate the racial discourse around Asian American bodies into their party strategies. In turn, party elites, recognizing the political danger posed to their party brand name by the discursive presence of "racialized outsiders" within the party coalition, must explicitly and aggressively expel Asian Americans if their party hopes to build and maintain a majority party coalition. Rather than promote inclusivity, two-party competition generates strategically motivated racialized hostility toward Asian Americans that places them even further outside the American polity. While individual party elites may hold anti-Asian animus, what is decisive to the political fortunes of Asian Americans are not irrational prejudicial attitudes or sentiments but the rational calculations of strategic party elite assessments of the political impact of racialized Asian Americans on the party's efforts to build a winning majority coalition. As a racialized minority group attempting to navigate the formal logic of the two-party system, Asian Americans will not only be unable to translate party coalition-building efforts into political power, they will actually endanger their own political interests by attempting to become important players in party politics. In other words, the problem rests not in the political strategies that Asian Americans might choose within the two-party system but in the structure of the system itself. Because the parties' hostility toward Asian Americans is promoted structurally, future efforts by organized Asian Americans to engage the two-party system as a vehicle for political empowerment will result in failure.

CHAMPIONS OF THE AMERICAN TWO-PARTY SYSTEM

The political disaster that befell Asian Americans in 1996 stands as a stark challenge to political scientists who have championed the American two-party system as an important and accessible vehicle for the political empowerment of immigrants and people of color.[13] With few exceptions, party scholars have consistently argued that two-party competition systematically assists these at times overlapping groups in their efforts to fully integrate into American civic life.[14] Two-party competition, the argument goes, at its best requires one or more of the major parties to appeal to an organized political racial or ethnic group, and at its worst ensures that "no group feels that it may at any moment have to drop everything else and defend itself against onslaught by some other group."[15] According to the conventional wisdom, two-party competition is fundamental to a democratic and egalitarian society in which politicians recognize and respond favorably to the mobilization and participation of organized political interests, including those of racial, ethnic, and immigrant groups.[16]

In response to those who champion the two-party system as a powerful vehicle for the empowerment of racial and ethnic minority groups and immigrant communities, I argue that the party competition inherent in the two-party system ultimately works against the interests of Asian Americans. Rather than help integrate them, two-party competition works to maintain the positioning of Asian Americans as perpetual foreigners to American society, outside the ideological mainstream. Rather than help generate a democratic and egalitarian society in which Asian Americans can participate as equals, two-party competition compels political elites to publicly reject and even become actively hostile to Asian American political interests, particularly when Asian Americans become most active within the two-party system. Not only is the two-party system ultimately closed to Asian American political interests, it represents a politically dangerous path for this particular interest group. Critically, the two-party system's hostility to Asian Americans is not a function of coincidence, bad luck, or simple anti-Asian prejudice but is rooted in both its *systemic logic* and the *racialization* of Asian Americans. In other words, the inexorable logic of two-party competition structurally puts Asian American political interests in a perilous position, and this problem is *specific* to Asian Americans. The two-party system will thus consistently fail Asian Americans.[17]

Champions of the two-party system will strenuously object to this characterization, arguing that "parties are, by nature, inclusive."[18] Seeing party competition as inherently positive, party scholars have not been able to grasp how two-party competition might lead directly to two-party hostility toward a particular racial, ethnic, or overlapping immigrant community. The logic of building a majority party coalition, they argue, means that parties simply cannot afford to alienate an organized racial, ethnic, or immigrant group that is largely up for grabs, or they risk losing that group to the opposition.[19] In contrast, I argue that it is precisely the demand to bring together a majority electoral coalition that generates a strategic incentive for party elites explicitly to ostracize Asian Americans who attempt to participate in the two-party system. The need to pull together a majority party coalition generates a structural logic that demands active and public hostility toward Asian American interests if the party hopes to protect its brand name. At structurally induced moments, party elites will conclude that failure to marginalize Asian American interests will significantly damage a party's political prospects.

PROBLEMS IN THE STUDY OF RACE IN
POLITICAL SCIENCE

Political scientists have generally approached race and racism by emphasizing their supposedly irrational, and thus exceptional, quality. This framing of race and racism as ultimately reducible to individual psychology has been a consistent theoretical orientation within the discipline, and follows the intellectual lineage of Alexis de Tocqueville, Gunnar Myrdal, and Robert Dahl.[20] Consistent with treating race and racism as largely attitudinal, today's leading behavioralists within the field are engaged in a continuing debate about whether racist attitudes are a thing of the past or whether they continue to drive policy positions against programs designed to advance the social, political, and economic conditions of people of color.[21] Whether these scholars argue that citizens are acting on conservative attitudes, instrumental self-interest, or prejudicial beliefs, all three camps in this debate assume that race and racism are merely psychological fictions that can be unlearned. By framing race and racism as standing outside "normal" and "logical" models and defining them as a function of "irrational" prejudice, the discipline has promoted theoretical models that do not adequately account for either race or racism.[22] Once the underlying prejudices of American society are "educated out" and everyone is "color-blind," so the assumption goes, the fundamental theoretical correctness of the models will be further revealed. Applying this approach to what happened to Asian Americans after the 1996 election, bipartisan hostility toward Asian Americans is understood as anomalous, and consequently as no hindrance to the basic integrity of models of two-party competition that demand inclusivity and generate democratic values.

In the party literature, Paul Frymer (1999) stands out as an important exception to the framing of race as exceptional and racism as irrational. After about one hundred years of American party scholars extolling the virtues of the two-party system, Frymer's incisive analysis is a long-awaited intellectual leap forward that has significantly advanced our national and scholarly conversation about race and party competition in America, and his breakthrough contribution has significantly informed the development of the analysis presented here. The genius of Frymer's model lies in demonstrating how party elite actions that result in the systemic disfranchisement of blacks, far from being the result of irrational individual prejudice, are actually quite rational responses induced by the logic of the two-party system. Antiblack animus among party elites is not nonexistent so much as it is irrelevant—whether or not party elites are prejudiced, the underlying logic of party competition continues to influence strategic decision making. Racism is logical and systemic rather than irrational, and race stands at the center of American politics rather than at the margins.[23]

Frymer asserts that racial cleavage between whites and blacks is a persistent and central feature of American politics that directly influences the political prospects of blacks by keeping them essentially "captured" in one party. Because both parties have made the strategic calculation that the electoral costs of "white flight" outweigh the benefits of maximizing black votes, neither party fully reaches out to blacks for fear of losing racially conservative white voters, and thus their chances for a majority coalition. The endurance of this racial cleavage in the electorate thus leads party elites to search for the median white voter rather than simply the median voter; two-party competition thus induces strategic, goal-oriented party elites to engage in a form of institutional racism. Blending this spatial analysis with a historical-institutional approach, Frymer further centers the role of white racism by pointing out that the developmental underpinnings of the modern two-party system, first devised in the antebellum era, are directly linked to efforts by the party elite to keep the divisive issue of slavery off the political agenda, and he traces the historical process by which Republican Party elites designed and executed strategies to maintain political silence on slavery. He goes on to delineate how the historical development of today's Democratic Party has been deeply influenced by party elite efforts in the post—Civil Rights Movement era to render black interests invisible in two-party competition. Frymer's historical-institutionalist approach allows us to see how party elites in different historical eras, in response to existing racial cleavage in the electorate, face systemic incentives to remove black interests from the political agenda.[24]

Consistent with his historical-institutionalist approach, Frymer's argument about party elite strategies and their racist outcomes is historically specific and contextualized. His treatment of *race*, however, is not. He does not address the reality that within American culture there is a constantly shifting discourse about race, and an ongoing struggle not only over the cultural representations of specific racial groups but over the meaning of race itself. Consequently, he does not incorporate into the analysis how and why the specific racial meanings of African American bodies have shifted in American popular culture, and whether these shifting meanings are important in determining the prospects for African American political gains. While party elites adopt different strategies at different historical moments, Frymer does not address whether this occurs in response to shifting cultural meanings of black bodies, nor are blacks themselves presumed to contest these racial representations in ways that might have been considered by these elites. Rather than highlight the political importance of discursive battles over racial meanings, his analysis leaves in place the implicit assumption that race is a transhistorical—and thus unchanging—phenomenon.

Consider, for example, his counterintuitive observation that black interests have been advanced at the national level when one party achieved national dominance immediately after the Civil War, when the Republican Party launched the First Reconstruction, and during the Second Reconstruction precipitated by the Civil Rights Movement. Frymer suggests that the ability of black interests to take advantage of a political opening that emerged when the logic of the two-party system broke down is indicative of how the two-party system can actually retard the development of racial policies that address long-standing antiblack racism. (Of course, he also reminds us that the southern experience of one-party domination should be enough to convince us that the solution to racism cannot be less party competition.)[25]

To understand the changes that took place during this period, it is critical to examine the intense cultural battles that occurred in the 1950s and 1960s over the racial meaning of black bodies. Frymer is exactly right to point to the political logic of the two-party system, but by incorporating the historical specificity of different racial representations during this period, it is possible to see how these shifting representations played a critical role in advancing black interests during the Civil Rights Movement, and later influenced the national government toward greater state repression of the Black Power Movement.[26] Within the dominant black-white paradigm that Frymer deploys, black Americans are not typically racialized as being potentially—and certainly not perpetually—disloyal subjects of the United States;

antiblack animus is thought to emerge primarily if not solely on the axis of white supremacy and black inferiority.[27] But African American political interests have often had to negotiate political charges that their activities are either controlled by or reflect the interests of illiberal, anti-American governments or interests, and the Second Reconstruction was no exception. As Thomas Borstelmann and Mary Dudziak have shown, key to the advances made by the Civil Rights Movement was its ability to take advantage of U.S. Cold War concerns about the consolidation and expansion of communist, and especially Soviet, influence around the world. Civil rights organizers understood that American efforts to build an internationally linked system of market economies were undercut by global perceptions that America sanctioned racist policies at home. By taking actions designed to underline the contradiction between American rhetoric abroad and American racial reality at home, the Civil Rights Movement forced the U.S. government to act against southern interests bent on maintaining the racial status quo: civil rights for blacks became the Cold War policy of the U.S. government. In response, southern interests consistently raised the specter of communist infiltration into black political organizations in an effort to discredit both them and national government responses that threatened white supremacy. Southern efforts were designed, then, to frame nonviolent actions in pursuit of racial reform as communist agitation in pursuit of Bolshevik revolution.[28]

Mainstream movement leaders must have been aware that the national government would be less likely to act if the South could successfully recast black political actions as designed to further communist objectives. Since they understood that the Cold War provided African Americans with political leverage, they must also have recognized that they could lose this leverage if they appeared to be on the wrong side of the Cold War. The potential for the Civil Rights Movement to achieve its goals was thus always implicitly dependent on black America's public rejection of communism. Once the Black Power Movement that emerged in the mid-1960s rejected the gradualist program of reform from above led by white politicians in favor of a radical revolution from below led by third world peoples of color, the charge of racial and national disloyalty to the United States was more likely to stick. In short, through both the Civil Rights Movement and the Black Power Movement, the backdrop of the Cold War meant that African Americans not only had to contest the enduring racial narratives of innate white supremacy and black inferiority, but they were also under domestic pressure to perform as loyal Americans who rejected a communist (and thus illiberal) way of life, and in competition with southern narratives that shaped the meaning of black protest activity as communist agitation.

Incorporating the significance of racial discourse as contested and produced in a specific milieu like the Cold War thus helps us understand why the Democratic Party felt compelled during its brief era of one-party dominance in the mid-1960s to pass the most important civil rights laws in almost a century. Frymer's argument, while appropriately emphasizing the structurally induced outcomes of the two-party system in disadvantaging black interests, also invites us to incorporate the significance of racial contestation over the meaning of bodies.[29] Scholarship on the political (dis)empowerment of racialized formations should not limit itself to an examination of the strategic decisions of rational, goal-oriented actors assessing the structural logic of institutions in light of unchanging cultural meanings accorded to racialized bodies. Acknowledging the fluidity and contestation of racial representations not only places African Americans at the center of their own political history as they contest the racial meanings of their bodies, it also moves us away from a transhistorical conceptualization of race.

Consistent with Frymer, scholars of cultural politics have been quick to point out that the framing of race as exceptional and irrational ignores the central role of race in American politics and society, as well as the reality that both private and public life are already highly racialized. But theorists working in the realm of culture have also insisted that conceptualizing race as transhistorical cannot account for the conflicted and contested nature of racial meaning. In their seminal text *Racial Formation in the United States*, Michael Omi and Howard Winant summarize this critique:

> Most racial theory fails to capture the centrality of race in American politics and American life. Most theories are marked by a tendency to reduce race to a mere manifestation of other supposedly more fundamental social and political relationships such as ethnicity or class....
>
> Instead of exploring how groups become racially identified, how racial identities and meanings changed over time, or how racial

conflicts shape the American polity and society, "mainstream" approaches consider race as a problem of policy, of social engineering, of state management.[30]

Race and racial categories are not static or given but are always fluid and negotiated, open to future historical movement even as they emerge from specific histories. Racial politics is broadly defined as the contestation over the creation, reproduction, and destruction of cultural representations of various racialized bodies, with the recognition that these racial discourses are a central, embedded, and continuing feature that permeates contemporary politics, economics, and society. Understanding racial politics thus entails understanding how racial representations are created, promulgated, perpetuated, and challenged, typically at different "sites" where "racialization" occurs via different modes of cultural production.[31]

To the detriment of both camps, political scientists and scholars of cultural politics have generally not been engaged in a rigorous intellectual conversation with each other. Scholarship on race in political science largely fails to incorporate the excellent work on racialization that has become canonized and taken for granted in the fields of cultural studies, American studies, ethnic studies, and Asian American Studies. While Tocqueville, Myrdal, and Dahl continue to be required reading for political science scholars of race, Omi and Winant's pioneering book on the theory of racial formation typically remains unassigned and unread in political science classes, even as it is widely engaged, expanded upon, and contested in virtually every other field that tackles race. With few exceptions, political scientists continue to take race and racial categories as given rather than as fluid and negotiated, even when they give a perfunctory nod to the significant advances in the theorizing of race. The result has been a theoretically impoverished political science literature on race—a point made emphatically by Michael Dawson and Cathy Cohen in their recent review of the state of scholarship on race and ethnicity.[32]

The serious theoretical shortcomings in political science are all the more troubling given that there is no shortage of sophisticated theorizing on race. On the topic of Asian American cultural representations alone, Elaine Kim, Lisa Lowe, Michael Omi and Howard Winant, David Palumbo-Liu, Claire Jean Kim, and Robert Lee, to name but a few scholars, have all written widely acknowledged texts that emphasize the critical role of racialization in structuring the opportunities for bodies racially marked as Asian in the United States.[33] Of these texts, only Claire Jean Kim's *Bitter Fruit* and Lee's *Orientals* have been acknowledged by the field of political science.

This illiteracy around the racialization of Asians in America speaks to a key problem of race scholarship in a field that fails to integrate the theoretical advances of other disciplines. Cultural scholars of race take for granted and insist upon scholarly analyses that take into account how different bodies (re)present and signify different cultural meanings. In simple language, what it means to be, say, black, is different from what it means to be Asian. What some cultural scholars term "racial common sense" about the meanings of bodies depends on whether the body in question is perceived to perform as Asian, black, Latina/o, white, and so forth, and this itself depends on the particular racial categories available at a particular historical moment.

That racialization proceeds on different historical trajectories projecting different racial meanings onto bodies is common knowledge for those who study the cultural production of race and racialization, and yet political scientists attempting to assess the prospects for political empowerment generally do not acknowledge, much less incorporate into their models, the notion that racial meanings are specific to certain bodies. A notable exception is the work of Claire Jean Kim on the racial triangulation of Asian Americans.[34] Kim proposes a theoretical framework embodied as a "field of racial positions" and argues that Asian Americans have been "racially triangulated" vis-à-vis whites and blacks in a particular field of racial positions that has endured since the mid-1800s.[35] Within this field, Asians in the United States are simultaneously constructed as superior relative to black Americans on cultural racial grounds, and "immutably foreign and unassimilable with whites on cultural and racial grounds in order to ostracize them from the body politic and civic membership."[36] Not only are Asian Americans, black Americans, and white Americans racially constructed and imbued with different cultural meanings, an investigation of this racialization undercuts the dominant black-white binary of race relations in the United States.

Efforts to incorporate the fluidity of racialized meanings in models of political empowerment should also be careful to distinguish between how apparently similar contestations on a particular dimension of difference (e.g., insider-outsider, superior-inferior) might play out differently depending on the historical trajectory of a particular racial formation. Consider, for example, how contestations over African American national loyalty are actually quite different from contestations over Asian American national loyalty. The former, I argue, is largely a question of whether blacks have tired of being disappointed by the promise of America. This framing of the debate means that blacks are constructed as having the *choice* to become disloyal to the United States. The racialization of Asian Americans, on the other hand, does not offer this choice of loyalties; Asian Americans are racially essentialized as *inherently*—and thus *perpetually*—foreign to American political and social values. They cannot choose to be disloyal to the United States because they were never really loyal in the first place.

As I argue in detail in Chapter 3, the kind of racial fear that was the political currency of the campaign finance scandal of 1996 was not an indiscriminate racial fear but one specific to infiltration, invasion, and takeover of the American body politic by foreign Asian bodies. And while Latinos in the United States have also had to deal with an enduring legacy of racialization as civic outsiders, contemporary Latino racialization, unlike Asian racialization, does not generally link Latinos to powerful governments and economies depicted as threats to American global hegemony.

RACIAL DISCOURSE AS DECISIVE, INSTITUTIONS AS IRRELEVANT

Scholars of racial and ethnic cultural politics generally premise their work on the notion that what really matters is the ability to engage in the politics of cultural production in order to influence the outcome of the contest over racial representations. In privileging as decisive the ability to enjoin and influence the cultural contestation over racial discourse, scholarship in this vein generally presupposes that the ability to control racial representation is the entire ballgame—control racial discourse, and you control the outcome.

Michael Chang's recent work on the dominant discourses of the campaign finance controversy is a good example of this kind of work. In attempting to explain how certain Asian American political interests were waylaid in the controversy, he notes that his "central organizing question is: What are the particular discursive and ideological shifts that occurred in 'Asian

Donorgate' that led to the racialization of the 1996 campaign finance controversy?" His book thus focuses on different discourses, including what he terms "the campaign finance scandal discourse," "the campaign finance reform discourse," "the foreign political influence discourse," "the threat to national security discourse," and "the Pacific Rim discourse."[37] As someone taking a cultural approach to politics, Chang is concerned with the ways that various political actors, working within historically grounded parameters, are able to shift cultural discourses through various modes of cultural production. He emphasizes the role of racial discourse in the disempowerment of people of color, as dominant commercial media outlets and political elites reproduced and perpetuated racist representations of Asians that effectively put Asian American political interests in the United States behind the eight ball.

Chang focuses on how the national Republican Party saw a potential for political benefit in hammering Clinton as a sellout to foreign powers, especially China. It is not difficult to conclude that the Republican Party would have been less likely to attempt to damage Clinton and the Democratic Party by tainting them as beholden to foreign powers were we talking about white European bodies representing European countries or corporations. And clearly the storm of negative propaganda against Asian Americans posed severe problems for a racial group that lacked the productive capacity to generate counterhegemonic discourses. However, insofar as scholars of culture and discourse privilege as decisive the production and consequences of racial representations, they almost invariably ignore the *institutional* settings or contexts in which cultural politics takes shape. That is, scholars of cultural politics fail to ask whether and how the formal "rules of the game" influence political elites to adopt particular kinds of strategies or tactics, largely assuming without discussion that the significance of cultural discourse is so great that it will simply trump any role that institutions might play.

I argue that this failure to take the institutional context into account is at philosophical odds with the emphasis in cultural studies to ground analysis within specificities rather than abstractions. Cultural theorists typically dismiss the theoretical modeling of political scientists because they view them as overemphasizing stable features such as institutional rules for the sake of elegant theoretical models; they criticize political scientists for failing to take into account the dynamic, shifting, and negotiated qualities inherent in the production of culture. In dismissing efforts to place politics within concrete, specified institutional contexts, however, cultural theorists paradoxically single out the institutional environment as the one dimension that they are comfortable ignoring as irrelevant to political outcomes. So, while on the one hand cultural theorists are much more attuned to the contextualization necessary to understand, say, how different bodies are racialized in different ways, and how this racialization is a function of both historical trajectory and the agency of actors engaged in the cultural production of racial discourse, they completely ignore what political scientists see as fundamental differences—namely, the different institutional contexts of political battles. Even as they insist on the necessity of integrating difference and context into scholarly analyses, cultural theorists do not differentiate between the specific rules of the game that dominate, say, the arena of congressional politics and the political machinations driven by the rules and logic of the two-party system. Instead, in privileging the importance of cultural production, cultural analysis trumps institutional analysis, and the question of how the rules might matter is left uninvestigated.

From the standpoint of someone trained to focus on the rules of the game, what is particularly striking about this type of cultural analysis is that it might as well be applied to every existing institutional context. Although we are talking about political actors seeking political gains through various stratagems and tactics, these political actors seem not to notice whether they are working within the institutional context of the rules that govern the congressional committee system, an electoral system of proportional representation, or an electoral system of single majority districts. The implicit assumption is that in no case do the rules matter, and that what really counts in every case is discourse.

This is all very frustrating for political scientists who take it for granted that not understanding the rules and how they operate is tantamount to being a political illiterate. After all, in order to understand why political actors deploy certain strategies and tactics, political scholars assume that they need to analyze the rules of the game, largely because they recognize that political actors, in rational pursuit of their goals, tend to be entirely aware of those rules and incorporate them into their strategic decision making.

To take a simple but powerful example, consider the argument of the "wasted vote" presented by a major American political party when it urges its "core" voters to vote not for a third party candidate but for the major party candidate least offensive to the voter's sensibilities. A vote for Green Party candidate Ralph Nader in 2000 or 2004, according to Democratic Party leaders, was a "wasted vote." Voting for Nader was tantamount to not voting, to throwing away one's vote, to helping the Republicans. This argument makes sense only in the context of a winner-take-all system in which the voter can cast only one vote for president; it would lose all cogency if the United States were to adopt the instant runoff voting system used by many other countries. Instant runoff voting (IRV) guarantees that the winner has a majority of votes, rather than a plurality. Under IRV rules candidates are ranked in order of preference. If one candidate receives a majority of the first-choice votes, he or she is elected; if not, the last-place candidate is defeated, and his or her votes are redistributed to the second-choice candidate on the ballot. This process continues until one candidate has a majority. If U.S. presidential elections used IRV, Democratic Party elites would not have had to spend a single dime urging ideologues not to "waste their votes," as Nader supporters could simply have ranked Nader first without worrying about handing victory to the Republicans.

DYNAMIC RACIAL FORMATIONS WITHIN INSTITUTIONAL FRAMEWORKS

That the rules matter is apparent to political scientists. This does not, however, mean that they should ignore the critical role of culture. In allowing institutional analysis to trump cultural analysis, political scientists typically see culture as unimportant or unmanageable, perhaps because it cannot be measured or is too fluid to incorporate into social scientific analysis. Irrespective of this, in prematurely assuming that incorporating the role of cultural—including racial—discourse into the study of politics is either impossible or undesirable, political scientists have ignored whether, when, and how political elites might take strategic actions whose logic depends on the existence of racial discourses that attach particular racial meanings to specific bodies and racial categories. At the same time, in declining to investigate how the particular rules that govern political elite actions might generate strategies and tactics that reproduce or rely upon racial discourse, scholars of cultural politics have ignored whether, when, and how political elites are systemically driven by the existence of particular rules of the game toward the adoption of strategies that generate the reproduction of cultural discourse.

Consider the process by which party elites incorporate various political interests in their respective party coalitions. Conventional scholarship tells us that an interest group—and particularly a racial or immigrant group seeking integration, will not face bipartisan hostility, because the winner-take-all electoral system requires parties to craft majority coalitions. Political logic dictates that if an organized interest with mainstream political values is attacked by one major party, the other party can and will absorb that interest into its coalition so as to build and sustain a majority.

Of course, parties do not target all groups equally, particularly given limited resources. Undecided "swing" voters, for example, get special attention.[38] Cost-benefit analysis often leads party elites to reach out to voters who already participate in the political system while ignoring habitual nonparticipants, who are more difficult to mobilize.[39] And a handful of party scholars have noted that institutional rules can provide structural incentives for party elites to privilege particular interests over others.[40]

Once we recognize that different interests are valued differently by party elites, we can analyze what makes an interest potentially valuable or disruptive, recognizing that this analysis will frame elites' strategic political actions in the future. I argue that in order for party elites to perform this analysis, they must take into account the interaction between racial discourse and institutional and organizational contexts. They can—and do—understand that bodies are racially marked, and that particular bodies mean different things in different institutional settings. In the case of Asian Americans, I argue that party elites recognize that the presence of racialized "perpetual foreigners" working within the party structure represents a political hurdle to building a majority coalition. They understand the political danger to their party brand name of being associated with an organized interest or with individuals perceived as having long-standing, culturally fixed attachments to foreign, "un-American" powers. Taking into account the popular representation of Asian Americans—especially in the context of international politics—as perpetual foreigners standing outside the American polity, party elites follow a structural incentive born of the logic of the two-party system to explicitly and publicly marginalize politically active Asian Americans, particularly if their racialized bodies are present in the party itself. Indeed, the more influence Asian Americans acquire or are poised to acquire within the two-party system, paradoxically, the more this interest is likely to suffer bipartisan attack.

Consequently, Asian Americans working today within the two-party system must do so with caution. Once we acknowledge that we are talking about Asian Americans *qua* Asian Americans, rather than as an anomalous group stigmatized by simple anti-Asian prejudice, their experience after the 1996 election can be understood as a systemic outcome of the inexorable political logic facing party elites that seek to create and maintain a majority party coalition. Once framed in this way, it will become clear that the problem for Asian American participation in two-party politics lies in the complex interaction between racial discourse about Asians in America and the institutional rules that govern two-party competition.

In emphasizing the role of racial discourse in structuring opportunities for Asians in America, I want to draw attention to the reality that racialized groups do not and cannot navigate formal political institutions and organizations as if they are any other political interest. In criticizing cultural scholars for ignoring a fundamental aspect of how contemporary politics operates through the civic institutions that govern our lives, I wish to draw attention to the reality that the rules of the game really do matter. While Asian Americans, like every other political interest, must work within formalized settings bound by institutional rules, Asian American political interests must also constantly negotiate "racial markers" specific to them that can be selectively magnified, minimized, or even altered for political reasons, and not necessarily by Asian Americans. And just as Asian Americans must take into account how they are perceived racially, scholars of Asian American politics must incorporate racial discourse about Asian Americans if they are to grasp how this political interest negotiates mainstream political institutions and the political logic they generate.

In making this argument, I want to pose a much broader challenge about the way scholars in multiple fields approach the study of racial and ethnic political empowerment. In a broad sense, I am arguing that advancing scholarship on racial and ethnic politics requires a transdisciplinary approach that truly synthesizes various fields of study. In order to assess Asian American prospects in American politics, it is not enough to focus solely on the institutional rules underlying the political logic that drives strategic actors to engage in particular behaviors, nor is it sufficient to remain solely on cultural terrain by analyzing the racialization of Asians in America, as if cultural representation is all that matters. Understanding the formal logic of governmental institutions does not mean that we understand whether and how racialized bodies might face unique or specific concerns when facing a particular set of formal rules, and focusing solely on racial representations ignores the reality that institutional rules structure the strategic direction and outcome of political processes. One must understand both the institutional rules of the game as well as the dynamic role of cultural discourse in order to assess how a racialized formation navigates the formal logic of an institutional setting.

This book thus deploys an analytical framework that emphasizes the existence of relatively stable rules of the game—both formal and informal—and their accompanying political logic, but insists that this more general, elegant, and stable framework be interwoven with the dynamic, fluid, and negotiated quality of racial discourse and racialization in the United States. The transdisciplinary approach taken here insists that scholars must understand the influence of different institutional rules on strategic elite behavior, and at the same time recognize that racial and ethnic groups are discursively represented in very different ways. Understanding when and how political elites in specific institutional settings strategically deploy specific racial meanings of Asian American bodies will allow an assessment of how institutional rules influence the reproduction of racial discourse in America. And understanding how the institutional rules influence racial discourse will in turn enable a more accurate assessment of the playing field for Asian Americans seeking political empowerment.

What Follows

By necessity, this book weaves together different theoretical approaches, not to mention different literatures, in making its argument. The challenge, of course, is to translate the insights of scholarship largely concerned with cultural discourse—impossible to measure quantitatively and perpetually renegotiated—into the political realities of a stable institutional framework where political strategies relentlessly take into account the formal rules of the political game. This book is an effort to face up to this challenge, and it focuses on the interaction between organized Asian American political interests and major political institutions of the United States.

What this book is not is a comprehensive treatment of how Asian Americans relate to all party organizations or forms. It is interested almost exclusively in the relationship between the national parties and Asian Americans, and not in the relationship between state and local parties and Asian Americans. When I speak of party elites, I am speaking about national party elites seeking to establish and maintain national political influence. Many Asian American individuals have become partisan officeholders over the past twenty-five years, especially at the local level, and scholars have effectively analyzed the relationship between local Asian American politicians and the communities they represent.[41] I do not, in any way, wish to diminish the importance of local politics or the importance of local party structures or leaders.[42] I am not claiming that Asian Americans should not engage in all forms of party politics; my emphasis is specifically on the relationship between organized Asian American political interests and national party coalitions as a vehicle for political empowerment. Nor is my intent to discourage Asian Americans from full and complete political engagement within the public institutions that dominate American life.

I am also not interested in engaging the ongoing debate about whether Asian American interests would be best represented by those who are understood to be Asian American.[43] While my argument clearly suggests that Asian Americans cannot hope to achieve substantive representation by pouring resources into the two-party system, I do not mean to suggest that Asian Americans should simply pursue descriptive representation, nor am I suggesting that there is something inherently problematic about political representation by those who do not claim Asian American identity. Rather, my concern is with whether substantive representation can be achieved via the two-party system given the political logic of marginalizing Asian American party-based efforts.

Finally, I do not engage the ongoing debate about whether opposition to any particular racial or ethnic interest suggests racist, ideological, or self-interested voters. This is not to suggest that this debate is unimportant, merely that my argument does not depend on taking a position on this debate. Indeed, it is not even necessary to claim that party elites have any anti-Asian or anti-Asian American animus. Rather, as I hope to make clear, I need only to show that party elites are rational, goal-oriented actors that, in pursuing their goals, take racial representations into strategic account. The focus of my analysis is not on attitudinal prejudice against Asians or Asian Americans, but rather on whether and how party elites factor into their strategic calculations their understanding of the constructed meaning of racialized Asian bodies within the United States.

Understanding how the two-party system operates is necessary in order to understand how organized Asian American political actions are both a product and a productive force within the system. Chapter 2 thus lays out the political and institutional logic of the two-party system, given its relatively stable institutional features. I begin by clarifying the assumptions that underlie each of three different theoretical approaches to the study of the political logic and institutional rules that support the American two-party system. I argue that each of these approaches to American party competition rests on the assumption that voters maintain similar core values; without this assumption of ideological homogeneity, two-party systems do not advance democracy within society. In the American context, the ideological homogeneity assumed by two-party models is often called the American liberal consensus, or *genus liberalism*, and it is marked by the values of individualism, government by consent, attachment to American political institutions along with a concomitant antipathy toward institutions and societies deemed not liberal, and belief in the economic system of capitalism. *Genus liberalism* functions as a boundary condition that requires majority-seeking parties to stake out positions squarely within its ideological confines and to be sensitive to associating with interests located outside those confines.[44] Interest groups discursively positioned outside the boundary condition of *genus liberalism* will ultimately find it virtually impossible to use the two-party system as a vehicle for political empowerment.

I then racially position Asian Americans vis-à-vis this two-party framework. I argue that party elites seeking to establish and maintain majority party power must incorporate existing racial discourse about Asian American bodies into their political strategies, and that this has a systemic impact on the prospects for Asian American political empowerment through the two-party system. Party elites are aware that Asian bodies in the United States can be discursively positioned outside the ideological boundaries of the

American liberal consensus. Because the party system requires political elites to build majority coalitions within the boundaries of *genus liberalism*, no rational office-seeking party can afford to have its party brand name associated with politically active Asians and Asian Americans racialized as standing outside those boundaries. Following the incentives built into the party system, goal-oriented party elites must sacrifice the interests of Asian Americans once the presence of their racialized bodies jeopardizes the party's ability to sustain majority-based coalitions. That is, the party competition inherent in the two-party system compels party elites to be explicitly and publicly hostile to Asian Americans, irrespective of whether party strategists hold any anti-Asian prejudice. The key political problem for Asian Americans seeking to attain political power through the party system is not attitudinal or individual anti-Asian prejudice. Rather, as a racialized formation maneuvering within an institutional environment of formal rules and rational, goal-oriented actors, Asian Americans—not to mention scholars of American politics—must confront structurally based racism.

Chapter 3 explores the implications of the argument presented in Chapter 2 by providing a detailed analysis of the strategic behavior of the two major parties during the campaign finance controversy following the 1996 election. Against the long-standing claims of party scholars who insist that the two-party system is a powerful vehicle for the political empowerment of racial and ethnic minority groups and immigrant communities, and that racism against these communities is equivalent to irrational prejudice that stands outside otherwise theoretically sound party models, I demonstrate that the party competition inherent in the two-party system drove rational, goal-oriented party elites to engage in specific strategic acts of racism against Asian Americans who found themselves an isolated minority facing bipartisan hostility. Against conventional wisdom, the approaching political ascendancy of Asian Americans within the party system led competitive parties not to integrate this interest group into party coalitions but to integrate the racial discourse about this interest group into party strategies. These party strategies simultaneously drew upon existing racial discourse while reproducing that discourse in publicly positioning Asian Americans as outside the American ideological mainstream and the American body politic. The logic of strategic racism hinged on party elite recognition that Asian bodies can and do maneuver through formal American public institutions in discursively specific ways.

Confronted by the structurally induced logic of the two-party system, nationally oriented Asian Americans should not look to it as a viable vehicle for political empowerment. In Chapter 4, through a discussion of the politics surrounding the "race question" on the decennial national census, I contend that organized Asian American political activity should instead seek an institutional environment that better facilitates countermajoritarian power, and that Asian Americans are far more likely to achieve political influence through the pursuit of congressional representation. The daily work of Congress is organized around a number of institutional rules and procedures that generate countermajoritarian tendencies that allow even a single member of Congress to aggressively pursue narrowly focused political goods. Particularly on issues where Asian Americans are the primary constituent group, their congressional representatives can take advantage of the formal rules of the legislative game to acquire meaningful political benefits for Asian communities. By influencing the content of the census race question, Asian Americans have improved their political prospects, helped bring important policy benefits to their communities, and intervened powerfully in the racialization that constructs the meanings attached to Asian bodies in the United States. That the institutional design of Congress enables Asian American political interests to take actions highly consequential to the material welfare and cultural construction of their communities indicates that advocates of Asian American political empowerment must take into account how the formal rules governing strategic behavior within American political institutions mediate the impact of racial discourse.

In Chapter 5 I analyze the political silence of Asian American communities on the campaign finance controversy. I contend that this silence is the result of the ways in which the Asian American political establishment has both pushed itself and been pushed by major party elites to focus on developing relationships with powerful politicians rather than on building community-based political power. In light of the time and energy invested by the political establishment in pursuing elite influence rather than building mass mobilization, one can hardly have expected Asian communities to do anything but ignore and distance themselves from an Asian American political establishment under attack. In a sense, Asian communities held their presumptive political leaders to account, and rightly called into question their legitimacy.

AL CONSENSUS

MERICAN

Y SYSTEM

IIS BOOK INVESTIGATES how Asian Americans as
ı racialized formation navigate the institutional setting of
a national two-party system populated with strategic, goal-
oriented political actors. The argument is grounded in both
the specific ways in which the two-party system operates and in the dominant racialized discourses surrounding Asian bodies in the United
States. I break with traditional political science scholarship in insisting
on the centrality and the historical particularity of racial formation in
determining the political outcomes for this group: I contend that Asian
Americans, because of the historical and specific way in which they have
been racialized, cannot successfully advance their political interests by
working within the party system. Moreover, their efforts to incorporate
themselves into one or the other majority party coalition paradoxically
push both parties to strategically ostracize Asian Americans where the
deployment of such a strategy may not previously have been necessary.

This chapter thus delineates the political and institutional logic of
the two-party system in order to assess how this relatively stable institutional environment interacts with popular racialization of Asian bodies in the United States. The theoretical framework adopted here
allows an analytical approach that both integrates the critical role

played by the institutional rules that structure strategic political behavior and takes seriously the critical role of race in influencing the prospects for political empowerment of racial and ethnic minorities in America. Incorporating the role of popular racial discourse around Asian bodies into the strategic calculations of goal-oriented party elites also makes possible a clearer assessment of the prospects of Asian American political empowerment via the two-party system, and allows one to assess more broadly the normative claims of party scholars who have consistently argued that the two-party system acts as a democratizing force vis-à-vis communities of color and immigrant populations.

After discussing the critical significance of the two-party system to the organization of modern democracy in the United States, I clarify the basic assumptions that drive the analytical and normative conclusions of conventional two-party scholarship. What becomes clear from this discussion is that in the American political context, most existing party scholarship is predicated upon an unspoken ideological consensus around classic liberal values, or *genus liberalism*. Because the liberal hegemony that binds the American body politic together endures over time, party scholars can integrate this ideological consensus into their theoretical models without losing any explanatory power. This in turn allows us to delineate the institutionally generated motivation of strategic party elite behavior vis-à-vis political minorities perceived as lying outside the American liberal consensus. Two-party elites seek to build majority coalitions in order to win elections, and must do so by drawing in multiple constituencies bound together by their membership in liberal society. Because no office-seeking party can hope to gain popular support from a liberal electorate if the party itself is seen as illiberal, party elites ensure that the party image remains branded in fundamentally liberal terms. Watchful party elites must thus take into strategic account any political efforts to associate the party brand name with illiberal political interests. They must assess whether and how the party's ability to win majority support might be influenced by the presence in the party coalition of political constituencies constructed in popular discourse as fundamentally and irreducibly illiberal. A political interest constructed as such will find itself structurally limited from successful participation in a major party coalition owing to wariness of damaging its party brand name through association with a political interest perceived as illiberal by a liberal electorate.

Were racial and ethnic communities just another interest group mobilizing to influence political outcomes, none of this would matter much. However, Asian American party-oriented efforts in fact face unique obstacles not encountered by any other political interest. Given their access to an unprecedented level of survey data about voter characteristics, parties clearly possess the necessary tools to take the measure of Asian American political interests and incorporate them into their respective party coalitions. But Asian Americans are not simply just another interest group with various policy positions to be surveyed and incorporated into party strategy, and party elites are not morally compelled to treat Asian Americans in the multiple and complex ways in which this racial formation understands and presents itself. Strategic party elites will, first and foremost, treat a political constituency in ways designed to further the party's interests. To that end, party leaders collect data on a political constituency not because they want to learn how best to serve this constituency, but because collecting and analyzing this data serves their party's interests. For party elites, what matters most may not be the various policy positions and political attitudes within Asian communities but the ways in which the broader liberal electorate understands the racialized meanings of Asian bodies.

Indeed, I contend that in their calculations, party elites incorporate the racial discourse around Asian bodies into their coalition-building strategies much more than they do actual Asian American policy positions, material interests, and political attitudes. Party elites may or may not be aware of the latter, but the electoral necessity of building a majority coalition in a liberal polity requires that they be aware of the former. The Asian immigrant has historically been racialized in dialectical opposition to the liberal citizen, with the consequence that Asian bodies have been framed as irreducibly illiberal alien foreigners that threaten the American body politic. Party elites recognize that a popular perception of racialized Asian bodies seeking power through active membership in a major party coalition can significantly damage a party's efforts to build a majority coalition. Strategic party elite behavior that attempts to racialize an opposition party through association with Asian bodies or seeks to distance a party's image from Asian bodies can be explained only if party elites are dealing in racial representations of Asian Americans as fundamentally illiberal and un-American rather than with the empirical reality of Asian American policy positions and political attitudes.

Because no party seeking to build a majority coalition in the United States can afford to be perceived as illiberal, party elites must be wary of associating the party brand name with Asian bodies racialized as illiberal in popular discourse, and will incorporate into their strategies the cultural meaning of Asian bodies, not because party elites are necessarily prejudiced, but because they are rational office-seekers that must build a majority coalition from within a liberal electorate.

That party elites are strategically if not morally sensitive to the impact of racial discourse on Asian bodies means that when a party's brand name runs the risk of becoming racialized through association with Asian bodies—Asian bodies racialized as immutably beholden to foreign entities—the institutional logic of two-party competition dictates that Asian Americans be politically ostracized by both parties. Two-party competition systemically drives party elites to draw upon and reproduce a historically overdetermined discursive representation of Asians as irreducibly illiberal, with enduring attachments to powerful "foreign" countries and powers. Moreover, Asian American efforts to integrate into the political mainstream by working within the national two-party system have the unintended consequence of reproducing existing racialized discourses of Asian bodies as illiberal threats to the health and legitimacy of the American body politic. A party's strategic incentive to promote this discourse increases as Asian American political interests become more and more visible in two-party politics, and the political benefits of strategically attacking the other party by associating the party brand name with the illiberal Asian become increasingly clear.

THE COMMON GROUND OF AMERICAN TWO-PARTY SCHOLARSHIP

Scholars of political science generally share the belief that the two-party system is rightfully central to the American political system because genuine competition between the two major parties leads to normatively positive outcomes that advance American democracy.[1] Even as the approaches to party scholarship have varied significantly over time, there is virtually no scholarly discussion of alternatives to the two-party system.[2] In 1950, E. E.

Schattschneider's Committee for a More Responsible Two-Party System proclaimed that "the two party-system is so strongly rooted in the political traditions of this country and public preference for it is so well established that consideration of other possibilities seems entirely academic." In the decades since Schattschneider's committee issued its report, whereas the public has increasingly lost its faith in political parties, political scientists have remained faithful to the central role and possibilities of America's two-party system.[3] Moreover, party scholars are not the only political scientists who believe in the two-party system; scholars in other American subfields consistently link the two-party system to the state of affairs in their own area of expertise.[4]

The two-party system clearly plays a central role in American politics; its institutional constraints serve to motivate strategic political behavior, reducing a great deal of uncertainty about the structure of everyday political life. Political parties are well suited to the demands of modern society, enabling politics to work on a grand scale, centralizing disparate interests and ambitions, and having the potential to impose discipline within their ranks.[5] Parties also "provide the electorate with a proper range of choice between alternative actions," facilitate the ability of voters to actually cast "rational" votes, allow for popular control over elected officials, and enable the peaceful and legitimate transfer of power.[6] A strong two-party system ensures that interest groups will not overpower the political system and cannot impose majority tyranny, as a single party might.[7] Unlike interest groups and wealthy individuals, parties as majority-seeking coalitions enable the many to overcome the otherwise superior resources of the few.[8] Meaningful competition between the two major parties is understood as critical to the American party system's health and vitality. So long as party competition exists, neither party can afford to ignore the political interests and aspirations of an organized interest group, and no such group should ever find itself facing a hostile and cohesive majority.[9] Goal-oriented parties that seek to win political office are constantly aware of the likelihood that the opposition party will appeal to susceptible groups in order to add to their numbers at the polls.[10]

Not surprisingly, then, party scholars consider the decline of parties a threat to American democracy. Concerned about the general decline of collective responsibility in national political institutions, Morris Fiorina declares that "the only way collective responsibility has ever existed, and can exist, given our institutions, is through the agency of the political party."[11] More generally, Gerald Pomper warns that "we must either acknowledge the mutual reliance of our parties and our democracy—or lose both."[12] John Aldrich sums up the position of American party scholars with the observation that, "as diverse as are the conclusions reached by these and other astute observers, all agree that the political party is—or should be—central to the American political system. Parties are—or should be—integral parts of all political life, from structuring the reasoning and choice of the electorate, through all facets of campaigns and seemingly all facets of the government, to the very possibility of effective governance in a democracy."[13]

THE SHARED ASSUMPTIONS OF TWO-PARTY SCHOLARSHIP

The scholarly conclusions about the U.S. two-party system are driven by several assumptions shared by American two-party scholars. First, party scholars assume the existence of a winner-take-all political prize via majority (or plurality) institutional decision rule. In plain language, majority rule means that a candidate or party that receives just more than 50 percent of the vote acquires 100 percent of the political prize; a second-place candidate or party with 49 percent of the vote acquires nothing. (Plurality rule means that the candidate or party with the most votes, even if it does not constitute a majority, is declared the winner.) Thus, although in the 2004 presidential election the Democratic presidential candidate, Senator John Kerry, received 48 percent of the popular vote and 47 percent of the Electoral College vote, he won nothing but a trip back to the U.S. Senate. By way of comparative contrast, a rule of proportional representation would mean that if one party received 52 percent of the vote and another party 48 percent of the vote, the first party would receive 52 percent, and the second party 48 percent, of the political prize. Voter preferences aggregated through the institutional mechanism of proportional representation generally lead to the rise of more than two parties, since a party can win far less than a majority or plurality of the vote and still gain significant influence within governing institutions. For instance, because even 2 percent of the popular vote wins seats in Israel's parliament, fifteen political parties are represented in the Knesset.

Second, party scholars assume that two-party candidates and parties are goal-oriented political actors seeking public office. This does not mean that the two major parties do not also want to make policy, simply that parties are composed of self-interested individuals who organize themselves into "teams" in order to seek elected office and, in the process, effectively organize electoral competition.[14] These office-seekers must use parties "because no collection of ambitious politicians has long been able to think of a way to achieve their goals in [American] democracy save in terms of political parties."[15]

Third, party scholars assume the existence of "uncertain voters," who by definition do not possess perfect or complete information on either party's policy positions, but instead are unsure where their own interests stand vis-à-vis the two major parties.[16] Politics can be a complicated business, concerned with countless issues, and voters are often unsure whether their policy preferences match up better with one party than another, or even what the issues are. For party differences to have an impact come Election Day, voters must be competent at relating party platforms to their own personal agendas. "Because uncertainty exists, voters need [informational] short cuts; so parties create them."[17] Most obviously and significantly, parties develop a "brand name" of partisan identification as a heuristic — an informational shortcut — by which voters can assess their political proximity to the respective parties. Given uncertain voters, party platforms move only incrementally over time, as parties remain relatively consistent in order to maintain the informational content of their brand name.

Finally, American two-party scholars typically assume a (roughly) normal distribution on a left-right ideological axis with a central conglomeration of voters clumped in the ideological middle.[18] This assumption is critical to the argument that the two-party system advances democratic values, a fact not lost on political theorist Anthony Downs, who writes: "It is clear that a basic determinant of how a nation's political life develops is the distribution of voters along the political scale.... [W]hether democracy can lead to stable government depends upon whether the mass of voters is centrally conglomerated, or lumped at the extremes with low density in the center; only in the former case will democracy really work."[19]

Rather than a single conglomeration of voters, imagine that the electorate is separated by one or more enduring internal cleavages. Relaxing the assumption of a normal distribution of voters is critical for Paul Frymer's argument that the two-party system structurally discriminates against African American political interests. He asserts that party scholars have largely ignored "the existence of a long-term, white-based majority interest in the United States."[20] Rather than a single conglomeration of voters, Frymer suggests a bimodal distribution that reflects an enduring racial cleavage between whites and blacks on racial issues. Because whites greatly outnumber blacks, and because politicians cannot win formal political power without the support of a majority of voters, party elites face systemic pressure to discount black political support—even when it is critical to political victory—leading to the "electoral capture" of blacks in one of the two major political parties, as both parties decline to reach out to them for fear of losing critical white swing voters. In the face of racial cleavage between whites and blacks, Frymer argues, party competition does not promote democratic inclusivity. Rather, the electoral incentive drives the two major parties to take up policy positions that account for this racial cleavage, with the effect of reducing African American party-based political power. In relaxing the assumption of a normal distribution, Frymer is able to argue that parties do not converge on the middle in search of the median voter so much as they converge on the median white voter.[21]

THE AMERICAN LIBERAL CONSENSUS

Taken together, the four shared assumptions outlined above lead conventional party scholarship to conclude that two-party competition typically leads party elites to move strategically toward the median voter in an effort to acquire a majority of the vote. Hence, the American two-party system translates into stable democracies as office-seeking parties take up positions in the middle to please voters, ensuring moderate party platforms that presumably translate into stability and moderation in governance. Because elections are decided by majority (or plurality) rule, political victory requires broad-based support from wherever and whomever it can be found; a competitive two-party system forces an office-seeking party to be remarkably hospitable to all interests and keeps party elites open to the involvement of groups previously uncommitted in politics.[22] In short, party scholars argue, the political and institutional dynamics of the two-party system inexorably lead self-interested individuals to pursue collectively beneficial goals.

In their effort to build an elegant, abstract model, American two-party theorists do not make any assumptions about the political values or other ideological positions of voters or parties. Presumably this is because even if the leading political values of the polity could be identified at a given moment, these values change over time, so a static understanding of dominant values would severely diminish the explanatory value of the two-party model as soon as the polity adopted different leading values.[23]

Notwithstanding the reluctance of American party theorists to incorporate ideology into their two-party models, it is clear that the ideological match between the content of a party platform and the broad ideological possibilities within an electorate clearly informs the chances of political success. Consider that socialist parties exist all over the world, including in the United States. But while socialist parties have had tremendous electoral success elsewhere and in many instances have become hegemonic, the political prospects of American socialists are perennially marginal at best. Indeed, two-party theorists can credibly claim that no party can openly tout socialist values and have a realistic chance to assume majority-based political power in the United States, because the lack of an ideological "fit" between socialist values and those of the American electorate prevents this outcome.

That socialism has not taken root in the United States as it has elsewhere suggests the existence of political values hostile to socialism in the United States that do not shift over time but endure as stable features of the political landscape. I am, of course, pointing to the obvious if often unstated reality that America is a liberal society—one that embraces the values of what Louis Hartz calls *genus liberalism*, manifested as individualism, the separation of public and private spheres, government by consent, and belief in the economic system of capitalism.[24] Liberal society demands "the unchallenged primacy of propertied individualism across the political spectrum ... [and] the independence of men, each from the other and from cultural, traditional, and communal attachments."[25] As a relentlessly individualistic ideology, "liberal democracy is suspicious of the demand to enlist politics in the preservation of separate group identities or the survival of subcultures that would otherwise not flourish through the free association of citizens," especially because societies deemed "illiberal" pose a severe threat to liberal identity.[26] Notwithstanding the emphasis on individualism, the assumption that liberal nation-states like the United States are essentially bounded, closed political communities is fundamental to liberal theorists ranging from John Locke to John Stuart Mill to John Rawls.[27] In short, liberalism as the hegemonic political ideology of the United States entails a fundamental attachment to American political institutions along with a concomitant antipathy toward foreign governments, societies, and communities deemed illiberal.[28]

This liberal ideological consensus does not exist in a single dimension or policy arena, but rather across countless dimensions or policy issues that may emerge at any given moment, yet it remains bounded within and by American society.[29] While the issues will vary and different aspects of liberal ideology will be highlighted more or less at specific historical moments, liberalism includes a set of enduring features and basic values shared by the vast majority of Americans, whether they call themselves—or are labeled—liberals, progressives, conservatives, neoconservatives, or libertarians. Liberal values in fact bind American society together and make it possible for two-party theorists to assume a normal distribution, with a centrally conglomerated mass of voters sharing a broad ideological consensus.[30]

It is tempting to see *genus liberalism* as the cause of the failure to build a viable socialist party in the United States. As a stable feature of the political environment, however, the American liberal consensus by definition cannot be a causal variable in any model that purports to explain the political behavior of parties. Something that is constant cannot causally induce anything—for an outcome to change, the inputs to that outcome must change as well. By way of example, some scholars have argued that the American welfare state is underdeveloped compared to European states because of the unusual strength and persistence of American liberal values. In this view, ideological conditions facilitate or delay action by a nation-state to promote social welfare policy and affect the content of that policy.[31] But this is not so much an argument as an account. It fails to explain how American welfare policy comes to exist at all, given liberal values, and it has little to say about why, for instance, social security was bifurcated from the rest of American welfare policy in the 1930s. Thus, although understanding American liberalism might be fundamental to understanding the ideological boundaries of American welfare policy, it cannot be understood as a causal variable that drives that policy.[32]

By way of comparison, consider the ideological diversity that exists in Great Britain, France, Italy, and Spain. Great Britain, where the Labour and Conservative Parties dominate the party system, still manages to have a competitive socialist agenda. France's socialist party continues either to hold power or to constitute a legitimate opposition. Spain saw its socialist party rise to power in 2004. And the Italian public regularly sends not only socialists but also communists, not to mention the inheritors of Benito Mussolini's fascist legacy, to its national legislature. In all four of these countries, it is entirely conceivable that the voting public will decide to significantly empower an illiberal party that could not possibly hope to compete in the United States because the dominance of liberal ideology of the American voting public effectively circumscribes what is politically possible.

Indeed, what Hartz calls a people's political tradition and what Alexis de Tocqueville terms a social state does not explain variation of outcomes in American politics so much as it explains continuity. Containing patterns that remain stable for very long periods, the ideological consensus around liberal values has been very effective in limiting American political development, precisely because "ideas and behavior, words and deeds have mutually constrained each other."[33] As an ideological force, American liberalism circumscribes what is politically possible in the United States, acting as a "boundary condition" that precludes illiberal politics and effectively reproduces the liberal status quo.[34] Applied to the two-party system, the hegemonic dominance of liberal ideology means that office-seeking parties operate within a particular ideological context that ensures that illiberal options and those constructed and represented as such are foreclosed to them. Unless forced to behave otherwise, parties do not choose to defend American liberal tenets in lieu of illiberal tenets as if the American liberal tradition is an independent variable—they simply assume, as party scholars do, that an ideological consensus exists around American liberalism, and then they make choices about options within the American liberal consensus. Note that while office-seeking parties have little choice but to adopt liberal positions, this hardly means that they do not make strategic choices within the American liberal consensus. Rather, within the ideological boundaries of liberalism there remains an enormous range of issues and policy differences that might be prominent at any given moment in two-party competition. That parties gain and lose ground over exclusively liberal terrain means that party competition does not threaten liberal hegemony. Indeed, the exact opposite is true—within the two-party system liberal hegemony begets liberal hegemony, as majority-seeking parties draw upon and appeal to existing liberal values in the polity, effectively reproducing those values in popular discourse and institutionalizing them in laws and political practices.

The winner-take-all institutional rule is fundamental in generating words and deeds that reproduce liberal hegemony in America. Because a leading party must fashion a majority coalition drawn from diverse yet inevitably liberal interests, it must simultaneously draw upon and reproduce liberal ideology in order to acquire majority support. Imagine, on the other hand, that political prizes were doled out by proportional representation rather than winner-take-all—to return to a previous example, a socialist (illiberal) party would be in a stronger position to counter liberal hegemony because there would be a political payoff if even a small minority of voters supported the socialist party. Moreover, if a socialist party had any kind of significant formal representation, speaking from the corridors of formal political power would put the party in a stronger position to challenge liberal hegemony because it would help to "legitimize" the party, enhance access to the electorate, and provide the opportunity to institute socialist values within and through formal legislation and political practices.

To be sure, liberalism has no shortage of variants and critics, yet among liberal theorists there is near-universal agreement about the basic values that mark liberalism's hegemony in American politics. Consequently, so long as two-party scholars are talking about the United States, *it is possible to incorporate the ideological consensus around liberalism in American society into theoretical models of the two-party system without losing any explanatory value*. Indeed, what was heretofore implied can now be made explicit—American two-party scholars who assume a normal distribution of voters are assuming the boundary condition of the American liberal consensus. Consequently, any office-seeking party will ideologically conform to American liberal values, identified as individualism, government by consent, separate public and private spheres, the economic system of capitalism, and attachment to American political institutions, along with a concomitant antipathy toward governments and societies deemed not liberal.

AMBIGUOUS, UNEQUIVOCAL, AND EXTREME POLICY POSITIONS AND THEIR RELATIONSHIP TO VOTER UNCERTAINTY

Two-party competition, then, given a winner-take-all political prize, places systemic pressure on parties to take up moderate positions. Party scholars have expanded on this by noting that party competition, given the assumption that there are uncertain voters, also leads both parties to cultivate ambiguity in their policy positions.

> This is because, as V. O. Key puts it, "the only way in which a party can form a majority is to draw further support from voters of all classes and interests ... party leaders cannot afford to antagonize any major segment of the population. A convenient way to antagonize an element is to take at an inopportune moment an unequivocal stand on an issue of importance. Similarities of composition, hence, contribute to two features of American parties: their similarity of view and their addiction to equivocation and ambiguity."[35]

Paradoxically, then, the presence of uncertain voters simultaneously promotes the development of a consistent party brand name and disinclines office-seeking parties to take an unequivocal stand on "an issue of importance" for a particular group, since this would potentially antagonize some of the group's members. Even when a politically unpopular interest group supports a party, parties typically do not find it necessary or rational to reject this political support without provocation or strategic reason. To be sure, parties typically do not publicly embrace unpopular interests, but this hardly means that when such an interest offers its political support, parties simply reject it out of hand. Rather, when both parties find it rational to be ambiguous about their policy positions and associations, "neither is forced by the other's clarity to take a more precise stand."[36] Instead, "political rationality leads parties in a two-party system to becloud their policies in a fog of ambiguity."[37]

A majority-seeking party's association with an unpopular or "extreme" interest group, however, does carry political risks. Given parties' deliberate ambiguity on certain issues, party support for extremist positions "may be the only way [for undecided voters] to tell the two parties apart ideologically, since most of their policies are conglomerated in an overlapping mass in the middle of the scale."[38] These "extremist" positions and "unequivocal" stands serve the same function—both reduce uncertainty in the electorate. Learning may occur both among the uncertain voters in the "extreme" interest group and among all voters.

Because a party's association with "extreme" groups often reduces voter uncertainty, both parties, not surprisingly, attempt to portray the opposition as beholden to unpopular "special interests" or groups on the political fringes. However, posing hypotheses for modeling strategic party behavior vis-à-vis "unpopular" or "extreme" interest groups raises the question whether a group qualifies as such. Because a particular interest may be quite popular at one time and quite unpopular at another, posing and then testing a hypothesis about the group's ability to negotiate the two-party system is pointless. Once a group's popularity shifts, previous conclusions about the group and its relationship to the two-party system are unfounded, and party scholars run into the difficulty identified earlier—of including specific issues, ideological content, or substantive preferences in models of two-party competition, given that issues, content, and preferences change over time.

However, once it is clear that the assumption of a normal distribution in two-party models is actually an assumption about an enduring and stable American liberal consensus, it is possible to model the reduction of voter uncertainty vis-à-vis interest groups positioned *outside* the liberal consensus. *Ceteris paribus*, voters within the American liberal consensus who know nothing about the two parties except that one is associated with illiberal values will decide that their ideological distance from that party is greater than their ideological distance from the other party. Consequently, no majority-seeking party appealing to a liberal electorate can afford to be publicly associated with a politically interest constructed as illiberal.

While parties have a strategic rationale for being ambiguous about their own positions, they also recognize the political benefits that can accrue from tying the other party's image to an interest or community popularly constructed as illiberal. This can greatly reduce voter uncertainty about the voter's ideological distance from the opposing party yet maintain ambiguity about one's own party's position. Given the pervasiveness of liberal ideology in American society and the need to develop a majority coalition to achieve political victory, parties have a strong incentive to associate the other party brand name with interests perceived to be a threat to liberal society. An office-seeking party must be wary of being closely associated with an illiberal interest group, since this association will invariably damage the party's prospects for victory. If one party succeeds in associating the other with an illiberal interest, party competition demands that the second party's elites must become publicly hostile to the illiberal minority, in a strategic effort to distance their party image from the illiberal minority image. The tenor and ferociousness of this hostility will probably depend on the degree of association between the party and the illiberal interest, as well as the perceived strength of the illiberal threat; the greater the association and the greater the threat, the more the party must actively and publicly direct hostility toward the illiberal interest if it wants to remain competitive within the two-party framework.

Because the two parties have a strategic incentive to link each other to illiberal minorities, a group perceived as illiberal seeking empowerment within the party system works under a constant threat of attack. Indeed, the more visible the role of the minority group within a party, the greater the likelihood that opposition party leaders will engage in a partisan attack. This in turn will systemically lead the illiberal interest group's own party to turn on the interest—rather than integrate the interest into the two-party system, party competition will subject the isolated minority to the attacks of a hostile bipartisan majority.

THE ILLIBERAL REPRESENTATION
OF ASIAN AMERICANS

Asian Americans are hardly illiberal ideological outliers from the American liberal consensus, nor, by any empirical measure, can they be considered extremists in the contemporary political environment. As a diverse racial formation with policy positions and political attitudes that fall predominantly within the American liberal consensus, Asian Americans should "fit" within the models of two-party systems posited by scholars of American politics.[39] Properly organized, Asian American political interests ought to find themselves in a tenable position to engage in the give-and-take of party coalition building. And so long as party elites engage Asian Americans politically in the multiple ways in which they see themselves and in a manner reflecting how Asian Americans actually participate in politics, there is simply no reason why both parties should become publicly hostile toward Asian American political interests.

The problem, of course, is that Asian Americans historically have not been perceived in accordance with either their political attitudes or their actions. Rather, Asians' lack of control over how they are popularly represented in the United States has been and continues to be a major sociopolitical challenge for Asian American communities. The inability of Asian Americans to exert enduring influence over racial discourse around Asian bodies in popular culture has particularly problematic consequences for Asian American efforts at mainstream political empowerment. As Lisa Lowe notes, "[i]n the last century and a half, the American *citizen* has been defined against the Asian *immigrant*, legally, economically, and culturally."[40] While racial representations of Asians in the United States have ranged from—at least—the pollutant, the coolie, the deviant, the yellow (or red or brown) peril, the model minority, and the gook, all of these representations, which "portray the Oriental as an alien body and a threat to the national family," position the Asian in America outside the liberal—and thus the normal and legitimate—polity.[41]

A rich historical and theoretical literature has developed around the racialization of Asian Americans either as perpetually foreign or as possibly assimilated yet never quite commensurate with the American citizen. Scholars who examine the formal-legal categorization of bodies from Asia living in the United States have demonstrated that they are represented and reproduced in the discourse of law and bureaucratic administration as racial minorities.[42] Moreover, Asian bodies in the United States are racialized as possessing deep and unchanging attachments to the communities and cultures of their countries of origin and consequently "become" perpetual foreigners in America.[43]

The availability of survey data on Asian Americans has led to a growing body of empirical research delineating the verifiably obvious diversity of Asian American communities along axes including but not limited to nation, ethnicity, language, socioeconomic class, partisanship, policy positions, and religion.[44] Despite the reality of Asian American heterogeneity, scholars have also increasingly documented the pervasiveness and continuity of cultural discourse that racially homogenizes Asian bodies as perpetual alien foreigners with national and cultural allegiances lying outside the United States.[45] Studies of visual media images have shown that Asians in the United States, when they are represented at all, are consistently portrayed as foreigners.[46] Racialized representations of Asians as perpetual foreigners are also quite prevalent in print media.[47] An illustrative investigation of whether and how newspaper coverage links international conflicts between the United States and Asian countries with Asian Americans arrived at the following conclusions:

> [I]n its agenda-setting function, the press focuses public attention selectively on international issues relevant to domestic concerns, and that this adds to and stirs the reservoir of images of Asians available to Americans in their relations with Asian Americans—identified by their Asian country origins and generalized as a racial minority group....
>
> The newspaper portrayal of Asian Americans disproportionately in their racial-minority status was unexpectedly strong. They are frequently depicted as resented outsiders—foreign newcomers—competing for employment, business opportunities, and political power, and as victims of this resentment in racial violence.[48]

Scholars who study the racialization of Asian Americans make clear that a constant flow of alien foreigner images exists for public consumption, and that this racial discourse around Asian bodies has endured for decades. Even as Asian Americans have made credible gains in overturning racist immigration laws and in acquiring formal-legal citizenship, these gains have not stemmed the enduring popular image of them as perpetual alien foreigners.[49] Asian Americans continue to face the unappealing prospect of what Neil Gotanda has characterized as "citizenship nullification," whereby their official status as "full" American citizens is denied in American culture and their bodies become contested sites in the popular racial imagination.[50] Citizenship nullification has ranged across national ethnic groups and over time, from the forcible revocation of American citizenship of immigrants from India after the infamous case of *United States v. Bhagat Singh Thind*, to the imprisonment of U.S.-born Japanese American citizens in concentration camps during World War II, to racially motivated hate crimes against Asian Americans today.[51]

Acknowledging that Asian bodies have been popularly racialized as perpetual alien foreigners in the United States does not deductively lead to the conclusion that the average American voter is irrationally prejudiced against Asians or Asian Americans. Nor does an empirical demonstration of anti-Asian attitudes demonstrate that these attitudes will necessarily be politically relevant or translate into anti-Asian American policy positions. In any case, it is quite difficult to make the causal connections between racist representations of Asian Americans and the actual attitudes and behavior of voters, given the dearth of targeted survey data on voter attitudes toward Asian Americans.[52] While scholarly investigation of the existence and degree of anti-black prejudice in the electorate has become an academic industry in survey-based research, the lack of data on Asian Americans means that very few studies exist that even attempt to link the barrage of negative images of Asian Americans to the actual attitudes and policy positions of the electorate. However, an inquiry into the existence and depth of prejudice against Asian Americans does not need to be made in order to show that racial discourse around Asian bodies matters in strategic two-party politics. This is not to suggest that irrational anti-Asian animus has disappeared in modern American society but rather to suggest that, for purposes of understanding party strategies, voter opinions about Asian Americans matter less than whether goal-oriented, rational party elites believe that Asian Americans are popularly understood or depicted as irreducibly alien foreigners. Acknowledging this racial discourse allows us to investigate whether, how, and under what conditions goal-oriented strategic party elites will—and must—incorporate the presence of racialized Asian bodies in their political strategies, and what this means for the strategic position of Asian Americans in two-party politics.

The political importance of racial discourse around Asian bodies not only trumps the relevance of anti-Asian attitudinal prejudice—it also trumps the very real Asian American individuals and organizations that have been endeavoring for years to empower Asian American political interests.[53] Whereas the racial discourse of Asians as perpetual alien foreigners is ubiquitous in the United States, it is highly doubtful that any politically meaningful portion of the national electorate could recall from memory even a single Asian American political leader or interest group.[54] This lack of public awareness means that party strategies cannot possibly incorporate voter perceptions of specific individuals and organizations; little meaningful information is available to an uncertain voter who sees either major party take a stand on those organizations or individuals. To illustrate by contrast, consider the tactics involved when party elites negotiate their party's image vis-à-vis African Americans. When the National Association for the Advancement of Colored People (NAACP) or the Reverend Jesse Jackson are invoked, party elites consistently behave as if images of the NAACP or Jackson are meaningful to voters, as they quite probably are, given their historical prominence and popular coverage in mass commercial media.[55] Consequently, when parties publicly interact with individuals and organizations well known "inside the beltway" of Washington, D.C., as political advocates of Asian American interests, what matters is not that the organization in question is the Japanese American Citizens League and not the Organization of Chinese Americans, or interest group leader Christine Chen and not Rodney Salinas—what matters is that their bodies perform as Asian in America.

Party elite recognition that voters are far more aware of racialized Asian bodies than they are of organized Asian American political activity means that when a party publicly engages this formation, its strategy will necessarily incorporate the racial representations of Asian Americans rather than the heterogeneity and competing claims that come from multiple Asian ethnic communities and Asian American leaders or organizations. As party elites incorporate the racialized representation of the illiberal Asian in America into their strategic decision making, it becomes clear that the parties are less concerned with the response of Asian Americans than they are with that of the broader liberal electorate.

Recall that voter learning can occur when a party takes a stand on a specific political interest. Party scholars typically privilege the learning that happens within the interest group in question as a means of concluding that parties cannot afford to alienate any potentially important group, since the interest group would be likely to move to the other party coalition; two-party competition thus ensures that no political interest will become an isolated minority that must endure bipartisan hostility. However, in this situation parties are not concerned with the learning that happens within the Asian American formation but with what non-Asian American voters are learning about each party's image as it becomes associated with a racialized representation of Asians. Because their target audience is not Asian Americans but the rest of the electorate, whether or not party elites recognize that Asian Americans are quite diverse will be irrelevant. Party elites will treat Asian Americans as homogeneous on the basis of their assessment of what the electorate "knows" about Asian bodies—their enduring loyalty to Asian political and economic institutions and their immutable adherence to un-American cultural values.

STRATEGIC PARTY ELITE BEHAVIOR AND RACIALIZED ASIAN BODIES WITHIN THE TWO-PARTY SYSTEM

Most of the time, Asian Americans do not make the news. Most of the time, political parties do not plot how to publicly distance themselves from racialized Asian American bodies. And most of the time, Asian Americans do not walk around wondering if non-Asian Americans think of them as "real" Americans. The challenges to their claims to American citizenship notwithstanding, Asian Americans can still vote, donate campaign funds, run for office, and contribute to American society. All of this is to acknowledge that while each individual may be inserted into a racialized world, the fact that the racial representation of Asians as perpetual foreigners has endured for more than 150 years does not mean that this illiberal racialization is all-powerful in lived experience. To be sure, the racialization of Asians as irredeemably foreign is not going away, but its impact is not deterministic. Rather, Asian American racialization has been and continues to be fluid and negotiated, as are the concept of race and racial categories themselves.

While the racialization of the Asian body in the United States has always proceeded along lines suggesting Asians' essentialized illiberal quality, the specificities of Asian American racialization have changed at different historical junctures, depending on the material situation at hand. When Chinese migrant labor became a threat to white male working-class entitlement and a weapon of the propertied class, the almost entirely male population of

Chinese in America were racialized as "coolies" who were "unfit for white work and white wives." The racial myth of the Asian American as the model minority emerged in the 1960s as a means of countering black demands emerging from the civil rights and black power movements. Constructed in opposition to unflattering cultural representations of blacks, Asian American communities suddenly found themselves being racially triangulated by whites who valorized them as possessing what amounted to essentialized "racio-cultural" values that predisposed Asian Americans to hard work, political silence, respect for authority, focus on the family, morality, and self-sufficiency.[56]

When neoconservative forces sought to undermine popular support for affirmative action policies in higher education, they discursively positioned Asian Americans as a model minority in contrast to "demanding" and "undeserving" blacks and Latinos. At the same time, neoliberals who favored affirmative action policies deployed Asian American "success stories" to prove that these policies worked, positioning Asian Americans as a benchmark for where other communities of color would be once they too had benefited from affirmative action.[57] In the 1980s, the economic dominance of Japan led to anti-Japanese depictions of a new "yellow peril," but since the 1990s the rapid rise of China in the global economy has raised fears of an anti-Chinese "red peril," "red" connoting communist China. In the post-9/11 era, the intense racialization of bodies seen to perform as Arab and/or Muslim is suggestive of a "brown peril."[58]

Racial discourse, then, does not emerge in a vacuum but out of the ideological needs of a concrete historical moment. Context matters. And looking exclusively at the institutional context facing Asian Americans seeking political empowerment, it is not hard to see why they might initially be drawn to the apparent promise of a two-party system in which their participation, under the logic of the system, ought to be valued. As a still untapped but increasingly ambitious political interest, Asian Americans would seem well suited to party politics, given their potential as an important swing vote in key states and their ability to donate meaningful amounts of campaign funds to national parties and candidates. Because Asian American political attitudes and policy positions generally fall well within the boundaries of the American liberal consensus, parties should not find it necessary to significantly alter their overall views or adopt new policy positions to appeal to Asian Americans who are not extremists by any measure.

Moreover, a disproportionate percentage of Asian Americans see themselves as independents or nonpartisans, and are generally found to be less consistent in policy positions and political attitudes than other Americans.[59] As a would-be party coalition bloc that remains "up for grabs," Asian Americans thus do not face a key problem that African Americans encounter in their efforts to use the two-party system to advance their political agenda. As a demographic that votes heavily Democratic, black Americans are often seen as among the most progressive voters in the United States, and as internally consistent on both policy positions and the priorities of the African American political agenda.[60] Scholars of African American involvement in two-party politics have argued that African Americans have been ill served by their overwhelming allegiance to one political party, and that this has been a factor in their failure to receive political benefits proportionate to their contributions.[61] The poor harvests that they reap in spite of their often decisive part in Democratic electoral victories has led some to suggest that African Americans would be better off organizing a third party, nominating a hopeless third-party presidential candidate, and generally attempting to position themselves as a "balance-of-power" player between the two parties.[62]

Indeed, if Asian Americans could be read as just another interest group, then they might expect as much of a welcome as any other interest group that provides resources for a party's success. After all, majority-seeking parties do not typically seek to alienate a potentially resource-rich and increasingly ambitious political interest for no good reason; both parties, acting rationally, would solicit and accept resources from Asian Americans, even as both kept their positions rationally somewhat ambiguous. An organized Asian American political interest that can deliver money and votes in key elections could make the difference, so the argument goes, between victory and defeat at the polls.

I contend, however, that Asian Americans are not just another interest group, nor can their bodies simply be interchanged in the analysis with other racialized bodies. Rather than simply measure the traditional markers of interest group influence, such as campaign contributions, votes, geographic concentration, partisanship, and so forth, scholars assessing the party prospects of Asian Americans must incorporate the historically and substantively specific ways in which Asian bodies in the United States have been racialized. Politically ambitious Asian Americans cannot stop at calculating when and where how much money and how many votes can be proffered to garner political influence within the party coalition. They must also anticipate how major party elites will incorporate into their party-building strategies the presence of racialized Asian bodies interacting with the two-party system. Asian Americans cannot rely on what the political environment looks like before their participation, but must assess what it will look like once their racialized bodies become active and visible within either or both of the major parties. While a reservoir of racial representations of Asian Americans as foreign agents is available for discursive deployment, in the absence of any direct, visible interaction with a major party, it is not obvious how reproducing this discourse would benefit a political party. While the historically enduring representation of Asian Americans as foreign and beholden to foreign interests can become a meaningful heuristic to uncertain voters, and thus a useful tool by which strategic elites can communicate information, it cannot be deployed in a vacuum but must be linked to concrete events in order to become politically relevant. In short, racial representations have to be connected to the decision making of party elites. In the absence of Asian American political involvement—in the absence of racialized bodies within party coalitions—no such political connection between bodies and parties can be exploited.

Visible Asian American participation within a major party coalition, on the other hand, provides a political opening for opponents to racialize a party brand name as associated with, and perhaps even beholden to, the illiberal and un-American interests that Asian bodies are purported to represent. And once racial discourse around Asian bodies turns toward the reproduction of such racialized representations, parties are no longer dealing with a typical interest group that can be assimilated into the two-party system.

Moreover, there are a number of reasons to believe that participation in the party system will help to reproduce and reinforce the racialization of Asian bodies as illiberal strangers. Recall that when party elites communicate information to the electorate vis-à-vis the party's relationship to Asian Americans, they deploy long-standing racializations of Asians in America. This means that when national party elites become publicly hostile toward Asian Americans in an effort to protect their party brand name, they will treat Asian Americans as if they are homogeneously illiberal because this is the most effective way to counteract voter concerns. And no strategic party elite in its right mind would, in an effort to dispute the connections between the party and Asian Americans, trot out Asian American party representatives to "educate" the populace as to why Asians are not homogenous, illiberal aliens. Given the fear that this would only reinforce the connection between the party and Asians, it is far more likely that if one party uses the other party's connections to Asian Americans against it, the other party's leaders will in turn become publicly hostile to Asian Americans in a strategic effort to distance themselves. Given both parties' willingness to traffic in racist, homogenizing discourses around Asian bodies, Asian American efforts to distance themselves from such racist constructions may also, ironically, end up reinforcing a bipolar racist discourse of "good" versus "bad" Asians.

Advocates of an assimilationist model of American society may object that the position of Asian Americans in the two-party system will change as Asian Americans become more fully integrated in the United States. As anti-Asian prejudice declines or is eradicated altogether, so the argument goes, Asian Americans will be able to negotiate the two-party system in ways similar to, say, Irish immigrants who initially faced intense anti-Irish sentiment but were able to maneuver through the two-party system in order to achieve political incorporation.[63] According to this assimilationist model, Asian Americans need only behave as "good Americans" and participate in American politics through legal and transparent avenues.

This assimilationist approach ignores the fact that, unlike the Irish and other immigrant populations that successfully "became white," Asian American political participation does not obviously lead to diminishing challenges to their claims of citizenship or membership in the polity.[64] Rather, political activity by Asian Americans is often read as consistent with, and evidence of, political corruption and immutable disloyalty to the United States.[65] Asian American participation in the two-party system not only fails to assist Asian Americans in the assimilationist project, it actually generates systemic incentives for party elites to reinforce and reproduce the very racialization of Asian Americans as perpetual alien foreigners that makes negotiating the two-party system so problematic for them in the first place. Asian American participation in the two-party system has an inevitable impact on the racial dynamics operating within this system, and in a manner that reflects how their bodies have been racialized. Racial discourse is both influenced by and consequently influences the political dynamics within stable institutional settings where systemic incentives exist for strategic party elites that motivate particular behaviors.

The assimilationist approach also fails to take into account how racialization proceeds vis-à-vis the construction of other racial bodies. Recall Lowe's assertion that the discourse of American citizenship is built in dialectical opposition to the construction of the Asian immigrant, whereby the popular understanding of who rightfully belongs within the polity depends on agreement about who does not, and can never, belong.[66] Recall also that party scholars inevitably assume liberal hegemony in the electorate in order to conclude that two-party competition for a winner-take-all political prize is a powerful democratizing force for integrating previously powerless racial and ethnic minorities into American society. This means that insofar as American citizenship is discursively embodied by the liberal political values that bind the polity together, the democratic inclusivity of the two-party system ironically relies upon the systematic political and cultural exclusion of Asians. Note that it is precisely this ideological consensus—built on the backs of Asian Americans—that works against Asian Americans, who must deal with historical representations of Asians as perpetual foreigners with illiberal attachments. The racialization of Asian bodies in the United States as a threat to liberal society thus plays a key role in understanding why Asian American party-based efforts are predisposed to end in failure.

Theorists who focus on culture might argue at this point that unless Asian Americans can influence their discursive representations as foreign, they will not be able to use the party system—or any other political avenue— as a means of achieving political empowerment. According to this argument, the degree to which Asian Americans can successfully inoculate themselves against charges of being un-American is likely to determine whether they can use parties effectively to advance their political agendas. From here it is but a small step to acknowledging the possible strategic deployment of the "model minority" myth in attempts to acquire mainstream political power. That the construction of Asian Americans as a model minority places them in a contingent racial position of favor vis-à-vis blacks suggests that the present and future of Asian American political empowerment includes the problematic question whether some Asian Americans will attempt to acquire political power at the expense of blacks, just as Irish, Italian, and other ethnic immigrants did before them in an effort to become white. It is conceivable that a conscious political strategy of implicitly presenting themselves as "anti-blacks" will enable Asian Americans to create political openings that depend upon the systematic political and cultural exclusion of African Americans from the body politic.

This possibility that Asian Americans can acquire political power by engaging in what amounts to white supremacist practices notwithstanding, it remains true that the racial representation of Asians as perpetual foreigners is about as likely to disappear as the institutional rules and political dynamics that govern two-party competition are. Consequently, Asian American party prospects at the national level remain quite dim. However, shifting discourse is not the only political game on the block, and the fact that Asian Americans face systemic obstacles generated by the formal logic of the two-party system, rather than simple anti-Asian prejudice, does not mean that they cannot effectively acquire political influence within American political institutions as a whole. It simply means that this particular national institutional setting is unfavorable to their political prospects, given the dominant tenor of their racialization as perpetual foreigners. Just as party elites take into account both institutional settings and racial discourse in situating themselves vis-à-vis Asian Americans, Asian Americans seeking political empowerment must do the same.

3

THE NATIONAL PARTIES, ASIAN AMERICANS, AND THE CAMPAIGN FINANCE CONTROVERSY

I N MAY 1996 THE SECOND ANNUAL fund-raising gala of the Congressional Asian Pacific American Caucus Institute (CAPACI) drew more than twelve hundred donors from around the country to Washington, D.C.[1] Keynote speaker President William Jefferson Clinton, who had also attended the previous year, extolled the important contributions that Asian Americans and Pacific Islanders had made to the United States, drawing some thirty-three rounds of enthusiastic applause. The bipartisan institute had also invited the likely Republican nominee, retired senator Robert Dole, who ultimately sent a letter of greeting in his stead with warm words for the contributions of the institute and Asian Pacific Americans more generally. The next day CAPACI donors listened behind closed doors as high-ranking Democratic National Committee (DNC) and Republican National Committee (RNC) party elites detailed to them their respective parties' strategy for winning the presidency, each emphasizing the key role that Asian Americans could play. Large donors were also rewarded with an exclusive White House briefing with Vice President Al Gore.

In 1996, the fact that both major parties at the highest level were actively seeking Asian American money and votes no doubt confirmed for many in the audience that Asian Americans were on the cusp of attaining real political power. Members of the audience were reminded that the Asian American population was growing at a remarkable rate, and that most of the growth was occurring in key Electoral College vote-rich states. The number of Asian American elected and appointed politicians had grown exponentially over the past two decades, and high-ranking Asian Americans were ubiquitous at what had become a key networking event for the Asian American political establishment. Many in the audience were also involved in what would ultimately become the single most successful national campaign ever mounted to get out the Asian American vote. The fund-raiser's events led *AsianWeek*, an important Asian American weekly journal, to announce, "it is clear that Asian Americans have begun their ascent onto the stage of national politics. As a political group, Asian Americans have arrived at a crucial moment in defining their role in public life."[2]

One year later, CAPACI held its third annual fund-raising gala. Down from more than twelve hundred the previous year, the 850 donors at the institute's May 1997 event neither applauded Bill Clinton nor received a briefing from Al Gore, both of whom were conspicuously absent. In fact, they did not see a single White House representative, leading CAPACI's executive director, Francey Lim Youngberg, to comment, "We were very disappointed that he wasn't able to send a cabinet-level person to come to our dinner and represent the administration. Especially this year when so many people are feeling like political pariahs, it would've been good."[3]

Asian Americans had indeed arrived at a crucial moment in their national political life, but their arrival did not happen as they had imagined it would. Rather, their watershed moment turned into a highly publicized train wreck that left politically engaged Asian Americans battered and bruised by the actions of both major parties. Prior to Election Day, the Republican Party alleged that the Democrats had accepted illegal campaign donations originating in Asia, attributing them to the Indonesia-based Lippo Group business conglomerate, headed by U.S. legal permanent resident James Riady, and various branches of the Hsi Lai Buddhist Temple.[4] The resulting campaign finance controversy led to what community leader and UC—Berkeley professor Ling-chi Wang called the single greatest setback to civil rights for Asian Americans in more than 150 years and without question the single most important national event influencing the political fortunes of Asian Americans in the post—World War II era.[5] During the controversy, a virtual *Who's Who* of Asian American politicians were investigated for alleged connections to illegal Asian money. The highest-ranking Asian American elected executive Democrat, Washington governor Gary Locke, and the highest-ranking Asian American elected executive Republican, California treasurer Matt Fong, were both subjected to attacks by their partisan opponents and to media scrutiny for alleged fund-raising improprieties.[6] Chang-lin Tien, a leading candidate for secretary of energy in Clinton's second administration, leading Asian American Democrat Michael Woo, and leading Asian American Democratic activist Maeley Tom also came under the media microscope for alleged fund-raising-related improprieties.[7]

The images of several leading Asian American political organizations were hurt as well. For example, the Clinton Justice Department subpoenaed the fund-raising records of the Organization of Chinese Americans (OCA), creating a cloud over a leading Asian American political advocacy group.[8] As for CAPACI, the organization that had held its second annual gala with so much promise less than six months before the November election, it was publicly criticized for having accepted funds from Asian American individuals who were later investigated, and for having named one of them, Charlie Trie, to a finance committee that had never formed.[9] The institute immediately disassociated itself from Trie.

Why did a year filled with political promise for Asian Americans turn into such an unmitigated disaster? How did a year that began with national party elites—including the presidential candidates—courting Asian American money and votes end with both parties publicly attacking Asian American political elites? In this chapter I analyze the strategic behavior of the two major parties during the campaign finance controversy, arguing that both parties followed institutionally generated incentives inherent in the nature of two-party competition when they actively ostracized Asian Americans following the November 1996 election. Party elites understood that public perception of an influential political presence of Asian bodies in a party coalition had the potential to significantly alter the racial dynamics of two-party competition. Because no majority-seeking party can afford to become associated with Asian bodies racially constructed as immutably tied to powerful Asia-based governments and corporations, party competition drove both parties to incorporate into their strategies the active and enduring racialization of Asians in America as perpetually foreign, illiberal aliens.[10] In attempting to signify to the liberal electorate that Asian entities and their agents in the United States controlled the Democratic Party, Republicans' exploitation of the campaign finance controversy necessarily drew upon and reproduced historically racist discourse that constructs Asians in America as fundamentally inassimilable aliens loyal to governments and cultures in Asia.

Because racialized Asian bodies posed a significant threat to party elites building and maintaining majority party dominance, it was out of the question for Democrats to defend Asian American political interests. Instead, the Democratic Party sought to demonstrate that Asian corporations and countries did not control it by publicly distancing itself from both Asians and Asian Americans and by arguing that Republicans were just as susceptible to Asian agents, thus perpetuating the very same racial discourse of Asian Americans as perpetual foreigners with alien allegiances. Asian Americans attempting to position themselves as key players in the two-party system thus found themselves in a politically untenable situation as a minority group facing a hostile and cohesive majority, with both parties rationally following institutionally generated incentives to marginalize them.

A BRIEF HISTORY OF ASIAN AMERICAN FUND-RAISING AND THE NATIONAL TWO-PARTY SYSTEM

Party elites have been reaching into the deep pockets of Asian American campaign donors for almost three decades, beginning with the 1976 election and peaking during the 1996 campaign.[11] Seeking to build a donor base in the Asian American community, the national Democratic Party began appealing in the 1970s to well-to-do Asian Americans by highlighting "anti-Asian discrimination as an issue that bridges the political and cultural divisions among immigrants from different parts of the Far East," and emphasizing the issue of immigration.[12] House Representative and DNC treasurer Robert Matsui (D-CA) recalled that during the Carter campaign, "there was one Asian at the Democratic National Committee who worked the [Asian American] community. In a few weeks, he had a million dollars."[13] At that time the party established a fund-raising arm known as the Asian/Pacific American (A/PA) Unit.[14] For the first time on record, a major party's presidential candidate, Democratic Party nominee Jimmy Carter, reached out to wealthy Asian Americans.[15]

The 1976 effort was followed in 1980 with $2.5 million in Asian American contributions to Carter's unsuccessful reelection campaign.[16] As wealthy elements of the Asian American political community demonstrated their financial clout in national political campaigns, along with the larger donations came greater political disappointment at their lack of political influence in party circles. Asian American frustration at failing to garner elite influence within the Democratic Party despite significant campaign contributions surfaced after the 1980 presidential campaign, resulting in the 1983 founding of the Asian Pacific Caucus (APC).[17] The caucus was considered by party elites to be the voice of Asian American Democrats, and Congressman Norman Mineta (D-CA) endorsed this party-based strategy as the "best vehicle to maximize [Asian Americans'] political role."[18] It became clear shortly after the 1984 election, however, that the APC would not be around long enough to play any significant role. Although evidence suggested that Asian American financial contributions to the Democratic Party in 1984 were second only to those of Jews among racial or ethnic groups, in 1985 party elites eliminated the APC, along with the gay and lesbian, liberal and progressive, and business and professional caucuses.[19] Following Democratic presidential candidate Walter Mondale's lopsided loss to Republican incumbent Ronald Reagan in the 1984 election, Democratic Party elites decided that the party's image was too closely linked to "special interests."[20] Newly elected Democratic Party chairman Paul Kirk commented that party interest groups' attitudes amounted to, "Got a cause, get a caucus. As a result, white male Americans say, 'Do we have to have a caucus to vote in the party?' Enough is enough."[21] On national television, Kirk called these caucuses "political nonsense" and promised to abolish them.[22] Rather than being the best vehicle for Asian American empowerment, the APC was implicated as one reason for Democratic defeat in 1984.[23]

Some Asian American Democratic Party activists inferred from the abolition of the APC that the party had made it clear that "[Asian American] concerns are meaningless, our vote is useless and our financial contributions are worthless."[24] Other Asian Americans joined a chorus of other racial groups in accusing the party of scapegoating minorities and of racism.[25] This did not, however, lead Asian Americans to get out of the party fund-raising game. Shortly after the APC was abolished, it was succeeded by the supposedly independent National Democratic Council of Asian and Pacific Americans (NDCAPA).[26] The NDCAPA's goal, according to co-chair and party activist Maeley Tom, was "to help mobilize, empower and unite an Asian Pacific Democratic constituency in order to impact a political process that has taken our dollars and votes for granted."[27] While the organization was advertised as the first-ever national independent organization of Asian American Democrats, an alternative explanation suggests that its founding allowed the Democratic Party to move organized Asian Americans outside the national party organization while maintaining the networks necessary to raise funds from this community. The NDCAPA's national convention in 1987 succeeded in bringing Democratic presidential candidates Jesse Jackson, Michael Dukakis, and Paul Simon (the only one who promised an Asian American cabinet member if elected) to make "splashy appearances, hoping to convince Asian Americans that their money, their votes, and their opinions are valued."[28]

The NDCAPA was not the only Asian American political organization launched between the 1984 and 1988 elections that brought funds into the party coffers. The Pacific Leadership Council (PLC) was founded in 1988 by Maria Hsia, a California Democrat who had been raising money in the Asian American community since the early 1980s for state and local races.[29] The objectives of the PLC were to raise funds and lobby for Asian American interests within the Democratic Party.[30] Hsia had initially come to the national Democrats seeking a way to channel more funds to California lieutenant governor Leo T. McCarthy's gubernatorial campaign, and she discovered that she could legally circumvent existing campaign finance laws, which restricted individual donations to a candidate, by having donors "tally" contributions to the Democratic Senatorial Campaign Committee (DSCC) for McCarthy's campaign.[31] The PLC acted as a fund-raising arm of the DSCC, pulling in close to $1.2 million from Asian Americans in 1988 to support Democratic candidates in the presidential and senatorial elections.[32]

In 1984 Republicans had resisted attempts by Asian American Republicans to create in the RNC an organization equivalent to the Asian Pacific

Caucus. Asian Americans were rebuffed by party chair Frank Fahrenkopf, who declared that such a caucus was "not necessary because we are all Americans."[33] Partly in response to the actions of both parties regarding Asian American party involvement, several prominent Chinese Americans created the bipartisan Interim Coordinating Committee for Chinese Americans (ICCCA). Its statement of purpose claimed that "Chinese Americans have made disproportionately large contributions of money ... yet, no Chinese American citizen has ever been appointed to any policy-making federal government position."[34] The ICCCA requested appointments in a number of specific policymaking positions in return for their votes and financial contributions.[35] The organization succeeded in getting all six major candidates to agree to their declaration and took credit for the appointment of John Tsu to the Bush transition team and a number of other appointments.[36]

In both the 1988 and 1992 presidential elections, Asian Pacific American contributions were estimated at more than $10 million, divided almost equally between Republican and Democratic candidates, and, as in 1984, were second only to those of American Jews in the amount of campaign money raised by an ethnic or racial group.[37] It is at best unclear whether Asian Americans and Pacific Islanders have accrued any meaningful benefits from their financial contributions to these national campaigns. William Wei has argued that "[f]inancial contributions have not gotten them greater attention to their needs and concerns or increased access to political decision making. Even when legislation or policy decisions that had special implications for Asian Americans were being formulated, their interests have often been ignored or overlooked."[38]

In the 1996 presidential election, Democratic Party officials decreed a $7 million contribution goal for Asian American campaign contributors.[39] John Huang and Hsia were two key party fund-raisers for the Asian American community, with Huang appointed as a DNC vice president of finance and Hsia active in the Democratic Party since the late 1980s as the co-founder of the PLC.[40] Huang emphasized a party strategy whereby Asian Americans would "bundle" their contributions through his DNC office.[41] Evidently Huang had indicated to DNC officials that an important title would enhance his credibility with potential Asian American donors and that this was necessary because he was older than most other fund-raisers.[42] Eventually Huang was instrumental in raising half of the estimated $10 million contributed to Democratic national party organizations by Asians and Asian Americans.

THE DEMOCRATIC NATIONAL COMMITTEE'S INTERNAL INVESTIGATION

After the 1996 election the DNC conducted its own internal investigation of alleged improprieties in its campaign fund-raising. The Democratic Party received approximately 2.7 million contributions from organizations and individuals in the election cycle between 1994 and 1996, and it examined more than twelve hundred of them.[43] The party's investigative efforts can be read as an instance in which strategic Democratic Party elites sought to contain a potentially damaging racialization of their party brand name in the face of Republican charges that the Democratic Party had been infiltrated by foreign agents representing Asian governments and corporations. Contradicting DNC co-chair Steven Grossman's claim that the party had engaged in a color-blind investigation that focused exclusively on campaign contributors who had been solicited by Huang, Asian Americans who had no relation to the Democratic Party fund-raiser and had never even heard of Huang reported being contacted by the DNC. The party investigation appears to have targeted individuals on the basis of whether their names contained racial signifiers suggestive of "foreign" identity, begging the questions of who decided what counted as "foreign" and what criteria were used.

It is rather fascinating to consider Democratic Party staff debating among themselves who could be safely categorized as a citizen and who needed to be investigated on the basis of the racial and national performance of their names. Names written originally in languages that do not use the Roman alphabet are often transliterated differently into English, resulting in the same name being given different spellings. Campaign donors whose names "performed" or "sounded" less "Asian" and perhaps more "American," such as "Young" rather than "Yung" or "Yang," were not selected for investigation. No doubt the "racial common sense" applied in selecting names was replaced by the "racial confusion" over surnames such as Lee, Park, and Young, all three of which are commonly held by Asian Americans and non-Asian Americans alike and thus potentially perform racially in multiple and contradictory ways.

That Democratic Party elites felt comfortable at all poring over their donor lists to search for "foreign" names indicates the unspoken confidence of party officials who assumed that they could generally identify who was and was not a suspect, and how this confidence is tied to popular cultural understandings of Asian bodies in America. Consider, for example, what would happen if Democratic Party elites suddenly charged that the Republican Party had been infiltrated by agents of France or Germany. It is ludicrous to think that Republican Party staff would go through their donor lists seeking out names like Cheney and Rumsfeld for further investigation, yet this is exactly what the Democrats did in attempting to separate out their Asian American donors. When we acknowledge the absurdity of looking for French and German names, it becomes clear that party elites implicitly imbue different bodies with different racial meanings and thus require different political calculations. Without even needing to articulate it, or perhaps even unconsciously, party elites operate quite clearly under the assumption that Asians in the United States are racially marked in popular culture as immutably disloyal.

Although the 1996 election left the DNC $13.4 million in debt as of mid-1997, the Democrats sought to return money to many donors with Asian surnames, and new donations by Asian Americans were not deposited immediately.[45] For instance, Noboru Isagawa gave the DNC $50,000, but in an unusual move the party held it for several months until it ascertained his citizenship as American.[46] The DNC voluntarily banned donations from legal permanent residents two months after the 1996 election, leading Matthew Finucane, executive director of the Asian Pacific American Labor Alliance, to declare that this DNC act and others like it "amounted to a giant sign on every campaign headquarters in the country saying, 'Immigrants not allowed.'"[47] The DNC never clarified how the ban was being implemented, a concern for Asian Americans who perceived that the implementation would follow guidelines similar to those of the internal investigation by focusing on "foreign-sounding" surnames. A year later the DNC lifted the ban.[48]

As of July 1997 approximately 172 of the 2.7 million contributions, representing .01 percent of the contributions received by the DNC, had been returned. The rejected contributions amounted to $2.83 million from ninety-three contributors, which came to approximately 1.3 percent of the money collected in the mid-1990s.[49] This does not mean that 172 contributions were illegal, simply that they were rejected by the DNC. In fact, former DNC finance director Richard Sullivan testified before the Senate Committee on Governmental Affairs that

> it's my sense that there are not very many that were returned that were deemed purely illegal. It's my sense that there were only two or three that were returned because they were illegal contributions. A number of those were returned because they were deemed to have insufficient information, and I truly believe that a great deal of those that were classified as ones without sufficient information was due to the fact—was due to the negative publicity surrounding the Asian American community. And I think that a number of those, of the 172, just chose not to respond to the audit that the DNC was conducting. I don't have a great opinion of the audit. I think it was a little intimidating. Therefore, a number of those were turned off by it.[50]

Donors who were investigated by the DNC were asked questions such as, "Is your income sufficient to afford this donation?" "What is your social security number?" "Would you sign a release for a credit check?" and "Are you an American citizen?"[51] If they declined to answer these questions, the DNC apparently threatened in some cases to release the contributor's name to the press as someone who was not cooperating with the investigation.[52] Many of the people investigated were no doubt aware of the existing racial discourse around Asian Americans as perpetual alien foreigners, and they must have suspected that the investigation into campaign improprieties would not have taken on the cast it did had it not involved individuals of Asian descent. In the face of a semipublic entity's attempting to decide their racial and national identity through potentially racist, xenophobic, and invasive questions, Asian Americans apparently responded in ways ranging from outrage to fear to indifference. More than a year later, fewer than thirty of the 172 contributions had been deemed illegal or improper.[53]

When faced with no discernible response or a blatant lack of cooperation from Asian American contributors, the DNC had simply returned their donations without ever ascertaining their legality.[54] That is, a national party organization $13.4 million in debt as of mid-1997 and gearing up its campaign apparatus for the next election cycle returned money to donors who might have been solicited again for more money, without knowing whether the funds were legally contributed or not, simply because it believed that the donors had Asian surnames. The Democratic Party's internal investigation appears to have been less concerned with whether campaign finance laws had been broken or with tending to their donor lists, at least when Asian Americans were involved, than with minimizing the political damage caused by Republican accusations that the Democratic Party had been shanghaied, as it were, by influential Asian money. Ironically, party elite concern over protecting the party brand name made it appear as though far more in illegal funds from Asians had been contributed than was the case.

Following the Democratic Party's lead, press accounts played fast and loose with the legal status of the $2.83 million in returned donations.[55] For instance, the *Washington Post* simply reported that the "DNC has returned about $3 million from 93 contributors, about 1.3 percent of the money collected in the mid-1990s. Most of the money returned was raised by Asian Americans," without commenting that most of these funds had not been determined to be illegal or improper.[56] Similarly, the *Los Angeles Times* reported that "the DNC has returned about $3 million in foreign-tainted contributions from the 1996 election," but did not acknowledge that much of the "foreign-tainted" funds were probably legal contributions from Asian Americans.[57] Press accounts also failed to point out that 79 percent of the money returned at that time had been raised by only three Asian American individuals—Huang, Johnny Chung, and Charlie Trie.[58] That the press did not present a more thorough account of the money returned by the Democratic Party is significant because it created the impression that far more illegal or inappropriate Asian money had been accepted by the Democratic Party than was the case.[59] Ironically, the large amounts of money returned by the Democratic Party were cited as evidence that it must have accepted illegal foreign funds from Asia and thus required an aggressive public investigation.[60]

HEARINGS BEFORE THE SENATE
GOVERNMENTAL AFFAIRS COMMITTEE

The Senate Governmental Affairs Committee began hearings on July 8, 1997, into whether illegal or improper activities had occurred in connection with the 1996 federal elections. Chairman Fred Thompson (R-TN) opened the hearings with the widely reported claim that his investigators had uncovered solid evidence of a "Chinese plan to subvert our election process" and to "buy access and influence in furtherance of Chinese Government interests." [61] Later in the day, Kansas Republican Senator Sam Brownback's opening statement alleged without evidence that Huang and other unnamed Asian Americans were "high-placed industrial spies" for Asian corporations.[62]

Also on the first day, the Senate committee's ranking minority member, Senator John Glenn (D-OH), insinuated a connection with McCarthyism, stating that "[d]uring the 1950s, we can all recall what happened to this committee, and I doubt anyone here wants to return to those dark days."[63] Robert Torricelli (D-NJ) compared the plight of Asian Americans to that of Italian Americans during the Estes Kefauver investigation of organized crime, and stated that "the pain ... that many Americans felt that day must not and will not be allowed to be visited on Asian Americans in the coming weeks."[64] Senator Daniel Akaka (D-HI), also a Japanese American, vocalized his concerns about "the negative impact that the allegations of fund-raising abuses have had on the Asian-Pacific-American community," and asserted that

> Asian Pacific-Americans have been targeted and misrepresented from the moment the press saw a good story in the allegations of foreign contributions to the 1996 elections. When the news of possible fund-raising abuse first broke last fall, the media was quick to toss around references to "Asian connections, Asian funds network, people with tenuous connections to this country," phrases applied equally to people who are American citizens and noncitizens alike....
> It is this lack of distinction by both the media, members of Congress, and the public that threatens to cast doubt on the integrity of Asian Pacific Americans.[65]

Akaka's prepared statement was two pages long. Concern from any Democrat over any possible negative impact on Asian Americans is not presented again until page 9561 of the 9575-page *Final Report of the Committee on Governmental Affairs of the United States Senate on the Investigation of Illegal or Improper Activities in Connection with 1996 Federal Election Campaign* (hereafter *Final Report*), and the defense is, not surprisingly, presented by Akaka:

> I continue to have serious concerns about the *manner* in which the investigation was conducted. On a number of occasions, in my view, the [Republican] Majority exhibited insensitivity to the effect of its actions and words on Americans of Asian ancestry.
>
> For example, in its discussion of the China Plan, the Majority Report confuses Chinese business and social connections of certain Asian American donors and fund-raisers with the possibility of their being "foreign agents." Seeds of doubt are cast out as to whether these individuals are loyal American citizens. Some of the subjects of the investigation may have violated campaign finance laws and some have been indicted by a federal grand jury. However, I am aware of no conclusive evidence that any of these individuals betrayed the United States. Absent stronger evidence, the Committee should refrain from making such damaging allegations.
>
> The Majority also exhibited insensitivity by blurring the important distinction between Asian nationals and Asian Americans....
>
> I am not just concerned that the Committee might have disparaged specific Asian Americans. I am also concerned about the effect that the allegations and insinuations of disloyalty may have on other Asian Americans.[66]

Only Senator Richard Durbin (D-IL) publicly shared Akaka's concern that Asian Americans had been wrongly accused.[67] Otherwise, committee Democrats were completely silent on the treatment of Asian Americans stemming from the campaign finance controversy. In addition to the *Final Report*, this includes ten volumes of hearings published by the Senate committee—another several thousand pages.

In noting the Democratic senators' unwillingness to associate with Asian Americans, I mean to point out that at numerous instances during the hearings Democrats could have made a strategic choice to defend this racial formation. Yet they declined to do so even when they could have gained a strategic partisan advantage. They could easily have confronted the racially insensitive comments made by Republicans. For instance, Senator Brownback commented on the subject of Huang's salary arrangements, "no raise money, no get bonus," and delivered it in a false Chinese accent.[68] Republican Senator Robert Bennett (UT), when commenting on an Asian American implicated in the scandal, stated, "In my opinion, Mr. [Charlie] Trie's activities are classic activities on the part of an Asian who comes from out of that culture and who embarks on an activity relating to intelligence gathering."[69] Apparently he was unconcerned that this comment might be interpreted as inflammatory or racist because a few minutes later he said, "my take on all of this is that Charlie Trie is a very typical Asian agent acting on behalf of his sponsor."[70] Meanwhile, the National Republican Senatorial Committee (NRSC) was using the name "Chinese Laundry" for their 1997 summer softball team.[71]

That the actions cited above are problematic is not in question; what I emphasize here is the general failure of Democratic Party elites to use them to partisan advantage. Nor do I claim that either individual Democrats or the party as a whole shared Brownback's or Bennett's assumptions about Asian Americans. But even if Democrats cared not at all about Asian Americans or the appearance of racism, political logic would seem to dictate that the party would attempt to reap partisan benefits from the public missteps of their Republican opponents. An obvious point of attack would have been to suggest that the racist comments of these senators demonstrated their unfitness to sit on a committee investigating Asian Americans. This was certainly an opportunity for Democrats to take organized Asian Americans into the party fold by symbolically reaching out to them.

Apparently Democrats did not believe there was much partisan advantage to be gained by accusing Republicans of making unsubstantiated and racist remarks. It was left largely to Asian American political organizations and leaders to officially criticize both senators' comments in a complaint to the U.S. Commission on Civil Rights, and Brownback and Bennett later apologized. One could argue that the Democratic Party did not attack Republican missteps because it perceived that such efforts would have no impact on a Republican Party bent on damaging the Democratic Party's brand name. But even assuming that there was no partisan advantage to be gained, why did Democrats fail to defend Asian American interests? That party elites failed to do so suggests not only that they perceived no partisan advantage in accusing Republicans of racial insensitivity, but that they believed that there were partisan disadvantages to strategically reaching out to Asian Americans that outweighed the political benefits of defending them.

National press accounts during the hearings consistently depicted the Democrats as having the upper hand over the Republicans.[72] The first witness, former DNC finance director Sullivan, proved to be far more combative than Republicans had expected, leading Lanny Davis, special counsel to Clinton and the president's "scandal control specialist," to exult, "I'm having fun."[73] Senate Republican sources, on the other hand, contended that Sullivan had been "turned."[74] In the first week, the *New York Times* reported that "much of what [Republican chair] Senator [Fred] Thompson ... stated as fact is a collection of theories that have been widely reported in recent months.[75] After two weeks of hearings, the *Times* concluded that "no testimony was offered showing that Mr. Huang had dealt in Chinese government money.... Nor was there corroboration of the suggestion by Senator Brownback ... that Mr. Huang and perhaps others were "high-placed industrial spies."[76] Thompson himself acknowledged that he could build only a circumstantial case that China had tried to influence the 1996 elections because the key players had refused to testify or had fled the United States.[77] Privately, Republican committee staff and aides acknowledged that the committee had failed to make a strong case for Chinese government involvement.[78] In short, as one Republican insider put it, they "blew it."[79]

The critical insight here is that Democrats had an opportunity to differentiate themselves from Republicans, this time on the issue of illegal Asian involvement in the American electoral process, but they did exactly the opposite. A week after the hearings began, Democrats announced to members of the national press that they agreed with Republicans about the connection between improprieties by Asian American fund-raisers and an illegal attempt by the Chinese government to influence the American electoral process. Senators Glenn, Joseph Lieberman (D-CT), and Carl Levin (D-MI) all agreed with Thompson that China had attempted to influence the 1996 congressional elections, though not the presidential election.[80] Senator Richard Durbin (D-IL) stated, "It's clear there was an effort by the Chinese to play a role in our political process. Whether it was confined to lobbying or went beyond that, I don't know," and implied that he shared the conclusions drawn by Lieberman and Glenn.[81] Despite the bipartisan declarations of the Chinese government's intentions to corrupt the American political process, three days later a front-page *New York Times* article stated, "In the case of the Chinese plot, the Republicans have been unable to prove that any of Beijing's money was actually put into any American campaign, Congressional or Presidential."[82]

Given the charges of a Chinese plot to influence the American electoral process, at first glance it appears inevitable that much attention would be paid to Chinese American fund-raisers Trie, Chung, and Huang, and Taiwanese American Hsia. This sense of inevitability, however, ignores the reality that the racialization of Asian bodies as perpetually alien is fundamental in having precipitated the investigation in the first place. Campaign finance violations by those not racialized or otherwise constructed as irreducibly illiberal may not have offered the political opportunity that Asian bodies presented. For example, consider that Americans with ancestral roots in Italy, Germany, Spain, and France are not generally constructed as having immutable political and social allegiances to their European roots. Tarring the opposition with the charge that their party contains the dangerous political force of powerful Europeans is not politically useful, even though there are literally millions of European socialists, communists, and fascists. Racial formation, after all, does not occur in a vacuum, but comes out of an existing racialized milieu, and those negotiating the meaning of racialized bodies and racial categories do so with the recognition that existing racial discourses must be contended with as meanings are reproduced or transformed.

In his concluding statement in the committee's report, Akaka admonished the Senate committee, "We cannot be guilty of selective harassment of those with Asian surnames because such actions only underscore the Asian American community's fear that they are being held responsible for the alleged crimes of some individuals who happen to be of Asian heritage."[83] Akaka's concern points to yet another opportunity that the Democrats had to strategically differentiate their party from Republicans. Many Asian Americans were concerned that they were being targeted because of their racial background. Democrats could have accused Republicans of selectively investigating the actions of Asian Americans such as Huang, Trie, Ted

Sioeng, Yogesh Gandhi, Hsia, and Chung—none of whom had either been indicted of a crime during the hearings or even fined by the FEC—while ignoring non-Asian individuals such as German national Thomas Kramer, who was fined $323,000—the largest fine ever imposed by the FEC on an individual—for illegally contributing to, among other organizations, the DNC, the DSCC, the NRSC, and the Florida Republican Party.[84] Kramer's attorney told FEC officials that no fund-raiser from either party ever inquired about his immigration status or refused funds from him because of his status as a foreign national. No doubt, Democrats would have been helped by the admission of the chief Republican counsel to the Senate committee, Michael Madigan, that no Republican looking into the campaign finance scandal actually believed that Huang was a spy, regardless of their public suggestions to the contrary.[85] Democrats might have made the strategic choice to accuse Republicans of unfairly scapegoating Asian Americans instead of investigating the broader dysfunctions of the campaign finance system.

Instead, Democrats replicated the Republican strategy of alleging connections between the Republican Party and Asian Americans or Asian nationals who had contributed to Republican candidates or Republican Party coffers.[86] When the GOP admitted for the first time that it had received illegal campaign contributions and was returning them, Democratic Party chair Roy Romer immediately responded, "For months, the Republicans have piously proclaimed their purity on campaign finance.... But the truth is out now—they have deliberately concealed receipt of foreign contributions."[87] Senator Glenn contended that former Republican Party chair Haley Barbour had participated in the laundering of illegal foreign money by way of Hong Kong national Ambrous Young, and that this money had helped Republicans win control of Congress in 1994.[88] Democrats accused Barbour of soliciting a $2.1 million loan guarantee from the Hong Kong businessman to the National Policy Forum (NPF), a policy arm of the national Republican Party, which then illegally laundered $1.6 million for the party.[89] By the end of the hearings, Senate Democrats had alleged links between elected Asian American Republicans Jay Kim and California state treasurer Matt Fong to illegal foreign money. [90] Other Asian Americans were also linked by the Democrats to the Republican Party as having facilitated illegal contributions.[91] In short, Democrats chose to defend themselves from accusations of improper or illegal interactions with Asian nationals by accusing

Republicans of the same transgressions. Given the Republican admission that the Senate hearings had not gone as they had hoped, and national press accounts that consistently gave the Democrats the upper hand, the Democratic strategy was apparently quite successful.

MATT FONG

California state treasurer Matt Fong's campaign for the U.S. Senate is instructive in the matter of how national Republicans handled the possibility of campaign fund-raising improprieties stemming from the highest-ranking Asian American elected executive in the Republican Party. When the Senate's *Final Report* was released and the House's Government Reform and Oversight Committee hearings were under way, Fong was in a difficult primary campaign in California for the Republican nomination for the U.S. Senate in 1998. The winner of the primary would face Senator Barbara Boxer, an incumbent whom Republicans had targeted as especially vulnerable to electoral defeat.

During the primary campaign, the House committee announced its plan to call Fong to testify about donations received from Ted Sioeng, an Indonesian national, and his company, Panda Estates Investments.[92] Republican members of the committee stated that they had no intention of embarrassing Fong in the middle of the Senate race. A senior committee staff member stated, "We will look into [Fong's alleged impropriety,] whether it leads to the DNC or whether it leads to Republicans.... If Matt Fong received money from Ted Sioeng, we intend to inquire."[93] Fong's potential trouble with the House committee led a spokesman for Fong's toughest primary opponent, Darrell Issa, to state, "Sure it hurts [Fong]."[94] The House committee eventually exonerated Fong on all charges, stating that it had "uncovered no evidence suggesting that Fong knew the contributions were improper, or that he knowingly solicited improper and/or illegal contributions," and that "[b]ased on the information developed during the course of its investigation, the Committee concludes that there is no evidence of improper or illegal activities on behalf of Fong."[95] In general, it appears, House Republicans were careful to avoid implicating Fong in the controversy.[96]

The same day that the House announced that it would call Fong to testify about his alleged improprieties, the Senate committee implicated Fong in illegal fund-raising in its *Final Report*. The committee's investigation of separate $50,000 contributions from Sioeng and Panda Estates Investments concluded that "at least a portion of one Sioeng contribution to Fong was made with foreign money"; $16,000 consisted of an illegal donation from Ted Sioeng.[97] The majority noted that according to Sioeng's U.S. business chief, Jessica Elnitiarta, the investigated contributions were the result of "some intense fund-raising appeals from Fong personally, and others on his behalf."[98]

Fong certainly recognized the political costs of being associated with "foreign" money. As soon as press reports linked Sioeng to the campaign finance scandal, Fong, stating that he wanted "absolutely no cloud, no suspicion, no doubt about my campaign conduct or my performance in public office," returned not only the allegedly illegal $16,000 from Sioeng but the entire $100,000.[99] Unfortunately for Fong, his attempt to protect himself from the charge of being loyal to Asian political and economic interests had its own negative consequences. Because distinctions between legal returned money and illegal returned money were generally not being made by either press or party elites, the voting public may have perceived that Fong had in fact received and returned $100,000 in illegal contributions rather than $84,000 in legal and $16,000 in illegal funds. In his attempt to erase doubts about his national and ethnic loyalties, Fong hurt himself in another way; his losing Senate campaign ran out of money just prior to the November general election.

In implicating Fong in illegal fund-raising, the majority used statements from attorneys for Elnitiarta and Panda Estates who were responding to Fong's attempt to put political distance between himself and Sioeng: In a letter dated May 27, 1997, these attorneys criticized "Mr. Fong and his campaign [for joining] in the shameful rhetoric directed at Asian-Americans."[100] The letter stated further that Jessica Elnitiarta had relied "upon the direct representations made by the Fong campaign ... that Panda Estates could properly contribute to Mr. Fong's campaign [for California treasurer in the 1996 election]."[101]

Interestingly, in no other place in the *Final Report* does any member of the Republican Party raise the issue of anti—Asian American rhetoric. Moreover, the text of the majority record never indicates that Fong is a

Republican, much less the highest-ranking elected Asian American Republican in the country. Fong's status did not protect him from charges of impropriety in the *Final Report*. By quoting Elnitiarta's attorney's accusation that Fong had engaged in "shameful rhetoric directed at Asian Americans," the *Final Report* implicitly suggested that the Republican Party was not responsible for the anti—Asian American sentiment expressed during the investigation.

The next paragraph of the letter implicated Fong for introducing Indonesian national Ted Sioeng to both Republican Speaker of the House Newt Gingrich and the NPF, which had been created and led by ex-GOP party chair Haley Barbour:

> On July 18, 1995, Panda Industries made a $50,000 contribution to the National Policy Forum (NPF). Exactly how this came about is uncertain, though it appears Sioeng's acquaintance with the NPF began with Matt Fong. Perhaps in gratitude for Sioeng's earlier contributions, Fong arranged in June 1995 for Sioeng to have his picture taken with Speaker Gingrich in Washington, DC. Later, Fong sent a letter in support of a Los Angeles badminton tournament that Sioeng underwrote, and arranged for Gingrich to send a similar letter.[102]

The majority presented no evidence demonstrating that Fong's initiative led to Sioeng's link to Gingrich, nor did it bring any evidence to bear on how or why Fong would have introduced Sioeng to either Barbour or the NPF. Two paragraphs after claiming that Fong appeared to be the link between Sioeng and Gingrich and the NPF, the majority completely exonerated the NPF and, by extension, Barbour: "The NPF was an independent 501(c)(4) organization created by Haley Barbour to serve as a grass roots organization for the Republican exchange of ideas. It had no PAC, donated no money, and did not advocate the election or defeat of any candidate. It was not legally prohibited from accepting foreign money."[103] The majority also downplayed any connection Gingrich might have had with Sioeng.[104]

The failure of the Republican Party to protect Fong is particularly striking for a number of reasons. First, as noted above, Boxer was considered vulnerable; moreover, she represented the liberal wing of the Democratic Party. Second, as a matter of practical policy, party elites generally avoid taking sides in primary contests, especially those without an incumbent nominee, unless they see a clear strategic advantage in doing so. (The very public Republican repudiation of former Ku Klux Klan grand wizard David Duke, who ran as a Republican for the Senate in 1990 and for the House in 1999, comes to mind.) When the *Final Report* was released, Fong was engaged in a bitter primary battle in California for the Republican nomination to the U.S. Senate against State Representative Frank Riggs (R-Napa) and car alarm magnate Issa. If Fong had not been a credible candidate, then his status as a sure loser could have led Republicans to believe they could damage Fong's image with no practical consequences to either Fong's chances of winning or the party's chances against Boxer in the general election. But Fong *was* a credible and competitive candidate—he won the Republican primary with a 45 percent plurality of the vote on June 9, 1998, despite any political toll taken by the fund-raising controversy.

In their political calculations regarding Fong's candidacy, Republican Party elites may have decided that larger interests were at stake. Obviously, any Senate seat is valuable, but one from the resource-rich and politically powerful state of California is particularly so. Yet Republicans strategically behaved in a manner hostile to Fong's primary and general election candidacies, failing to insulate the highest-ranking elected Asian American Republican from potentially damaging accusations. Given the political office involved, it is impossible to imagine that Republican Party elites were unaware that Fong was engaged in a competitive campaign against the progressive Democratic incumbent, Barbara Boxer.

The failure to shield Fong was not, of course, about principled conviction that an important politician was haphazardly breaking federal laws or in the grip of Asian governments and businesses. Consider how the Republican Party defended its national chairman, Haley Barbour, from similar accusations during the hearings, despite evidence that he had been both aggressive and successful in pursuing foreign money.[105] Submitted into evidence was a letter that Barbour had written to Jason Hu, an official Taiwanese representative to the United States, thanking him for his willingness to financially underwrite the work of the NPF.[106] The president of the NPF, John Bolton, had also acknowledged receipt of "generous contributions" in a letter thanking Michael Hsu, a special assistant at the Taipei Economic and Cultural Representative Office (TECRO), which was widely known to represent Taiwan as its unofficial embassy in the United States.[107] The NPF's successful solicitation of campaign funds from Taiwan stands as a clear example of a foreign government contributing to a national political party.[108]

Barbour also successfully sought out a $2.1 million foreign loan guarantee for the NPF from Ambrous T. Young, a Hong Kong businessman. According to another former RNC chairman, Richard Richards, Barbour had made it clear that the loan guarantee would relieve the $3 million debt owed to the Republican Party by the NPF, and would thus assist in the election of sixty potential new members of Congress during the 1994 House campaigns.[109] Indeed, $1.6 million of the loan went to repay money the NPF owed the RNC, and that sum was spent as "soft money" in states with competitive congressional races.[110]

To ensure the legality of transferring funds from Young to the NPF to the RNC, the NPF had to make clear that it was not under the control of the RNC. However, before the Young loan guarantee was consummated, the head of the NPF, Michael Baroody, informed Barbour that he was resigning because of the difficulties in maintaining that the NPF was an officially nonpartisan organization and not simply under the control of the RNC.[111] According to Baroody, even before Barbour's dealings with Young, the NPF's operations were being blurred with the party's committee's "in such a way as to conceivably jeopardize" its application for tax-exempt status.[112] The IRS eventually denied the forum tax-exempt status, stating that the NPF's "activities are designed to promote the Republican Party and politicians affiliated with the Republican Party.[113] Baroody added that the NPF's operations were so tightly controlled by Barbour's party aides that it "has become increasingly difficult to maintain the fiction of separation."[114]

Prior to the loan guarantee, Barbour had personally written Young's attorney, "As Chairman of the R.N.C., I will ask the Republican National Committee to authorize me to guarantee and pay off any National Policy Forum debts."[115] Despite Barbour's assurances to Young, after the 1994 election the former chair proposed in 1996 that the NPF's loan guarantee be forgiven with the financial losses imposed on Young.[116] The NPF eventually defaulted on the Signet Bank loan guaranteed by Young's money, and the Hong Kong businessman lost $800,000. Finally, according to Barbour's aides and to Richards and Young—that is, according to everyone but Barbour himself—he had been told several times that the money providing the loan guarantee was foreign, though not necessarily illegal.[117] Yet evidence that Barbour had sought foreign funds from Young, not to mention the government of Taiwan, was largely ignored by the majority, which concluded that Barbour had not violated any campaign law or even acted improperly.

In the final analysis, Republicans staunchly defended Barbour, a white American, although he had been both more aggressive and more successful than Fong in soliciting illegal money from sources in Asia. The vigorous Republican defense of Barbour is also notable in its contrast to the Democratic Party's race to deny its association with party fund-raisers like John Huang and Maria Hsia. That Barbour was the national party chair and thus had a very tight institutional relationship with the party clearly played a role in rallying Republicans to his defense, but Barbour's racial performance as white rather than Asian cannot be ignored.

It might appear at first glance that Barbour was fiercely protected while Fong, Huang, and Hsia were publicly rejected because of simple racial prejudice on the part of party elites. However, I contend that *whether or not* those calling the shots in both parties were prejudiced against Asian Americans, political strategy in the interest of their party's brand name pushed them to behave in just this way. Consider a hypothetical situation in which Barbour's body performs in popular culture as Asian rather than white. Democrats would still have attacked him, but their attacks would inevitably have incorporated the racial meaning of his Asian body into their partisan hostility. Just as Republican elites were able to charge that Democratic Party fundraisers John Huang and Charlie Trie were actually the loyal agents of Asian corporations and governments, Barbour's racial performance would have allowed the Democrats to make the far more damaging accusation that the head of the Republican National Committee was actually a loyal agent of an Asian government or corporation. Far from being an enlightened act, declining to similarly accuse Barbour the Asian would have been an act of political disarmament.

In short, what counts is not individual prejudice but the ways in which party elites necessarily incorporate the racialization of bodies into their political strategies. Indeed, Barbour's whiteness is incorporated into both parties' strategies—a reality revealed as soon as we acknowledge that party strategies would have been different if he had been Asian. Democrats devised political attacks that incorporated Barbour's racial performance as white, largely limiting their accusations to illegal campaign activity rather than suggesting that his true loyalties lay elsewhere. Republicans no doubt did not worry that Barbour's race could be used against him, feeling safe in the implicit white privilege afforded him.

What party elite behavior toward Barbour, Fong, Huang, and other campaign finance violators indicates is that Asian American charges of racism, however justified, cannot be addressed by emphasizing their unfair treatment at the hands of individual bipartisan elites suspected of racial prejudice. However racially enlightened party elites may become, reforming or replacing them will not solve the problem, because the underlying political logic of the two-party system will remain the same. Office-seeking parties must still cobble together a majority coalition from a liberal electorate, and party elites cannot simply ignore the political opportunities afforded by the powerful communicative value of Asian bodies within a party coalition. Ultimately, Asian American political empowerment strategies must simultaneously incorporate the impact of institutional settings and the rules that govern them, while always acknowledging how Asian Americans are uniquely racialized in the United States.

PASSING CAMPAIGN FINANCE REFORM

In response to Republican accusations of corruption and foreign influence in the DNC, Democratic elites adopted the strategic response that any campaign finance abuses or improprieties that occurred were common to both parties and that the goal should be to change campaign finance laws.[118] After a month of hearings, Democrats "spun" the abuses as proof of "how corrupt the whole campaign finance system had become, and that reform was needed."[119] Some Republican elites were concerned about Chairman Thompson's predilection to push for campaign reform on soft money and the campaign fund-raising system generally, fearing that the spotlight would move away from the violations of individual Asian American Democrats.[120]

In 1997 members of the U.S. House introduced a total of nine bills prohibiting campaign contributions by legal permanent residents. At the time, 37 percent of Asian Pacific Americans were noncitizen legal permanent residents, compared to 6 percent of the entire U.S. population.[121] Other proposed bills would have made it illegal for noncitizens to write letters to politicians, volunteer their time, or even talk to their neighbors or co-workers about political issues.[122] In an era in which campaign finance reform has stubbornly resisted virtually any attempt to limit fund-raising, the House passed HR 34, the *Illegal Foreign Contributions Act,* by an overwhelming bipartisan vote of 369 to 43. The act denied legal permanent residents the right to contribute to political campaigns.[123]

Asian American political leaders perceived that the sudden bipartisan consensus in the House on campaign finance reform was linked to the scapegoating of Asian Americans. Before the House had passed the provision on legal permanent residents, Stewart Kwoh, executive director of the Los Angeles–based Asian Pacific American Legal Center, stated that "there is no doubt that campaign finance reform is necessary and overdue. But it's much easier to place the blame on Asians for the abuses of the system rather than overhauling a system that benefits both Republicans and Democrats."[124] After the vote, Bob Sakaniwa, the Washington, D.C., representative for the Japanese Americans Citizens League (JACL), declared,

> Our campaign finance reform nightmare came true last night ... that one of the only provisions of the [campaign finance] reform bill to pass would be the ban on [legal permanent residents] and political contributors. This First Amendment right of legal permanent residents has been obliterated with no real concern by the 369 members of Congress who voted in favor of H.R. 34. Rather than pass meaningful campaign reform, Congress is putting a "no immigrants allowed" sign on every political party office in the country.[125]

No corresponding campaign finance reform bill came out of the Senate that year, and campaign finance legislation died for the congressional session.[126] In September 1999, the House passed HR 417, the *Bipartisan Campaign Finance Reform Act of 1999.* During floor debate, the House voted in favor of an amendment that would prohibit legal permanent residents from making campaign contributions to federal elections. The ban on contributions by legal permanent residents was not passed by the Senate, however, and legal permanent residents continue to contribute legally to U.S. political campaigns.

THE RESPONSE OF THE ASIAN
AMERICAN POLITICAL ELITE

In response to what they saw as racially biased treatment of Asian Americans by party elites and commercial media during the campaign finance controversy, a broad coalition of Asian American political leaders and organizations asked the U.S. Commission on Civil Rights to investigate their claims of widespread bias against immigrants and Asian Americans. In September 1997 a coalition of prominent advocacy groups and individuals alleged that Congress and top national party organizations had racially discriminated against Asian Americans.[127] They decried the hostile attitude toward their communities as a function of actions taken by members of Congress, both Republican and Democratic party organizations, and the mainstream commercial press. Regarding party elites, the coalition declared,

> The DNC, in response to allegations of improper fund-raising, institutionalized a voluntary policy more restrictive than existing federal law, barring legal permanent residents of the U.S. from contributing to the DNC, banning their attendance from White House or DNC Finance events and even having photographs with the First Family. In its investigation into allegations of improper fund-raising by three Asian Pacific American individuals, the DNC conducted an audit which singled out for invasive and humiliating interrogation donors of APA ancestry in 1996 and 1997, including many who had little or no connection to the individuals under investigation.
>
> The NRSC has also contributed to anti-Asian sentiment through xenophobic mailings and statements. In a recent fund raising letter, the NRSC claims the White House was "sold for ILLEGAL FOREIGN CASH" including money from "Red China, which still considers itself a Communist country!" The letter, together with other public statements made by Republican leaders alleging APA involvement in a Chinese conspiracy, serve to reinvigorate the fears of the Red Peril posed by the Chinese and other foreigners, and threaten to create an unfounded hysteria about foreign influence in American politics.[128]

Outside the commission, Asian American political elites asserted that the campaign finance controversy had helped create an environment of fear and dismay among many Asian Americans. For instance, Albert Chu, head of the Asian American Political Coalition in New Jersey, described experiencing "a kind of chilling effect. All of a sudden people are getting in trouble, and people are afraid."[129] Governor Gary Locke, a leading Asian American politician, expected long-term repercussions and noted that he had already witnessed fallout in potential Asian American candidates' discussing their reluctance to run for office.[130]

Some Asian American political elites argued that the appropriate response to the past year's events was to be especially careful to follow campaign finance laws. As Chinese American Governor Locke, put it, a critical lesson from the campaign finance controversy was that Asian Americans had "to be extra careful in dotting the i's and crossing the t's" of campaign finance laws.[131] The best defense against future charges of "foreign" influence or "tainted" contributions would be to follow the guidelines of campaign finance law strictly, and thus prove through their model behavior that Asian Americans were above suspicion.

This political tactic reflects the awareness that Asian bodies are already racialized in ways that compel Asian American into racial performance as model would-be American citizens. For this kind of advice to make any sense at all, it must acknowledge in the first place that someone will be watching, turning the normal process of abiding the law into racial theater. It signifies the reality that even when race may not appear to be present, Asian Americans implicitly understand that they are negotiating the racial meanings of already racialized Asian bodies while they are navigating the abstract, "color-blind" laws that govern America's dominant political institutions. In the parlance of Omi and Winant's theory of racial formation, one can read Locke's advice as a "racial project" whereby Asian Americans attempt to stop damaging racial discourse about Asians before it begins, by shutting off political incentives to draw upon and reproduce that discourse.[132] By performing as model law-abiding citizens following the letter of campaign finance law, Asian Americans seek to control the meaning of their racialized bodies, hoping that this will help bring about the distribution of political benefits such as high-profile government appointments. Broadly speaking, this tactic is consistent with the ubiquitous strategy of Asian Americans racially performing as the model minority in an effort to avoid being suspected as racial aliens immutably disloyal to the United States.

Following campaign finance law to the letter clearly presupposes that there is an important political distinction between legal and illegal money. But this tactic's effectiveness hinges on the assumption that party elites believe that the electorate can and will distinguish Asian American citizens and legal permanent residents from noncitizens of Asian descent who cannot legally donate money. Consider that an Asian American political organization cannot prevent ineligible Asians from making illegal campaign contributions to either or both of the major parties; at best, they can control their own networks of political fund-raisers, though even this is highly doubtful.[133] That there are strong incentives for Asian governments and corporations to attempt to influence American politicians is obvious. For example, two business groups based in the United States with close ties to the government of Taiwan illegally spent more than $230,000 from 2000 to 2004 to fund trips for members of Congress to meet with high-ranking Taiwanese officials.[134]

Financially backed efforts by foreign governments and corporations to acquire influence in U.S. government will not end anytime soon, and freelancers like Trie and Chung will continue to seek access or influence in national politics. So too will politically and economically established Asian Americans, who are increasingly positioning themselves as the ideal go-betweens between Asian and U.S. corporations and governments.[135] What happens when Asian American political elites in the know, as it were, follow Locke's advice and behave as the model minority, but other individuals of Asian descent do not? Would the national parties respond differently to Asian Americans on their best behavior working within the two-party system, while political agents of Asian governments and corporations broke the rules?

I think not. Consider that Locke's suggestion to perform as a model minority in an effort to control public discourse speaks to the broader inability of Asian Americans to control the cultural discourse that effectively racializes their bodies as perpetual alien foreigners. This political reality was quite clearly demonstrated by the commercial mass media feeding frenzy over the campaign finance controversy.[136] Studies have shown that press coverage concentrated on the legitimacy and loyalties of Asian American citizens, legal permanent residents, and nonresidents alike. Analyses of mainstream news reporting have demonstrated that descriptive adjectives evoking historically racist stereotypes of Asians as mysterious and inscrutable foreigners were used repeatedly.[137] Ninety percent of all stories on allegedly illegal campaign donations mentioned Huang, despite the relatively paltry amount of illegal money he had raised.[138] News accounts also repeatedly alleged or implied illegal and influential actions by Asian American campaign donors. To top things off, the Asian American outcry that Asian Americans were being unfairly attacked because of their race was met with very stiff resistance and with the counteraccusation that they were "playing the race card."[139] Asian Americans clearly had very little if any control over the reporting of the fund-raising scandal.

Significantly, national newspapers consistently blurred the lines between Asians and Asian Americans, and between different Asian countries. In one prominent example, Pulitzer Prize winner Bob Woodward of the *Washington Post* wrote that FBI files "indicate that Maria Hsia—a Taiwanese American immigrant who for a decade has raised money for Democratic causes—was 'doing the bidding' of Beijing as a Chinese agent."[140] Woodward failed to distinguish between the People's Republic of China (PRC) and Taiwan despite the difficult political relationship that the island has had with mainland China since the Maoist revolution. He also failed to acknowledge that Hsia's parents had fled from the PRC, and that Hsia was the daughter of a politically well-connected Taiwanese family.[141] As such, Hsia was unlikely to be working as an international agent for a country determined to eventually assume full governance over Taiwan.[142]

Press coverage also failed to make distinctions between established Asian American political actors and the self-appointed Asian American freelancers who had tapped into personal relationships—*guanxi*—to raise money from mostly ethnic Chinese capitalists and even from Asian immigrant nuns.[143] Aside from Huang and Hsia, the Asian American fund-raisers most deeply implicated in the controversy were strangers to Asian American political elites and inside-the-beltway politicians.[144] Not surprisingly, politically aware Asian Americans did not identify with Huang and other prominent figures in the controversy, even as they decried the racist and xenophobic undertones of the country's conversation on the scandal. No established Asian American political leader or advocacy group defended Asian American citizens who had engaged in corrupt fund-raising.[145] In short, journalists failed to make important factual points or distinguish between Asians and Asian Americans, or between Asians who claimed different countries of ancestry (including the United States). Although Asian Americans took great pains to distance themselves from the individuals who had been implicated in the controversy, the *Washington Post* criticized unnamed friends and backers of Huang for "playing the race card," effectively conflating Asian American political elites critical of Huang, who were also charging anti-Asian bias, with supporters of the discredited Democratic Party fund-raiser.[146] The inability to control the racial discourse around Asian bodies meant that Asian Americans' own political efforts were reinterpreted to work against their own interests.

Performing as the model minority and adopting what one might call a "hyper-legal" or "hyper-American" approach rests on the dubious assumption that parties will behave as if there are important distinctions between Asians and Asian Americans, and not just between legal and illegal money. It also ignores the fact that the political conundrum that has often faced Asian Americans has not been their illegal participation in mainstream politics but rather the racialization of their political participation as a peril to the health of the American polity. If party elites perceive that the electorate generally does not make clear distinctions between Asians and Asian Americans, then it makes no difference whether Asian Americans dot all their i's and cross all their t's. Party elite strategies will still be driven by the concern to maintain the party brand name, and this will drive them to distance the party not only from Asians but also from Asian Americans who may have engaged in perfectly legal behavior.

Since some campaign donations came from sources in Asia, Asian American political activity within the Democratic Party provided the political incentive for Republican elites to accuse their partisan opponents of being on auction to Asian corporations or governments. In response, the Democratic Party still had the incentive to distance itself from the perception of Asian corporate or government influence. For instance, Vice President Al Gore's response to being linked to Hsia was to distance himself from his longtime friend and political fund-raiser, saying, "It had nothing to do with me." Gore's office simply stated, "The matters for which Ms. Hsia has been indicted do not involve Vice President Gore."[147]

THE BILL LANN LEE NOMINATION

In November 1997, President Clinton nominated Chinese American Bill Lann Lee for the office of assistant attorney general for civil rights. His nomination was not without political risks to the Clinton administration, being the latest in a series of nominations for the position that had caused political controversy. The president's first attempt to fill the position in 1993 had ended badly for him and the progressive civil rights community, and he was forced to withdraw his support for Lani Guinier after conservative Republicans attacked her in racially veiled language as a "Quota Queen" who held "extreme" policy positions. At first glance, then, the nomination of an Asian American as the highest-ranking civil rights attorney in the Department of Justice appears to be a significant political victory for an Asian American political establishment that was desperately in need of political resurrection.

Indeed, Lee's nomination had tremendous symbolic value in the eyes of Asian American political elites, and their disappointment was acute when social conservatives, disillusioned by Lee's position on affirmative action, succeeded in preventing a Senate Judiciary Committee vote on the nomination, effectively scuttling it before the full Senate could consider his candidacy.[148] In response, leading Asian American political organizations made a major push to pressure Clinton into giving Lee an unusual recess appointment.[149] In addition to calling on their constituencies to send letters and make phone calls to the White House and the members of the Senate Judiciary Committee, the organizations held press conferences publicizing what they saw as Lee's impeccable legal record.[150] In December 1997, rather than give him a recess appointment, Clinton named Lee acting assistant attorney general for civil rights, to the dismay of Senate Republicans who argued that their constitutional prerogative to advise and consent on executive nominations was being usurped.[151] Delighted by this development, Asian American political elites called it a major political success after the disappointments of the previous year.

It is not clear, however, that Asian American lobbying was responsible for Lee's appointment, as there were several other political factors at play. Indeed, I contend that the Lee case reveals the limits of Asian American party-based power in cases where much larger strategic interests are at play. Clinton's appointment of Lee came in a highly partisan environment, with heavy hitters both within and outside Congress weighing in with an eye to Clinton's civil rights approach in his second term and the impact of the case on the 1998 midterm elections. The nomination also framed an institutional debate between the Senate and the president over the Senate's constitutional power to advise and consent on nominations to executive posts. Democratic Senators were hesitant or openly unwilling to support their president because such support might increase executive power at the expense of the legislature.[152]

Perhaps most significantly, Asian Americans do not appear to have been Lee's most important political backers. Interest groups in the United States, and particularly racial and ethnic groups, often have similar or aligned interests and work together as a means of maximizing political power.[153] While it is not possible to assess with certainty what impact Asian American efforts had in pushing Clinton to stick with Lee, it seems unlikely that Lee would have been appointed had it not been for the larger coalition of civil rights groups endorsing Lee's nomination, and especially the support of the NAACP.[154] The battle over his appointment was not so much a victory for Asian Americans as it was the outcome of an ideological struggle between the increasingly conservative Republican Senate and the NAACP over the future of affirmative action.[155] Lee, like the previous three Democratic nominees for the position of attorney general for civil rights, was a leading attorney with the NAACP.[156] As the western regional counsel for the organization's Legal Defense and Educational Fund, the civil rights law firm founded by the late Supreme Court justice Thurgood Marshall, Lee's record fell squarely within the mainstream of the civil rights establishment. African American political elites, perhaps still smarting over Clinton's political retreat on Guinier nomination, mobilized in defense of a nominee who was not only one of their own litigators but was also being labeled by social conservatives the "Quota King," in an attempt to link him to Guinier's failed candidacy.[157] When Clinton finally appointed Lee to the post of acting assistant attorney general, newspaper accounts scarcely mentioned Asian American political efforts, noting instead the pleasure of African American leaders like Jesse Jackson and the continued hostility of prominent social conservatives like Clint Bolick.[158]

When Lee came up for reappointment as acting assistant attorney general in 1999, Asian American political elites told Republican senators that their repeated refusal to confirm Lee would be seen as a partisan rejection of the Asian American community and a partisan attack on civil rights.[159] Along those lines, Stewart Kwoh, executive director of the Asian Pacific American Legal Center, referred to "incidents where the Republicans and Democrats essentially shot themselves in the foot. On the Republican side, a lot of Asian-Americans saw them as anti-immigrant, anti-minority, and they've continued to oppose popular figures like Bill Lann Lee for Assistant Attorney General for Civil Rights. On the other hand, the Democrats overreacted to the [campaign finance] scandal, basically distanced themselves from Asian-Americans."[160] Kwoh's claim that both parties had made significant political miscalculations in inadvertently alienating Asian American communities is implausible. It is much more plausible that party elites, as rational political actors, recognized that Asian bodies move through American political institutions with racial markers, and that ignoring these racial markers would not have been an act of color-blindness so much as an act of political stupidity. No major party seeking to ascend to national political office can fail to incorporate the presence of racialized Asian bodies in the two-party system into their party calculations. In turn, Asian American political strategies must anticipate how their own racialized bodies will significantly shift the racial currents they attempt to navigate.[161]

According to conventional theories, two-party competition is supposed to ensure that when a candidate constituency for incorporation into a party coalition comes under attack, the electoral necessity of building majority coalitions virtually compels a major party to reach out to that constituency. Parties have often attacked a political interest group, but this does not mean that the interest group cannot work within the party system. In this case, at the very least, a major party might be expected to appeal to Asian American communities simply by presenting itself as not hostile to them, and perhaps by attacking the other party's conduct as obviously opposed to Asian American interests, whatever they might be. This appeal would cost the party no valuable resources, since it would rely purely on symbolic appeals without making any promises about access, policy, or patronage. Given the hostility of the opposition party, a symbolic approach would probably be effective in drawing a substantial number of Asian American voters and donors into the party coalition.

But party elites do not treat Asian Americans as just another interest group. Rather, they recognize that Asian bodies in the United States are imbued with racial meanings that can be deployed to communicate politically relevant information to potential voters. Because Asians in America are racialized as having immutable and enduring loyalties outside the United States, their visible presence in a party coalition can significantly threaten a party's chances to build a majority coalition out of a liberal electorate; an office-seeking party cannot afford to be perceived as a political vehicle for illiberal Asians in America. Strategic party elites will consequently distance their party from Asian Americans by trafficking in the racist discourse that Asian American political actors find so distressing to their political fortunes. This means that not only will party elites fail to halt anti-Asian racist discourse once it gets started, they will be under systemic pressure to reproduce it.

So long as Asian Americans work visibly within the two-party system, their participation provides a political opening for one party to associate the other with illiberal Asian bodies, giving parties an incentive to reproduce the racially homogenizing discourse of Asians in America as perpetually alien strangers. Not only is two-party scholarship incorrect in concluding that working within a competitive two-party system will propel the assimilationist project forward, Asian American party-based efforts actually lead backward into further political and civic ostracism. Only by reducing their visible presence within a party coalition is it possible for Asian Americans to minimize the political incentive for parties to reproduce this racially homogenizing discourse. After all, racial discourse does not in and of itself communicate important political information to an uncertain voter—the discourse must be linked to the party brand name if it is to influence how strategic party elites calculate the racial dynamics within party coalitions. The greater the visibility of Asian Americans in the party, and the more political power they can credibly be claimed to possess, the greater will be the political incentive for parties to draw upon and reproduce the racist discourse that continues to plague Asian American political interests. Not only are Asian Americans uniquely blocked from successfully participating in party coalitional politics, nonparticipation in the national two-party system must be considered a means of protecting this racial minority from a potentially hostile majority.

What is so striking about the Democratic Party's response during the campaign finance controversy is the difficulty of imagining any other viable option for a major party seeking national power. Faced with the possibility that the party brand name would become associated with a powerfully illiberal and foreign image, the party's actions were entirely predictable within the logic of the two-party system. In response to Republican rhetoric about Asian influence over the Democratic Party, Democrats had no choice but to publicly repudiate anything with an illiberal Asian tint. The evidence does not suggest that the Democratic Party engaged in consciously racist behavior in an attempt to deny Asian Americans their political due. Rather, it suggests that party elites saw Asian American political fortunes as a necessary and unavoidable sacrifice. Race matters not because party elites are prejudiced—though they well may be—but because, as rational political actors, they necessarily incorporate into their political strategies the ways in which Asian bodies can be deployed for political gain or loss.[162] A failure to incorporate the fact that racialized Asian bodies change the racial dynamics within the two-party system—and throughout American politics—is thus not a color-blind act so much as it is one of willful intellectual and political blindness to racial reality.

4

ASIAN AMERICAN CONGRESSIONAL REPRESENTATION

COUNTING AMERICANS BY RACE is at least as old as the United States itself. Its institutional roots can be found in Article I, Section 2, clause 3 of the U.S. Constitution.[1] The Founding Fathers mandated that every ten years a comprehensive enumeration of the American population would take place. In and of itself, this did not force government counters to separate by race, but because the founders deemed enslaved blacks, euphemistically described as "all other persons," only three-fifths of a person, and because each state was apportioned a number of seats in the U.S. House of Representatives based on the official count of its population, the Constitution effectively required census takers to distinguish between free whites and enslaved blacks. For good measure, government enumerators threw in the category of "all other free persons."[2] From the beginning, then, officially recognized racial population statistics have been a cornerstone of political power.

Every census in American history has counted the population by race, and racial population statistics continue to have important political consequences today. But while the 1790 census recognized free whites, all other free persons, and slaves, respondents to the 2000 census were given the following options when asked to select their race or races: (1) White, (2) Black, African American, or Negro, (3) American Indian or Alaskan Native, (4) Asian Indian, (5) Chinese, (6) Filipino, (7) Japanese, (8) Korean, (9) Vietnamese, (10) Other Asian, (11) Native Hawaiian, (12) Guamanian or Chamorro, (13) Samoan, (14) Other Pacific Islander, and (15) Some other race.[3] What immediately stands out, of course, is that while blacks, whites, and Native Americans are each represented by a single box, and Latinos are not represented at all, the race question lists eleven different ethnic categories covering the Asian and Pacific Islander communities.[4]

How did the national government come to list so many Asian and Pacific Islander options on the census? The extensive listing is particularly striking given that so few people in the United States identify with some of the offered options. On the 2000 census, for instance, about three-tenths of 1 percent of all respondents checked any of the boxes representing any Pacific Islander category, meaning that four of fifteen listed categories were devoted to enumerating the ethnic and national status of fewer than four hundred thousand persons in a population approaching 300 million. Listing so many different Asian and Pacific Islander categories is certainly not cost-efficient, and the Bureau of the Census has made no secret of its antipathy to this practice.[5] Yet, despite their opposition, census officials have not been able to halt the dramatic increase since the 1970 census in the number of Asian American and Pacific Islander (API) categories listed, even as they have successfully rebuffed the demands of other groups such as Cape Verdeans and Arab Americans for more variation in the racial categories listed.[6]

That Asian American communities have somehow scored an important political victory is clear, especially considering the significant political and policy benefits accrued by their communities from being listed on the census. Disaggregated listings are a tremendous boon to API communities for a number of reasons, not least of which is that they lead to higher official counts. Census figures provide the raw data that state legislators use to draw district lines for federal, state, and local elections, and generally have the effect of enhancing the political prospects of larger communities. Higher counts also increase the likelihood for eligibility in government programs. When individuals are not counted through the national census, their communities can miss out on potential funds and general assistance from government programs. For instance, approximately forty thousand Cambodians in Long Beach, California, were not counted in the 1990 census, and the undercount was sufficient to disqualify the entire Cambodian community there from an important federal housing grant program.[7]

Census data on API communities are also quite valuable because, until the 1990 census, national and statewide survey data on disaggregated communities of Asian Americans were essentially nonexistent.[8] Census data allowed policy analysts to concretely identify the socioeconomic needs of specific Asian ethnic communities, in turn leading to more cost-effective solutions tailored to address these communities' concerns, especially in geographically coherent concentrations.[9] Using census data, scholars of Asian American studies are now able to conduct important statistical research in a number of areas, including but not limited to employment discrimination, housing patterns, education levels, and intermarriage rates. Census data have also been used to investigate whether public and private entities have illegally discriminated against Asian Americans in housing, employment, health care, and other vital areas.[10]

In this chapter I demonstrate that Asian American political successes in influencing the content of the census race question are largely attributable to their political relationships with a handful of members of Congress. National legislators working with Asian American constituencies have leveraged the institutional rules that underlie the organization of Congress and allow even a single member to wield significant authority on issues uniquely important to specific constituencies. Because congressional incumbents have significant advantages and are remarkably consistent in getting reelected, they can often aggressively pursue narrow political objectives without fear of being sanctioned by party leaders. Consistent with this theme, I close this chapter with a discussion of how the successful appropriation of American tax dollars to recompense Japanese Americans forcibly interned in concentration camps during World War II hinged on the ability of the representatives of Japanese American interests to leverage the countermajoritarian authority allowed by the formal rules of Congress.

THE COUNTERMAJORITARIAN
TENDENCIES OF CONGRESS

Members of Congress are faced with a workload as complex as it is enormous. A typical tax bill, for instance, is thousands of pages long and filled with arcane technical minutiae. In order to accomplish its many objectives, both the Senate and the House of Representatives have developed a number of institutional rules that organize their daily operation. Because it serves their purposes, many of these rules have a decidedly countermajoritarian bent that benefits individual legislators—and their specialized constituencies—at the expense of stronger parties. These rules, along with the many advantages of incumbency, also allow individual legislators to flex congressional power whether or not they are in the legislative majority.[11]

The origins and consequences of these rules have been discussed and debated elsewhere in great detail, and I limit myself to brief remarks necessary here. In order to divide labor, build institutional competency, and help legislators achieve their political and policy goals, Congress is divided into a system of largely autonomous committees and subcommittees where the bulk of the daily work is accomplished. Individual legislators can acquire a great deal of institutional authority, often at the expense of party leadership. Some committees are more important than others, and members of those committees are, accordingly, more powerful than members of others. Legislators often have some influence over their committee assignments, and they generally find assignments that will help them get reelected, helping to insulate them from the demands of both their own and opposing party elites.[12]

The longer a legislator is on a particular committee, the more powerful he or she tends to become. Because the committee system generally, though not always, follows the rule of seniority, senior members generally have more power than junior members; committee and subcommittee chairs are the most powerful of all, and are typically quite senior.[13] A legislator can also develop expertise in committee affairs over time, and build influential relationships with the various bureaucratic agents that work with the committee. All of this helps him or her to amass political chits that can be traded in for unrelated favors.[14] In short, the committee system enables legislators to acquire significant congressional authority and to become insulated from the demands of party leaders.

This structural tendency toward countermajoritarian power is further enhanced by the ability of congressional incumbents to get reelected repeatedly. National parties have never had much influence in nominating candidates for Congress, owing largely to primary elections in which individuals are largely responsible for their own political fate.[15] Members take advantage of an array of resources available to them as incumbents to stack the deck in favor of their reelection against less well-equipped challengers.[16] Partisan and racial gerrymandering throughout the American states has ensured that the vast majority of House districts are now dominated by the voters of one party; only a small fraction of elections for Congress are competitive. Safe seats often translate into greater freedom for legislators seeking to advance particular agendas, making it more likely that they can substantively represent a constituency of their choice. Inasmuch as individual candidates can get nominated, elected, and reelected without having to rely on the party, they will have the political latitude to pursue an independent agenda.

By way of contrast to the countermajoritarian power generated by the institutional rules and procedures of Congress, consider that for a society and government that prize the rights of the individual and emphasize the protection of minority rights, the two-party system is remarkably majoritarian. The winner-take-all political prize of presidential elections means that even a significant minority of the final vote does not translate into any political power, forcing any office-seeking party to win majorities at all costs. Of course, an individual legislator's power is closely tied to whether or not his or her party is in the majority, and minority power tends to be more effective in blocking than in passing legislation. Nevertheless, countermajoritarian rules combined with control over reelection can enable even a single legislator or organized minority caucus to wield significant congressional authority and insulate the member from party demands. Not surprisingly, African American members of Congress, virtually all of whom are Democrats from districts with large black constituencies, support the rule of seniority, committee autonomy, and racial gerrymandering despite their recognition that all three hurt the overall coherence and power of the Democratic Party.[17]

The ability of individual members of Congress to pursue a specialized constituency's agenda can also depend on the nature of the political goal. Because congressional party leaders want to be in the legislative majority, scholars who have examined party involvement in congressional campaigns have concluded that party leaders generally encourage individual legislators to put their own political interests first.[18] On specific issues that fly under the radar, and where Asian Americans are the primary constituent group, their representatives in Congress should be able to exercise disproportionate influence simply by exploiting institutional rules that engender countermajoritarian power. However, when party leadership in Congress does identify a specific issue or policy arena as having national significance for the party, they are far more likely to bring party elite pressure to bear on rank-and-file members of Congress than when an issue does not have national significance.[19] Legislative advocates of Asian Americans will probably not be able to influence the course of events significantly when political issues bring in major political players, be they party elites or powerful interest groups.

Following a brief introduction to the history of the census race question and its relationship to Asian America, I discuss four issues related to the decennial national census to explore the possibilities and limits of flexing Asian American political muscle through congressional representation. First, I discuss how Asian Americans were able to get so many different Asian ethnic groups listed on the census forms of the last three decennial censuses. Second, I explain the role played by congressional advocates of Native Hawaiians in the creation of a new racial category for the 2000 census. Third, I analyze why Taiwanese Americans are unlikely to succeed in their attempts to get listed on the census as a category separate from Chinese. Finally, I assess Asian American political efforts to influence the political debate that occurred over whether and how to officially recognize multiracials/multiethnics through the census race question.

A BRIEF HISTORY OF THE CENSUS AND ASIAN AMERICANS

Historically, social and political interest in monitoring a changing American demographic landscape has encouraged changes in the content of the census question regarding one's race.[20] At times, the shifting racial classifications of Asians in America have been the outcome of dynamic negotiation between state interests and politically organized Asian American challenges. At other historical moments, U.S. government treatment of Asians as undesirable and inexorably foreign has led the state to deploy the race question in an effort to track Asian communities.[21] The census deployed its first Asian classification in 1870, when the national government listed "Chinese" as a category for the race question (see Table 4.1).

TABLE 4.1: ASIAN/PACIFIC ISLANDER CATEGORIES IN THE U.S.
CENSUS: 1870 TO 1990

YEAR	CHINESE	JAPANESE	OTHER ASIAN OR PACIFIC ISLANDER	OTHER
1870	Chinese			
1880	Chinese			
1890	Chinese	Japanese		
1900	Chinese	Japanese		
1910	Chinese	Japanese		Other + write in
1920	Chinese	Japanese		Other + write in
1930	Chinese	Japanese Korean	Filipino, Hindu, out in full	Other race, spell
1940	Chinese	Japanese	Filipino, Hindu, Korean	Other race, spell out in full
1950	Chinese	Japanese	Filipino	Other race, spell out
1960	Chinese	Japanese	Filipino, Hawaiian, part Hawaiian, etc.	
1970	Chinese	Japanese	Filipino, Hawaiian, Korean	Other (print race)
1980	Chinese	Japanese	Filipino, Hawaiian, Korean, Vietnamese, Asian Indian, Samoan, Guamanian	Other (specify)
1990	Chinese	Japanese	Filipino, Hawaiian, Korean, Vietnamese, Asian Indian, Samoan, Guamanian, Other Asian or Pacific Islander	Other race

Source: Edmonston and Schultze (1995: table 7.1).

Note: The 2000 census broke apart the "Asian or Pacific Islander" category into the two separate categories of "Asian" and "Native Hawaiian or Pacific Islander." For the first time, it also allowed multiple check-offs to the race question.

The government's decision was a response to political pressure from white male Anglo-Americans concerned that Chinese workers needed to be monitored and controlled. Their sense of entitlement similarly inspired the listing of Japanese as a racial category in 1890, although both Chinese and Japanese immigrants represented a minuscule percentage of the population. When anti-Japanese hysteria arose during World War II, the director of the Census Bureau flew to California with 1940 census data to help the U.S. military round up and incarcerate Japanese Americans in concentration camps.[22]

In the 1960s, government motives for gathering data on its citizens based on race came under increasing suspicion, and the race question came under fire as an unnecessary and even dangerous tool—unnecessary because race was increasingly being seen as a fiction rather than a biological reality, and dangerous because of the ways in which "racial science" had been deployed in the name of genocide, slavery, and other acts of social injustice.[23] Had it not been for the passage of civil rights legislation during this time, the race question might not have appeared in the 1970 census.[24] Civil rights advocates who had previously decried government abuse of data on communities of color recognized that the new laws could not be enforced without racial population statistics that demonstrated inequalities and disparities of treatment and opportunity. Concern over whether these data would be abused was ultimately overwhelmed by the desire to enforce civil rights laws and provide policy analysts and academic researchers with an important national dataset.

Consequently, even as a hegemonic understanding of "race" was being attacked and discredited, racial population statistics were becoming ever more important and prevalent.[25] The scholarly and popular confusion over the meanings of race and different racial categories, combined with the obvious importance of racial population statistics and the persistence of racism, gave organized interest groups both the incentive and the rationale to put political pressure on bureaucratic officials. Census Bureau officials became engaged in an inherently messy and complex intellectual and political process that opened them up to attack from political interests keenly interested in whether and how data on their communities would be collected.

ASIAN AMERICANS, CONGRESSIONAL PRESSURE, AND THE 1980 CENSUS

In January 1973 a lengthy process to ensure that the U.S. government properly culled racial population data began when the U.S. Commission on Civil Rights sharply criticized federal agencies for failing to produce the racial and ethnic data that would allow national civil rights laws to be enforced.[26] In May 1977, in response to both criticism from the U.S. Commission on Civil Rights and increasing pressure from organized communities of color, the U.S. Office of Management and Budget (OMB) announced new guidelines for collecting and tabulating racial and ethnic data. The OMB's Directive 15 officially recognized five standardized racial and ethnic categories that all federal agencies would be required to use in administrative reporting and statistical activities. Four categories were considered "racial": American Indian or Alaskan Native, Asian or Pacific Islander, Black, and White, while one — Hispanic — was considered "ethnic." An Asian or Pacific Islander was defined as "a person having origins in any of the original peoples of the Far East, Southeast Asia, the Indian subcontinent, or the Pacific Islands."[27]

While Directive 15 proposed that individual responses be aggregated into the five basic racial/ethnic categories, nowhere did it mandate the collection of additional, more detailed racial and ethnic data. Given the tremendous internal diversity of Asian American populations, aggregating all people who claim to be Asian — or Pacific Islander for that matter — into a single category would inevitably gloss over significant cleavages within the Asian American racial formation and make it impossible to target policies and programs for specific Asian communities in the United States. Advocates claiming an Asian American interest were also deeply concerned that the offering of only a single panethnic "Asian or Pacific Islander" category on official census forms was likely to depress their official count, inasmuch as individuals from different Asian countries claimed their ethnic or national identity rather than identify with the Asian American racial formation.[28] Because Directive 15 required that APIs be tabulated and reported as a single category, disaggregated listings that allowed individuals to identify with a particular subgroup, nationality, or ethnic community would paradoxically be more likely to translate into higher numbers once their checkoffs were aggregated into a single panethnic category. Each ethnic community also had a strong incentive to ensure that the race question listed that community as an option, because each had its own political goals and policy issues and wanted to learn more about its community. The promise of listings was that it gave both ethnic-specific and panethnic Asian American interests the benefits of individual responses to the race question, since those responses could be aggregated for panethnic purposes and disaggregated for ethnic-specific ones.

The Census Bureau generally sponsors focus groups, performs statistical tests and dress rehearsals, employs demographic researchers, and organizes academic conferences in an effort to craft a successful race question for the decennial census. In preparation for the 1980 census, for the first time, the national census also involved local officials, civil rights activists, academics, and members of Congress who demanded to be included in the census planning process.[29] Congressional committees held more than forty hearings on the 1980 census, and political pressure from racial and ethnic interest groups led the bureau to establish minority advisory committees to make recommendations on the content and conduct of the census.[30] For the first time, individuals with no scientific or technical expertise, acting simply as representatives of their communities, were a formal part of the discussion over how to frame the race question.[31] To the dismay of Asian American political interests, however, the bureau refused to charter an API advisory committee. In response, Asian American political interests lobbied three Asian American members of Congress—Representatives Patsy Mink (D-HI) and Norman Mineta (D-CA) and Senator Spark Matsunaga (D-HI)—to put political pressure on the bureau. Responding to congressional and interest group pressure, the bureau changed its mind and chartered the Census Advisory Committee on the Asian Pacific American Population for the 1980 Census.[32]

In the 1970 census, five Asian American groups had been identified in the "color or race" question, while other Asian Americans were relegated to the "other" category (see Table 4.1). Asian Americans and Pacific Islanders, supported by members of the Census Advisory Committee, sought to get more Asian American groups listed on the race question, arguing that many individuals from Asia, particularly those with limited English-language skills and new immigrants, might not identify with the

Asian American category.[33] In opposition, the Census Bureau testified in congressional hearings that it preferred a single blanket category of Asian or Pacific Islander with a write-in space for subgroups.[34] Not only did the bureau lose this fight, but it ultimately ended up adding Asian Indian, Vietnamese, Samoan, and Guamanian to the five groups in the 1970 census, theoretically enabling a count of approximately 95 percent of all Asians and Pacific Islanders in the United States.[35]

ASIAN AMERICANS, CONGRESSIONAL PRESSURE, AND THE 1990 CENSUS

Like the 1980 census, the 1990 version was preceded by a number of quantitative analyses and statistical tests. Based on their research, the OMB and the Census Bureau promoted the conclusion that results from the short version of the race question, with its "write-in" space for Asian Americans and Pacific Islanders, were at least as good as, if not better than, test versions of other race questions that listed detailed Asian and Pacific Islander categories.[36] It became clear that the bureau was planning to announce a return to the format it had initially promoted in 1980 but had abandoned in the face of political pressure. The intended format required a checkoff in the summary group of "Asian or Pacific Islander," and then a write-in response for a specific subgroup.[37]

Asian and Pacific Islander political elites and community leaders remained concerned that the changes in the race question would influence the final tabulations of their numbers. They were also concerned about when and how any write-in responses would be tallied, as 1980 census results on Asian Americans and Pacific Islanders had taken as long as eight years to publish. The bureau also announced that neither it nor the OMB planned to tabulate the write-in responses for census short forms, and in congressional hearings, Census Advisory Committee member Dr. Trong Chai testified that bureau staff members had indicated that only 20 percent of the Asian American population who answered the longer census form would be counted by group.[38] Other representatives of the Asian American and Pacific Islander community criticized the bureau for failing to solicit them in the planning process and claimed that the bureau had decided on the format of the race question even before the advisory committees had begun to meet.[39]

In early 1988, to the dismay of Asian American political interests, the bureau announced that it would indeed return to the checkoff system.[40] It became clear that Asian American political interest groups alone could not force the bureau to change its mind. After meeting with the bureau one last time, Henry Der, the head of the National Coalition for an Accurate Count of Asian Pacific Americans (National Coalition), concluded that "the Census Bureau has gone as far as it will go.... We have to go to a higher authority."[41]

That higher authority was Representative Robert T. Matsui (D-CA). First elected in 1978, Matsui had quickly won a position on the powerful House Ways and Means Committee. In response to the bureau's plan not to count all write-in responses, Matsui remarked in congressional hearings that "Asian and Pacific Americans are being told to write in their subgroup even though the Bureau plans to ignore their answers."[42] The congressman initiated legislation that would force the bureau to count all write-in responses rather than only a sample, as planned. Responding to congressional pressure, the bureau relented and agreed in March 1988 to hand count every single census form returned by Asian Americans.[43]

Matsui was not finished. As a member of the Appropriations Committee, he was able to get a spot on the conference committee set up for the purpose of reconciling differences between the House and Senate versions of the appropriations bill for fiscal year 1989, which governed the budget of the Commerce Department and by extension the Census Bureau. Matsui was able to insert a provision mandating that the bureau not only return to the 1980 checkoff format but also add at least two more Asian Pacific Islander groups to the list.[44]

Matsui's ability to deliver political goods to Asian American political interests and communities reflects how Asian American political interests can be powerfully represented by even a single well-positioned member among the 435 representatives in the House. Appropriations bills are virtually certain to pass because of the tremendous work involved in getting them to their final legislative stages, and once Matsui succeeded in placing the provision in the bill, it was destined to become law. Although neither the House nor the Senate version of the Commerce Department's budget had passed this provision, and in the face of the bureau's opposition, Matsui was able not only to get what he wanted but to do it through negotiating with his congressional colleagues behind closed doors. Because the negotiations must reconcile two versions of the same appropriations bill, one passed by the House and the other by the Senate, once Matsui succeeded in getting his provision in the final bill, he effectively cut off the possibility of further debate.

Matsui also pushed a second bill directing the bureau to use the 1980 categories, at the very least, for all future censuses, but after Congress passed this bill President Reagan declined to sign it and pocket-vetoed it in November 1988.[45] In the days between the pocket veto and the bureau's announcement, Matsui kept the pressure on and reintroduced this second census bill, while Asian and Pacific Islander groups intensified their lobbying efforts. Finally, in January 1989, the bureau's resistance collapsed. The General Accounting Office (GAO) explained the bureau's reversal in bluntly political terms: "The Asian and Pacific Islander community succeeded in gaining congressional attention for its concerns.... Responding to congressional direction and pressures from the Asian and Pacific Islander community, the Bureau reconsidered its original decision and chose to include in the 1990 census a version of the race question with prelisted [checkoff] Asian and Pacific Islander categories."[46] The bureau further announced that it would include an "other Asian or Pacific Islander" category, allowing for the first time a 100 percent count of all individuals identifying in any way as Asian Americans or Pacific Islanders.[47] From the perspective of Asian American political elites, the "other API" category's most important function is that it boosts the total numbers of Asian Americans.

The bureau's collapse in the face of congressional pressure came extraordinarily late in the planning process for the 1990 census, indicating its unwilling participation in the turn of events. Later evaluations of the 1990 census emphasized the late change in explaining the census's dysfunctionality, and the uncertainty over the race item was considered a significant part of the census's unexpectedly high cost.[48] The change came after the bureau and the OMB had engaged in an expensive special research and testing program on the race question in an effort to build a scientific and political consensus that was ultimately not nearly as relevant as Matsui's relentless congressional pressure. From his perch as a powerful incumbent with almost no chance of losing office, and a member of the House Appropriations

Committee to boot, Matsui was able to aggressively and successfully represent Asian American political interests.[49]

THE CREATION OF THE NATIVE HAWAIIAN OR PACIFIC ISLANDER CATEGORY FOR THE 2000 CENSUS

The failure of the bureau to run an efficient operation for the 1990 census, as well as its demonstrated inability to hold fast to its decisions in the face of political pressure, probably encouraged a number of interests to seek to influence the categories of the 2000 census.[50] Joining multiracials/multiethnics, Arab Americans, and Cape Verdeans were Taiwanese Americans and Native Hawaiians who sought to have their claims recognized by the OMB and the bureau. In July 1993 the OMB published its proposed changes for the 2000 race question.[51] A key change had to do with how to address the growing social movement around those who were identifying increasingly as multiracial/multiethnic. While rejecting a "stand-alone" multiracial/multiethnic category option, the OMB recommended allowing individuals to check off multiple boxes in their response to the race question. The OMB declined to recognize the other interest groups that had been seeking recognition, among them Native Hawaiians seeking to move out of the Asian or Pacific Islander category and into the American Indian/Alaskan Native category and Taiwanese Americans attempting to establish a clear political and legal distinction from "mainland" Chinese in America.

In the early 1990s Senator Daniel Akaka's (D-HI) office began receiving requests for assistance from families of Native Hawaiian students and alumni of Kamehameha High School who were having difficulty getting admitted to college and paying for college tuition.[52] Akaka traced the influence of Directive 15 as it traveled from the OMB to the Department of Education to colleges and universities, and ultimately into the path of Native Hawaiian students. He discovered that university administrators and financial aid officers, following Directive 15, considered Native Hawaiians within the encompassing panethnic category of Asian American, and that this rendered them ineligible for most higher education affirmative action programs. Native Hawaiians suffer from a very difficult socioeconomic position as a class in both Hawaiian and the broader American society, but their inclusion in the "Asian or Pacific Islander" category per Directive 15 was effectively disguising the manifest social and economic hurdles specific to the Native Hawaiian experience.

In 1993 the senator initiated a conversation with OMB Director Leon Panetta, and shortly thereafter Akaka proposed in congressional hearings that Native Hawaiians be placed in a category with American Indians and Alaskan Natives. He was backed by the Hawaii congressional delegation, Hawaii's governor, John Waihee, Native Hawaiian organizations, and the panethnic National Coalition.[53] After the OMB published its new proposed categories in July 1997 without the requested change, the Hawaii congressional delegation applied intense pressure to the OMB, conducting a simultaneous outside and inside lobbying campaign during the two-month interregnum between the publication of the OMB's proposed decision and its final decision.[54] Akaka also asked members of the Senate Governmental Affairs Committee to pressure the OMB. The congressional advocates who backed the switch also flooded the OMB with statistical and social-scientific evidence indicating the merits of taking Native Hawaiians out of the summary Asian or Pacific Islander category. Outside lobbying efforts generated approximately three hundred letters and seven thousand individually signed preprinted postcards sent to the OMB. Akaka also organized a meeting between all the major Native Hawaiian service organizations and Clyde Tucker, a central figure in census decisions at the Bureau of Labor Statistics in the Department of Commerce, and Nancy Gordon, the bureau's liaison to the OMB.

Congressional advocates for the switch also lobbied the White House to pressure the OMB. However, Asian American congressional pressure on the White House was apparently counteracted by the caution being urged by the National Congress of American Indians and their congressional representatives, who were concerned that moving Native Hawaiians into a category with Native Americans would negatively affect their legal relationship with the U.S. government.[55] Given the competing interests, White House staff apparently asked OMB officials to resolve the situation without alienating the members of Congress actively engaged in representing either Hawaiian or Native American interests.[56]

Shortly before the OMB made its final decision on where to place Native Hawaiians, the Hawaiian delegation arranged a meeting with OMB administrator Sally Katzen, chief statistician Katherine Wallman, and her chief deputy, Suzanne Evinger. Faced with competing demands from different racial and ethnic groups as well as congressional pressure, Katzen proposed a diplomatic compromise that had not been seriously considered until then: The new directive would group Native Hawaiians and other Pacific Islanders together in their own separate category. The compromise meant that Native Hawaiian numbers would not be swamped by other Asian subgroups and that Native Americans would continue to be legally separate from Native Hawaiians.[57] The end result thus satisfied the concerns of the congressional representatives of both Native Hawaiians and their mainland counterparts. In October 1997, less than three months after they published their initial proposed changes, the OMB announced its reversal: The Asian or Pacific Islander category would be separated into two categories—"Asian" and "Native Hawaiian or Other Pacific Islander."[58]

> Asian. A person having origins in any of the original peoples of the Far East, Southeast Asia, or the Indian subcontinent including, for example, Cambodia, China, India, Japan, Korea, Malaysia, Pakistan, the Philippine Islands, Thailand, and Vietnam.
>
> Native Hawaiian or Other Pacific Islander. A person having origins in any of the original peoples of Hawaii, Guam, Samoa, or other Pacific Islands.[59]

There is little doubt that the shift in categories would not have happened had it not been for the intervention of Daniel Akaka and the rest of the Hawaii congressional delegation. But again, this is not an individual story so much as it is an institutional one. Ultimately, what is revealing about the eventual creation of the new Native Hawaiian or Pacific Islander category is the rather mundane process by which it came about. A handful of legislators, alerted by one of their electoral constituencies, lobbied the relevant bureaucracies in order to achieve a policy goal that aligned with their electoral incentives. Indeed, in addition to being a case study in Asian American politics, this could just as easily be a case study in how members of Congress address a constituency's needs. The OMB and the Bureau of the Census, faced with congressional pressure from the Hawaii delegation and coordinated interest group lobbying, engineered a political compromise that addressed the concerns of Native Hawaiians—a group that otherwise should have had no reason to believe it would be able to flex any political muscle. Thus did the concerns of Native Hawaiian high school students eventually translate into a significant shift in how the state racially categorizes its population.

TAIWANESE AMERICANS

Like other Asian American ethnic subgroups, Taiwanese Americans have both lobbied Congress and presented their concerns directly to the Census Bureau.[60] Since its inception in 1985, the Taiwanese American Citizens League has come out strongly in favor of listing Taiwanese as a separate category in the census race question. Unlike other Asian American groups, however, Taiwanese Americans have been completely unsuccessful in getting any bureaucratic movement on this issue.

It is instructive to consider why Native Hawaiians succeeded while Taiwanese American efforts have been met with unflinching resistance. In the Native Hawaiian case, a small, nationally unimportant constituency was seeking a policy shift that was far more significant to them than to anyone else. Their only opponents were Native Americans, who may have outnumbered Native Hawaiians but were by no means a major national or international political player. Even so, bureaucrats found a way to address the needs of Native Hawaiians without imposing costs on Native Americans. Native Hawaiian interests could be aggressively pursued, behind closed doors, by congressional legislators who were more likely to die in office than be defeated at the polls.

Taiwanese Americans face a very different political situation because of the serious international implications of recognizing them as separate from mainland Chinese Americans.[61] Official U.S. recognition of Taiwan in any way carries with it the not insignificant political risk of upsetting the government of the People's Republic of China (PRC), which insists that Taiwan is part of the PRC. Providing greater formal recognition to those identifying as Taiwanese is thus not about a slight adjustment in numbers or a simple matter of adding another checkoff box to the census race question, but fundamentally affects how the United States relates to the rising global presence of the PRC.

Consequently, it comes as no surprise that when the Census Bureau rejected Taiwanese demands to be listed in the 1990 census race question, it cited U.S. State Department concerns that relations with the PRC might be harmed by such an action.[62] International concerns may have also played a role in President Reagan's pocket veto of Representative Matsui's bill spelling out API categories for the 1990 census race question, as the bill would have listed Taiwanese as a category. When the Census Bureau capitulated to congressional pressure and spelled out more than a dozen API categories, it left out Taiwanese Americans.[63] The bureau rejected Taiwanese American demands for listing in the 2000 census for the same reason.[64] In short, Taiwanese American attempts to get a separate listing on the census run smack into a complex conversation between powerful national and international actors concerning what many foreign policy experts consider the greatest challenge to American global dominance in the coming decades. In this political context, leveraging the countermajoritarian rules of Congress is unlikely to help this community achieve its goals.

THE MULTIRACIAL/MULTIETHNIC CATEGORY AND ALLOWING MULTIPLE RESPONSES TO THE RACE QUESTION

In 1993 Thomas Sawyer, chairman of the House Subcommittee on Census, Statistics, and Postal Personnel, held four hearings that were dominated by the question of whether to add a multiracial/multiethnic category for the 2000 census. Emphasizing the importance of protecting the civil rights of those who claimed more than one racial or ethnic heritage, Project RACE (Recognize All Children Equally) and the American MultiEthnic Association (AMEA) led the political push for official state recognition of those who claimed heritage from more than one officially recognized racial or ethnic category.[65] Project RACE pushed for a "stand-alone" multiracial category to the exclusion of all other considerations, while AMEA pushed for a combination of a multiracial/multiethnic category and multiple responses.[66]

The "stand-alone" checkoff box was strongly opposed by most of the existing civil rights establishment, including prominent African American

and Asian American political groups and all four census advisory committees for minority populations.[67] These groups anticipated that most of the
individuals who might, if given the opportunity, select a stand-alone category would otherwise check a nominally monoracial classification.[68] Allowing a stand-alone category would thus lead to a decrease in nonwhite racial
population numbers that would in turn lead to a decrease in the political
power of communities of color as well as influence their eligibility for various government programs.[69] The statistical effect of allowing individuals to
check off a multiracial/multiethnic box appeared to be particularly significant in diminishing Asian American and Pacific Islander numbers. While
tests of a multiracial/multiethnic category had been ambiguous for its impact
on African Americans, Roderick Harrison, chief of the Census Bureau's
Racial Statistics Division, noted that "clearly, the statistical effects [of a mul-
tiracial/multiethnic category] are much more likely to appear in the Asian
Pacific Islander Population and in some segments of the Native American
Population."[70] Indeed, the numbers of those marking "Asian or Pacific
Islander" in tests were consistently depressed when respondents were offered
a multiracial/multiethnic option. Among Asian Americans, as many as 11.8
percent considered themselves as belonging to more than one racial category,
and as many as 3.1 percent indicated they would opt for a multiracial/multi-
ethnic category were it available.[71] Such a drop in numbers would have a powerful political and policy impact on their communities, and Asian American
political elites and community leaders expressed their deep concern.[72]

Leaders of civil rights organizations were also suspicious of what they saw
as bare-knuckled socially conservative political interests supporting the mul-
tiracial/multiethnic movement. Robert Hill, then chair of the Census Advisory Committee on the African American Population, remarked that "the
people who are against affirmative action are the same people who are pushing this."[73] The head of Project RACE, Susan Graham, came under particular scrutiny because of the Georgian's connection to Republican Speaker
of the House Newt Gingrich (R-GA). In congressional hearings, Gingrich
linked his support of the multiracial/multiethnic category to a larger
neoconservative vision that foresaw the end of programs like affirmative
action that explicitly acknowledged race.[74] Skeptical of the contention that
the movement was only about "treating all children with equal respect," as
Project RACE maintained, the civil rights establishment perceived that the

drive for a new category was a backhanded way to attack race-based programs that could not be administered without consistent racial population statistics. Noting that existing civil rights laws and programs were premised largely on exclusive membership in a racial group, opponents of a multiracial/multiethnic category argued that those who marked themselves as such might lose the legal protections afforded by those laws as well as their eligibility for various government programs.[75] Civil rights lawyers also worried that changing the allowed responses to the race category from one census to another effectively meant that individuals could and probably often would shift from one category to another every ten years, thus making it more difficult to rely on racial population statistics in civil lawsuits to prove that racial discrimination had occurred.[76]

The OMB ultimately decided not to add a multiracial/multiethnic category, but it did propose allowing multiple responses to the race question.[77] Befitting the importance of the issue, the Clinton administration actively attempted to allay congressional concerns on both sides of the debate, reassuring members that multiple responses would not artificially inflate the number of racial minorities through "double counting" or jeopardize civil rights enforcement, because those protections would be extended to all who considered themselves at least partially a member of a racial minority group.[78] The decision generally pleased the civil rights establishment because it avoided the possibility that individuals would only check off a multiracial/multiethnic box, effectively disappearing from the nominally "monoracial" categories. On the other hand, the OMB's decision disappointed Gingrich and Graham, who called it "half a loaf."[79]

When the multiracial/multiethnic issue first surfaced in congressional hearings held in 1993, only one leading Asian American political interest group, the Japanese American Citizens League, came out in support of government recognition of multiracials/multiethnics.[80] While careful to acknowledge the claims of multiracials/multiethnics, other Asian American organizations, including the National Asian Pacific Legal Consortium and the National Coalition for an Accurate Count of Asians and Pacific Islanders, lined up in staunch opposition to the creation of a multiracial/multiethnic category.[81] Despite the near-unified organized Asian American opposition and the statistical data showing the possible depressing impact on Asian American numbers of counting multiracials/multiethnics, it is doubtful that their efforts had much political influence over the Census Bureau's decision to allow for multiple responses to the race question. Heavyweight political figures, including the very powerful Republican Speaker, and major African American political interests were engaged in the debate, largely because of the outcome's potential influence over the political power of black interests and the future of affirmative action and other civil rights programs.

Census respondents checking a multiracial/multiethnic box might have led to a significant redistribution of individuals away from existing categories, no doubt with serious repercussions for the design of racial and partisan gerrymandering in areas with significant black populations. In contrast to Native Hawaiian efforts to effect a policy shift that would have a far greater impact on their community than on anyone else, the battle over counting multiracials/multiethnics brought in powerful actors tussling over significant political considerations. The relatively narrow concerns of Asian America's congressional representatives could not dominate the political landscape, no matter how important the issue was to their communities.

REPARATIONS FOR JAPANESE AMERICAN INTERNMENT DURING WORLD WAR II

The power of congressional countermajoritarian norms was quite clearly displayed by the passage of funding for the 1988 Civil Liberties Act (CLA), which promised reparations and a formal apology to Japanese Americans who had been incarcerated in concentration camps during World War II under suspicion of disloyalty without evidence, without even a trial. The journey of the act's passage stretched over four and half decades, and it is a remarkable testament to those Japanese American political elites, activists, and communities that made it happen.[82] But when President Ronald Reagan signed the CLA into law, there was no guarantee that former Japanese American internees would actually ever receive the authorized funds. As with every U.S. law that promises federal funding, the authorization to spend must be followed by another congressional action that specifies the amount, timing, and manner in which the money will be appropriated. If such an appropriation is either not made or significantly underfunded, then the original authorization bill effectively becomes a mere symbol.

Indeed, the early signs did not look good for thousands of Japanese Americans, many of whom, having been interned in the 1940s, were dying in the 1980s. President Reagan's proposed budget plan for fiscal year 1989 allocated only $2.1 million for administrative costs related to executing the CLA. The Democrat-dominated Congress went along, and when the 1990 budget proposal suggested that $20.3 million be allocated for reparations — about 1.6% of what had been authorized — proponents of reparations could not have been pleased. Moreover, without a set schedule of disbursements in place, advocates would have to fight the same battle over money every year, with uncertain prospects.

Ultimately, those who had fought for so long to pass the CLA had to rely on a political insider skillfully operating within the quintessentially insider game of appropriations:

> For us there is one person with the internal institutional clout to put a bigger redress number on the table, and that person is Daniel K. Inouye: the powerful number two Democrat on the full Senate Appropriations Committee, the Chairman of the Senate Defense Appropriations subcommittee ... and most important, the number two Democrat in the Appropriations Subcommittee where the Senate decision on redress money will be made.... Senator Inouye is the man of the hour.
>
> Our community must recognize that at the appropriations stage, politics is not patty cake or public relations, but inside, subcommittee hardball. This means that a single individual inside the relevant subcommittee must champion our cause.[83]

Champion it he did. As a former captain in the U.S. military and a highly decorated World War II veteran who had lost an arm in the European theater, the Japanese American senator's personal credibility in the matter was beyond debate. As a senior member of the Senate Appropriations Committee, Inouye's institutional power could not be ignored. Calling in a number of political chits accrued over a Senate career that had begun in 1962, the Japanese American senator from Hawaii shepherded through the appropriations process a disbursement schedule beginning in fiscal year 1991 that legally bound the U.S. government to appropriate the entire amount authorized by the CLA over the next four years. Inouye also delivered a powerful emotional speech drawn from personal experiences on the floor of the Senate that received wide media coverage. In the fall of 1990, almost fifty years after being imprisoned under suspicion of disloyalty to the United States, the first Japanese Americans received a formal apology, along with $20,000 for each living internee, from the U.S. government.[84]

Senator Inouye's role in attaining reparations is undeniably heroic. No doubt, had Inouye not stepped in to create an entitlement program, the appropriation of funds would have come much later, if at all.[85] However, an emphasis on Inouye the person has the potential to individualize what is fundamentally an institutional story. Certainly the senator's personal commitment and political skills were a factor in the process, but his very ability to put these into practice was a function of the ways in which Congress has organized itself as an institution to empower even a single member to exercise significant influence on targeted issues. The process of shepherding a pet project through the congressional appropriations process relies heavily on the power of legislators who have obtained seats on important "power" committees like Appropriations, developed long-term relationships with other members of Congress and the executive branch, and have plenty of political chits to call in. Inouye qualified on all three counts. He was also, at the time, a thirty-seven-year incumbent with virtually no chance of being defeated in future Senate elections, and privileged with all the numerous advantages of incumbency. Because the rule of seniority moved him into a more and more powerful position on the committee as time passed, his long tenure both in the Senate and on the Appropriations Committee translated into even greater institutional clout. Inouye the individual could have cared all he wanted to about redress, but what ultimately mattered for the appropriation of money was that, as one of one hundred senators, he was sitting on a remarkably powerful institutional perch from which to influence the course of events. That Inouye successfully enacted an entitlement program for a small, relatively powerless Japanese American community at a time when both the national debt and the national deficit were rapidly increasing suggests how the institutional framework of Congress can be leveraged to pursue Asian American political goals more fruitfully than via the national two-party system.

CULTURE, INSTITUTIONS, AND
ASIAN AMERICAN RACIAL FORMATION

Cultural theorists rightly emphasize the significance of the racial representation of Asian Americans in arguing that they face a unique situation in mainstream American politics. However, a singular focus on cultural discourse would lead us to overlook a great deal of important political negotiation that occurs within the institutions that dominate American political life. Analysis of cultural representations provides insight into the ways in which Asians are racialized in any given situation, but it cannot adequately explain different political outcomes across political contexts. Successful congressional advocacy of Asian American interests demonstrates that variance in institutional design can drive political actors to adopt different strategies and even generate different outcomes. Whereas Asian Americans negotiating the two-party system are structurally disadvantaged by the political logic of party competition, the countermajoritarian rules that organize the daily political work of congressional incumbents provide an institutional framework within which Asian American interests can be aggressively pursued by even a single legislator. Strategizing the future political development of Asian America requires attention to the distinct institutional rules that govern the different roads to political empowerment.

Meanwhile, when political scientists emphasize the inevitability of the political logic followed by goal-oriented actors within defined institutional frameworks, they too often ignore the relationship between the rules of the game that structure strategic behavior and the reproduction or contestation of cultural discourse. The temptation to claim that the only thing that matters is how political elites engage in instrumental rationality when faced with formal rules runs up against the reality that popular racialization of Asian bodies is precisely why Asian Americans must analyze the structure and political logic of different institutional settings if they are to advance their objectives. Were it not for the unique ways in which Asian bodies are racialized in the United States, Asian American political interests would not need to ask how these racializations might interact with particular institutional frameworks. Because Asian Americans are potentially racially marked as they negotiate institutional settings, they must anticipate whether and how their bodies will be culturally constructed and deployed for strategic reasons in different institutional settings.

I argued in Chapter 2 that, because an office-seeking party must build and maintain a majority coalition in a liberal society, party elites cannot help but incorporate into their political strategies how Asian bodies are racialized in American popular discourse as immutably illiberal. As Asian Americans become more active and potentially powerful within a major party coalition, the systemic logic of two-party competition forces party elites to draw upon and reproduce historically racist representations of Asians that have endured throughout America's history. Here I contend that congressional activity that occurs largely out of public view on behalf of Asian American interests illustrates how the countermajoritarian rules that govern the daily work of Congress can be exploited to the great benefit of Asian American communities. By leveraging the institutional rules and procedures of Congress, a handful of incumbent legislators were able to assertively advance Asian American political interests without the threat of party hostility or attacks from commercial mainstream media. Because institutional norms empower individual legislators to wield disproportionate influence on issues of concern to a specialized constituency, congressional advocates of Asian American communities were able to bring about critical changes to the census race question.

Of critical importance, Asian American success in influencing the census race question not only enhanced Asian American political prospects and helped Asian American communities acquire significant benefits in a number of policy areas; it also suggests how Asian American interests can powerfully influence the racial formation of Asian America. Consider that the census race question is a key site of Asian American racial formation: Shifting classifications of Asian bodies, along with the contestation over these classifications, not only influence the formation of public policy and have important policy impacts but indeed play a fundamental role in creating, defining, and transforming the Asian American racial formation as such. Asian American political influence over the census race question has thus played a critical role in influencing the content and shape of Asian American identity.[86]

Although Directive 15's racial classifications were intended to be limited to providing consistent categories on race (and ethnicity) for national government purposes, its categories were quickly adopted by a range of state and local agencies as well as the private and nonprofit sectors, both because the categories had official government recognition and because the population data existed and were organized through these categories. Because national and statewide datasets on Asians in the United States remain quite rare, census data are an absolutely critical resource for research on this formation, and this means that census classifications directly and deeply influence the development of popular understandings of Asian bodies. For example, consider how census data are used to intervene in the discursive narrative of the Asian immigrant as a model minority that overcame racial disadvantages to assimilate into American society.[87] This narrative generally makes no distinctions between Asian American ethnic subgroups, and it has the effect of simultaneously disguising Asian American internal heterogeneity and encouraging the perception that all Asian Americans meet or exceed the standard indicators for socioeconomic success.[88] Using census data, researchers have powerfully attacked this narrative by demonstrating that wide variations exist both between and within Asian American ethnic subgroups, and that the vision of an assimilated minority group that has overcome racial bias is suspect at best.[89]

Advocates of cultural politics consistently frame Asian American efforts to represent and influence the construction of their multiple identities as a matter of whether and how cultural interventions can influence the discursive meanings attached to Asian bodies. Yet Asian American political success in influencing the census race question tells us that the ongoing cultural struggle over racial representation can be enjoined through quintessentially political insider battles that occur behind closed doors between political elites. The broader political lesson here is that those who are serious about Asian American political empowerment must develop strategies and tactics that take into account both the institutional rules of the game and the dynamic role of cultural discourse in assessing how a racialized formation can successfully navigate the formal logic of an institutional setting.

5

SILENCE, MOBILIZATION, AND THE FUTURE OF ASIAN AMERICAN POLITICS

I N 1994 A MAJOR POLITICAL BATTLE of national and international resonance was fought in California over Proposition 187, a statewide initiative intended to prevent undocumented residents from utilizing state services such as public education and various forms of medical assistance.[1] Proposition 187 enjoyed the support of a majority of voters throughout California and was especially but not exclusively popular among conservatives.[2] Most Latinos in California and nationwide, not to mention Mexicans on both sides of the border, understood Proposition 187 to be anti-Mexican and anti-Latino.[3] The initiative was fiercely fought, not least because incumbent Republican governor Pete Wilson, suffering badly in the polls and up against a tough Democratic challenger, decided to hitch his reelection campaign to it.[4] Wilson saw his poll numbers go up, especially after his opponent Kathleen Brown refused to take a firm stand on the initiative until very late in the campaign.[5] Brown apparently anticipated that coming out against Proposition 187 would damage her among conservative and moderate voters, but she also recognized that supporting the initiative would cost her in immigrant communities of color. When she came out in opposition to Proposition 187, it was far too late to influence the outcome of the election.

During the campaign, an impassioned grassroots mobilization of citizens and noncitizens of Mexican descent took place in California schools and communities. This mobilization culminated on October 16, 1994, when more than seventy thousand opponents of Proposition 187 marched in downtown Los Angeles, many waving Mexican flags.[6] Campaign consultants on both sides of the fence knew immediately that the election was over when television news programs broadcast images of the demonstration. Proposition 187 had been losing ground to its opponents, but the march of so many Latinos under the banner of Mexico was popularly seen as backfiring on the marchers, leading to a backlash by voters incensed that Mexican nationalism would be publicly expressed in California, particularly given that the protestors were marching in opposition to an initiative that presumably would deny undocumented Mexicans in California access to state services.[7] Proposition 187 passed shortly thereafter with 59 percent of the vote, in the face of widespread mass antipathy to the measure in Latino communities.[8]

For political strategists envisioning the future of Latino politics, the situation was more complicated than this. On the one hand, they clearly desired the defeat of Proposition 187, and they well knew that as soon as Mexican flags were broadcast on television, victory for Proposition 187 was ensured.[9] On the other hand, although the gap had been narrowing in the final weeks of the campaign, Proposition 187 was still seen as quite likely to pass by a majority, regardless of whether Latino communities marched in the streets.[10] Moreover, most legal analysts had already gone on record saying that Proposition 187 would be found largely unconstitutional if passed, and indeed that turned out to be the case.[11] Most important, the terrific groundswell of grassroots opposition to Proposition 187 coming out of Latino communities was a precious asset to the future of Latino political power.[12] Had Latino political leaders followed the advice of anti—Proposition 187 campaign consultants and urged their communities to avoid publicly affirming their Mexican identity because it might upset white Californians, this would hardly have endeared would-be Latino political leaders to these communities, who probably would have ignored them anyway. Indeed, given that the Latino population had been called the sleeping giant of California politics since the 1950s, attempts by the Latino political elite to stifle this grassroots mobilization would have been rather dumbfounding.[13] The anti—Proposition 187 movement lost decisively despite massive mobilization efforts, yet rather than being a low point for Latinos, the campaign has come to represent a watershed event for Latino political power.[14] Powerful Latino voting blocs emerged throughout California, and as a consequence their support propelled Latino legislators into a dominant position in the state legislature, and thus in state politics.[15]

In the thirteen years prior to the battle over Proposition 187, the National Association of Latino Elected Officials had concentrated its efforts on helping Latinos acquire U.S. citizenship. For twenty years the Southwest Voter Registration Education Project had focused exclusively on getting Latino citizens registered to vote. When the battle over Proposition 187 occurred, this political infrastructure was already in place, ready to naturalize new citizens and enroll new Latino voters anxious and angry about Proposition 187. During the campaign, Latino opponents of 187 had burned Governor Wilson in effigy, and after the election his face became a symbol in Latino voter registration drives of anti-Latino racism and xenophobia.[16] In short, the emergence of Latino political power after Proposition 187 had everything to do with the long-term emphasis that the Latino political establishment had placed on mobilization efforts and its ability to take advantage of the tremendous political energy stirred up by the 1994 campaign.

In light of the grassroots outrage over Proposition 187 and the concomitant mobilization of Latino communities, consider the reaction of Asian American political elites and communities to the campaign finance controversy following the November 1996 election. Asian American political elites were in despair over the tremendous political damage inflicted by this controversy and the response of Asian American communities, calling it, among other things, "a major setback," "a year of feeling battered, abandoned and discriminated against," and the single worst political retreat for Asian American civil rights in 150 years.[17]

By contrast, if Asian American communities recognized the political cost of the controversy, they did not show it. Despite overwhelming evidence of anti-Asian actions and attitudes, there was no apparent widespread or sustained discussion among ordinary Asian American voters; the outrage was generally contained within circles already politically active in electoral politics. The vast majority of Asian Americans were apparently only dimly aware of the nationally televised Senate hearings on the campaign finance scandal, a media maelstrom that only Bill Clinton and Monica Lewinsky could outdo, the dashed hopes of a watershed year, and the organized response of politically active individuals and interests who had positioned themselves to speak and act on behalf of Asian American communities.

Why were there such starkly different responses to the controversy from Asian American political elites and the communities they claimed as their constituents? And how do we interpret the silence of Asian American communities in response to a highly public controversy in which anti-Asian rhetoric was ubiquitous? Many explanations were circulated after the 1996 election. It was said that Asians are somehow naturally apolitical, that they live under a historical legacy of social and political anti-Asian discrimination that depresses their political involvement, that their political activity is concentrated in other areas, that collective action, given the internal diversity of Asian America, is impossible, and so on and so forth.[18] In this concluding chapter I contend that the silence of Asian communities in the United States on the subject of the campaign finance controversy is a function of how the Asian American political establishment has both pushed itself and been pushed by major party elites to focus on developing relationships with powerful politicians rather than on building community-based political power.

Much scholarly work on conventional Asian American politics has focused on the internal heterogeneity that marks this racial formation and creates barriers to collective political action. At times, the study of mainstream Asian American politics seems to begin and end with a demonstration of diversity along axes of ethnicity, ancestry, language, religion, partisanship, ideology, levels of political participation, generation, and socioeconomic class. Demographic studies concentrate on socioeconomic differences, language barriers, age, immigrant status, geographic mobility, and other social-structural factors, while studies on levels of participation, political behavior, and public opinion focus on the heterogeneity of views, the importance of ties to respective home countries, varying partisan affiliations, poor voter registration levels, and politically divisive cultural differences.[19] While a handful of countervailing studies have suggested that Asian Americans are perhaps more consistent across ethnic subgroups than was previously believed, scholars have also documented how Asian American ethnic groups sometimes actively attempt to "disidentify" from one another.[20]

The diversity of Asian America obviously calls into question whether it is even possible to talk about "Asian American political interests," something

I have done throughout this book. Clearly the interests of Chinese Americans, Vietnamese Americans, Indian Americans, and so on, cannot be monolithic, nor does it make sense to treat, say, all Japanese Americans as if they are the same. The Asian American racial formation, like all other formations, is made up of differently situated communities and classes that negotiate their position not only vis-à-vis broader society but also within Asian America, and it is not unusual for particularized interests within Asian America to claim to speak for the entire racial formation when this is clearly impossible.

Internal diversity undoubtedly poses numerous challenges to effective political organizing. But a narrow focus on centrifugal forces frames the problem of collective political organization as something negotiated wholly internally among the communities within this racial formation. The reality is that negotiations within the Asian American racial formation are not strictly internal at all, but are themselves directly influenced by the broader cultural and strategic contexts within which politics occurs. Indeed, the very idea of inquiring whether and how very diverse people from different countries and backgrounds have internal commonalities finds its origins in racial discourse throughout American history, which has culturally constructed these peoples as somehow monolithically "Asian" in values, behavior, and attitudes.

Scholarly investigation of the internal diversity within Asian America is hardly "natural" but is rather a culturally constructed research agenda that emerges in the first place because of the dominant and enduring racial discourse in the United States around Asian bodies that sees them as fundamentally homogeneous.[21] The paradox is that the study of diversity among Asian Americans occurs only because this formation has been racially constructed as sharing fundamental values, attitudes, and behaviors. In the absence of this historic racialization of Asians, the question of their supposed diversity would not need to be posed.

This means that when scholars investigate whether an Asian American political interest exists, even when they focus exclusively on the political negotiation that occurs among different Asian American communities, they necessarily take into account how external political actors and society at large typically fail to distinguish effectively among different Asian ethnic communities, both between and within officially or popularly recognized Asian classifications. It is critical to acknowledge that the emphasis on empirical differences within and among Asian American communities ultimately rests on a singular notion of Asians that is culturally constructed. Otherwise, the study of Asian American diversity legitimates an essentialist reading of Asian American bodies, and the assertion that no coherent political interest can possibly exist because of their internal diversity has the ironically paradoxical effect of promoting an essentialist conception of Asian Americans as such.

Consider, for example, how Asian American interests have rallied around the collective political goal of preventing anti-Asian violence and discrimination. Throughout the communities that have constituted Asian America over time, individuals from one ethnic background have felt the hostility of attackers whose actions are motivated by animus toward a different Asian ethnic community. An oft-cited example is the murder in 1982 of Chinese American Vincent Chin by two white Americans who racialized, nationalized, and gendered Chin as embodying the male Japanese threat to white male America.[22] Because a culturally imposed identity can make them targets of verbal and physical violence, not to mention unwarranted state deprivation of liberties, Asian Americans have often come together to militate for the shared political objective of being able to live without fear of anti-Asian hostility. This political goal is culturally constructed: It would not exist if most of the citizenry distinguished easily and ubiquitously among different Asian nationalities and ethnicities—as in fact occurs in most Asian countries.

As the example of hate crimes suggests, a racially homogenizing discourse can act as a powerful counterbalance to the centrifugal forces within Asian America, motivating disparate groups to unify. But the existence of such a discourse does not mean that Asian Americans must simply accept it. As with any racial formation, Asian Americans have historically contested the cultural meanings of their racialized bodies.[23] Consider, for example, how Asian Americans have challenged the ways in which they are represented on the U.S. census as discussed in the last chapter. To achieve maximum political effect, Asian American political and community interests combined under a panethnic banner to influence census politics. Rather than simply embrace a monolithic racial category, however, these diverse interests sought policy guidelines that would allow individuals to identify by ethnicity, thus generating data on their specific communities. Counts of the different communities were then aggregated into a single panethnic category that could benefit panethnic efforts. Operating as a panethnic political player at the national level facilitated significant gains without compromising the needs of specific ethnic subgroups.[24] By leveraging the congressional authority of a handful of legislators, Asian Americans became powerfully involved in influencing both the official classifications and the cultural representations of their bodies.

When Asian Americans define their own political interests and make strategic decisions, whether they are conscious of it or not, these decisions are always linked to the racial discourse around Asian bodies in the United States. The decision to try and coalesce as an organized national interest is itself influenced by calculations about the future racialization of Asian bodies in the United States, and this necessarily takes into account how Asian bodies have been and are racialized today. Decisions about whether to pool resources across geographical, generational, and cultural borders can not only influence the size of the Asian American political coalition and the resources it can bring to bear, they can also have an impact on future negotiation of Asian American identities. For instance, embracing and utilizing panethnicity as an enduring moniker may have the effect of encouraging others to recognize the staying power of the panethnic classification; collective actions among diverse Asian American actors may in turn reinforce panethnic identity.[25]

In short, treating this racial formation as if it is just another political interest group is simply wrong. Asian Americans seeking to empower a coherent political interest must incorporate into their political calculations how Asian bodies have been racialized in American culture as well as the tremendous "internal" diversity that this racialization has paradoxically wrought. Finally, an investigation of whether there is a coherent political interest within Asian America must avoid naturalizing the entity of Asian America itself, even while acknowledging that decisions that have a tremendous impact on Asian American communities are made all the time by mainstream political elites within American governing institutions, and that goal-oriented Asian Americans seek to intervene in those decisions.

My analysis thus far has focused on the instrumental calculations and cultural negotiations involved in organizing as an Asian American political interest. Note, however, that organizing a coherent political interest is not the same as actually succeeding in politics. Organized political interests are collective actors that are subject to institutional constraints, and strategic decision making necessarily anticipates and incorporates the preferences of other political actors. Political success ultimately demands an awareness of the external political environment, including the actions, goals, and strategies of other political actors, how mainstream political institutions operate, and the cultural or ideological context within which political struggles occur. Failure to understand these factors may lead even a well-organized interest to ineffective or even politically dangerous mistakes that not only stall political progress but leave the interest in a worse position than before.

Simple ignorance about Asian Americans can play a role as well, and in leaving discussion of this out of this analysis, I do not mean to suggest that it does not exist. For instance, some mainstream political elites may truly believe that all people from the countries popularly understood as Asian are somehow alike, and this may factor into their political interactions. But, as I have argued previously, to focus on ignorance that would presumably be eradicated by educating the political establishment is to miss the fundamental reality that mainstream politicians are propelled not only by their knowledge and assumptions but also by their strategic motivations when dealing with Asian Americans.

Ignorance about Asian Americans does not change the fact that a politician would rather deal with a single panethnic group that can offer combined political assets than with individual ethnic groups, each offering a smaller set of resources. By waiting for a number of different communities to come together under a panethnic banner, a politician can both avoid the organizational costs involved in coalescing the panethnic political interest and reduce the transaction costs of negotiating with smaller groups of Asian Americans. Insisting on a panethnic presentation can also allow the politician to avoid alienating one ethnic group by privileging another.[26] And it is more efficient to satisfy a single panethnic interest with symbolic gestures, such as attendance at cultural events, token appointments, the occasional public use of Asian words, and the conspicuous consumption of ethnic food. More tangible, limited benefits such as political patronage can then be reserved for more resource-rich and politically savvy interests. An ethnic group thus faces a situation in which the probable success of an independent, go-it-alone strategy is not simply a function of its cohesion, resources, and mobilization, but also of a politician's preference to see the ethnic group join with other Asian American ethnic groups in providing political resources and making demands.

Party elites not only prefer that Asian Americans organize panethnically, they also have strategic reasons to prefer that this racial formation focus on acquiring national influence through campaign financing rather through local mass mobilization efforts. Consider that if Asian Americans were to plan strategies for mobilization, the need for efficient use of resources would probably dictate targeting a geographically dense concentration of people. Because of existing demographic patterns, mobilization efforts would thus almost certainly end up targeting a particular ethnic subgroup. Not only would this work against a politician's preference for panethnic organizing, it would probably (and more significantly) generate Asian ethnic political candidates who see their political chances grow as their constituency becomes politically integrated. The possibility that any rapidly emerging constituency would have the power to promote a competitive challenger is not likely to be a welcome development to an existing political establishment that wants to maintain power.

The rise of Asian American voting blocs and candidates would also threaten the political establishment because it would have a significant impact on campaign fund-raising. Over the past thirty years, Asian Americans have become an increasingly important source of funding political campaigns, with millions of dollars going to non-Asian American, primarily white candidates.[28] Asian American candidacies have also become much more frequent over this period, and they attract a disproportionate amount of campaign funds from Asian American donors.[29] Because Asian Americans typically prefer to donate to Asian American candidates, and especially to candidates of their own ethnicity, the proliferation of Asian American candidacies running competitive campaigns for higher office will necessarily cut into the percentage of campaign funds available for non-Asian American politicians. And these politicians thus cannot help but see the rise of Asian American candidates as politically threatening.

Non-Asian American political elites are thus invested in keeping ambitious Asian American political interests focused on the short-term promise of elite influence rather than the long-term development of a political infrastructure that includes homegrown Asian American politicians clearly attached to Asian communities in the United States. I contend that one key way that parties keep Asian American dollars coming is by encouraging what amounts to expensive Asian American "candidacies" to appointed offices. For example, Asian Americans hoped that their financial contributions to the 1996 reelection of President Bill Clinton would win them a cabinet position in the second Clinton administration.[30] Via large campaign contributions to the Democratic Party, Asian American political elites essentially "ran" for a powerful appointed office. This is a not uncommon strategy for interest groups seeking to place one of their own in the inner circles of the White House, and it is not all that surprising that the Asian American political establishment sought to have a "mirrored" face in the cabinet. After all, cabinet positions do come with significant authority and political prestige. From the perspective of party elites that require large and continuing infusions of campaign contributions to fund increasingly expensive national campaigns for elected office, appointed office can be quite valuable.

However, investing in the already politically powerful rather than pursuing power through grassroots organizing has steep costs. Campaign contributions allow Asian Americans to participate in politics in the short term but inevitably hinder long-term efforts to develop a political infrastructure within Asian communities.[31] Even if Asian Americans were to achieve their short-term goals, a strategy that depends on giving money to national party organizations does not provide even indirect resources for advancing grassroots mobilization and politicization efforts within Asian American communities. Inasmuch as the campaign finance game diminishes the ability of Asian Americans to pursue other strategies, it would necessarily decelerate the push for lasting, independent Asian American political power.

Consider what would happen if Asian American donors took the money they have invested in the major parties over the past thirty years and redirected it toward electing candidates grounded in Asian communities in the United States. Funding campaigns, even losing ones, that focused on naturalization, voter registration, and political mobilization would arguably leave Asian American communities with far brighter prospects for acquiring lasting, independent political power. On the other hand, pursuing elite influence through campaign contributions may lead to the development of a "gatekeeper" model of politics, whereby a select few Asian American elites are able to forge long-term relationships with established mainstream political actors.[32] Rather than having multiple tiers of political actors providing many points of access and a nonhierarchical flow of information, information would have to go through these Asian American elites. These elites would dominate the Asian American political landscape by dint of their access to and influence over powerful actors located within the governing structure of the United States.

It should come as no surprise that some Asian Americans would also prefer to focus on building relationships with powerful establishment politicians rather than invest in long-term mobilization efforts. Wealthy corporate elites within Asian America will not put resources into building a base among working-class Asian immigrants concerned about economic issues affecting their lives, such as a living wage or the enforcement of labor laws.[33] The push toward building elite, influence-based relationships rather than mobilizing at the grassroots level is also motivated by Asia-based multinational corporations that attempt to sway American economic policies in concert with selected Asian American political actors. Not surprisingly, all of the individual Asian Americans investigated for illegal or inappropriate fundraising for the 1996 election were directly linked not so much to Asian communities in the United States as to transnational and multinational corporate interests.[34]

In response to the political devastation wrought by the campaign finance controversy, both scholars and advocates of Asian American political life urged this racial formation to move toward greater integration between Asian communities and conventional politics rather than trying to curry favor with party elites.[35] For these commentators, the lesson was that without mobilization and strong community-based institutions to rely upon, powerful elites would be able to maintain an influence-based relationship with Asian Americans until it became politically expedient to jettison them. Presumably, were Asian Americans politically mobilized, parties would not have treated them with such hostility, because these communities could have imposed political costs.

Grassroots mobilization has not been a major part of Asian American political strategy.[36] There are, of course, many historical reasons for this, tied to racist practices that were codified in U.S. law. [37] Restrictive immigration laws that rested on anti-Asian sentiment allowed only a trickle of immigrants from Asia until the passage of the 1965 Immigration Act, significantly depressing the political development of Asians in America, both in numbers and in terms of acquiring political experience.[38] The Asian immigrants who did come to the United States were denied political rights and generally prevented from participating as members of the nation's polity.[39] Their political preferences were irrelevant to the political process because they could not partake of mainstream politics, and they could not partake of politics because they were not and could not become naturalized citizens until the passage of the 1952 McCarran-Walter Act.[40] The lack of basic political rights also meant that it was more difficult for Asians to protest their civil deprivations; as noncitizens with no political rights, their position in the United States could be more easily terminated without penalty to either their employers or the U.S. government.[41]

The Asian American acquisition of political rights was a long time coming, and today there is no question that Asian Americans are in a much stronger position to register their political preferences through the normal political process. But exercising political rights is not the same thing as having meaningful political power. Sometimes a very small constituency can have a great deal of power through voting. At other times, a very large constituency can have very little power. The difference can rest on how voter preferences are mediated through institutional design. Consider, for instance, how parties are allocated seats via election to the Israeli parliament. Two percent of the total national vote can lead to a party member's election, and this has led to the proliferation of parties offering candidates. The rise of so many parties has in turn made it very difficult for one party to gain a majority of parliamentary seats, and this in turn has allowed small parties with very few representatives to wield disproportionate power as the larger parties try to woo them into joining their coalition. On the other hand, in the 2004 American presidential election more Americans voted for Democratic senator John Kerry than had ever voted for a presidential candidate in U.S. history—save one: Republican incumbent George W. Bush, who received even more votes in the same election.[42] Because the presidential election is run by majority rule with a winner-take-all prize, the single largest outreach and mobilization effort in Democratic Party history led to 48 percent of the vote and no formal political power.[43]

Asian American political advocates have suggested that if their communities had mobilized as a voting bloc in 1996, this would have positively influenced the behavior of party elites. Mobilization has been offered as a long-term strategy that might even lead to Asian Americans becoming a poten-tial swing voting bloc that could tip a minority coalition into a majority one, thus making them a sought-after electoral commodity.[44] I believe that this is a misreading of the political logic of the national two-party system, and that this misreading occurs because it fails to incorporate how the presence of racialized Asian bodies influences party elite strategies. Whether or not Asian American communities had been highly mobilized for the 1996 national elec-tion, party elite behavior would not have changed. As we have seen, an office-seeking party must build a majority coalition, and the presence of racialized Asian bodies within such a coalition can undermine this goal. Greater mobi-lization of Asian Americans would not have changed the structural necessity of building a majority coalition, nor would it have lessened the danger to the party brand name of being associated with Asian bodies racialized as immutably loyal to corporations and governments based in Asia. The threat of a strong Asian American electoral base would not have stopped party elites from making the strategic decision to distance themselves from Asian bodies through publicly hostile acts, regardless of whether Asian Americans made up 1 percent of the electorate or 10 percent. Indeed, an argument could be made that perceptions of a strong electoral base of Asian Americans might actually have heightened party elite concerns about being associated with them.[45]

This is not, by any stretch, to say that mobilization does not matter. Rather, it is a reminder that if Asian American political interests are to pri-oritize mobilization, they need to critically evaluate how the political par-ticipation of Asian communities will travel through institutions governed by formal rules and populated by strategic political elites. Indeed, I believe that mobilization would have made a tremendous difference after the 1996 election, but not because party elites would have behaved any differently at the time. Rather, as the example of Latino mobilization against Proposition 187 demonstrates, there could have been other important political advances.

Asian American political development has a long way to go, and the cam-paign finance controversy was obviously a major setback. But more than that, I contend that the disconnection between Asian American political elites and Asian American communities, and not the campaign finance controversy itself, represents the contemporary nadir of Asian American political devel-opment. The 1996 election could have been the watershed event the Asian American political establishment anticipated, not for the acquisition of elite influence but for sparking the development of long-term community-based political power. The campaign finance controversy was a missed opportunity to forge meaningful ties between the Asian American political establishment and Asian communities in the United States.

In an interview with the Public Broadcasting System (PBS) for a special *Frontline* report on the campaign finance controversy, longtime Asian American fund-raiser David Lang pinpointed just how far removed Asian American political elites were from the communities they claim to represent in Washington, D.C.

> FRONTLINE: *Were there Asian-Americans who were appropriately rewarded by the [second] Clinton administration?*

> LANG: Oh, of course, yeah, I think, because if you look at the list of Asian-American appointees ... there were close to 200 of them. Most of them are very well qualified. Most of them have served the Administration well. A lot of them got to the kind of position they wanted. Of course ... we didn't have a Cabinet secretary, so that was a major disappointment, but on the other hand we also realized that our history of political involvement is relatively short compared to other candidates, so maybe we need to invest more time and get more involvement before we can reach that level yet.
>
> I think the Administration has paid attention to us.... We're happy....

> FRONTLINE: *You attended [Clinton's second] presidential inauguration. How would you describe it?*

> LANG: It could have been a crowning achievement for the Asian-American community, but unfortunately that wasn't the case. So far, we haven't seen any major appointments in the Asian community.... I don't want to use the term going down the drain, but I think our involvement at the national level has a serious setback. I think it's a serious setback.[46]

Besides the apparent contradiction in being happy about a serious setback, what is remarkable is how Lang equates the number and prestige of the political appointments given to Asian American political elites as the measure of political success for the Asian American community.[47] That he does so calls into question who he is talking about when he speaks of the Asian American community.

I do not mean to lay undue blame on Asian American political elites; as I hope I have shown, the ultimate responsibility for the political demobilization of Asian communities in the United States is located in different histories, elite strategies, and political goals, and cannot be neatly parceled out. To single out Lang and other Asian American political elites simplifies, individualizes, and ultimately disguises the institutional and cultural forces that continue to direct conventional Asian American politics. But I do believe that had Asian American political elites been better prepared to take advantage of the strategic opportunity afforded by the outpouring of public hostility toward racialized Asian bodies, Asian American political development could have taken a major step forward. Instead, in light of the time and energy invested by the political establishment in pursuing elite influence rather than building mass mobilization, one could hardly have expected Asian communities in the United States to do anything but ignore or distance themselves from an Asian American political establishment under attack. In a sense, Asian communities held their presumptive political leaders to account, and rightly called into question their legitimacy.

The central problem facing Asian American political development today is not the presence of a few individuals, like the fund-raisers John Huang, Maria Hsia, and Charlie Trie, who break campaign finance laws and potentially hurt innocent people in the process. Nor is it that someone like David Lang does not speak for the Asian American community. After all, if the community he identifies as his own is satisfied with placing Asian Americans in key appointed positions in the executive branch of the national government, then it makes little sense to demand that he pursue other goals. Rather, the challenge is for Asian American communities, however they define their identities and interests, to design and execute political strategies that take into account how cultural constructions of race are mediated through different institutional settings.

NOTES

CHAPTER 1

1. U.S. Bureau of the Census, Population Division, Population Estimates Program, "Resident Population Estimates of the United States by Sex, Race, and Hispanic Origin: April 1, 1990 to July 1, 1999, with Short-Term Projection to November 1, 2000" (Washington, D.C., January 2, 2001).

2. U.S. Bureau of the Census, "California Leads States and Los Angeles County, Calif., Tops Counties in Asian and Pacific Islander Population Increase," Census Bureau Reports, September 4, 1998, http://www.census.gov/Press-Release/cb98-161.html (accessed August 12, 1999).

3. On Asian Americans as potential swing voters, see Pei-te Lien, *The Making of Asian America through Political Participation* (Philadelphia: Temple University Press, 2001); Don T. Nakanishi, "When Numbers Do Not Add Up: Asian Pacific Americans and California Politics," in *Racial and Ethnic Politics in California*, vol. 2, ed. Michael B. Preston, Bruce E. Cain, and Sandra Bass (Berkeley: Institute of Governmental Studies Press, 1999), 3–43; Don T. Nakanishi, "The Next Swing Vote? Asian Pacific Americans and California Politics," in *Racial and Ethnic Politics in California*, vol. 1, ed. Michael B. Preston, Bruce E. Cain, and Sandra Bass (Berkeley: Institute of Governmental Studies Press, 1991), 25–54; and Bruce Cain, "Asian American Electoral Power: Imminent or Illusory?" *Election Politics* 5 (1988): 27–30. On the rising number of Asian American officeholders, see Don T. Nakanishi and James Lai, *1998–99 National Asian Pacific American Political Almanac* (Los Angeles: UCLA Asian American Studies Center, 2000).

4. Susan Berfield and Stuart Wolfendale, "A Political Status Symbol: Asians Now Have It—Their Own Lobbying Group," *AsianWeek*, September 26, 1997.

5. Asian American Government Executives Network, press release, December 1996. See http://www.aagen.org.

6. Frank Wu, "Pressure on the Jobs: CAPACI Pushes for Cabinet Appointments," *AsianWeek*, December 6–13, 1996.

7. For further details and documentation, see Frank Wu, *Yellow: Race in America beyond Black and White* (New York: Basic Books, 2001); Ling-chi Wang, "Race, Class, Citizenship, and Extraterritoriality: Asian Americans and the 1996 Campaign Finance Scandal," *Amerasia Journal* 24 (spring 1998): 1–21; Ling-chi Wang, "Campaign Finance Scandal and Anti-Asian Exclusionism: Historical and Contemporary Perspectives," statement before the U.S. Commission on Civil Rights, December 5, 1997; Helen Zia, *Asian American Dreams: The Emergence of an American People* (New York: Farrar, Straus and Giroux, 2000); and Michael Chang, *Racial Politics in an Era of Transnational Citizenship: The 1996 "Asian Donorgate" Controversy in Perspective* (Lanham, Md.: Rowman & Littlefield, 2004).

8. For the most comprehensive analysis of media coverage of Asian Americans during the campaign finance controversy, see Frank Wu and May Nicholson, "Have You No Decency? Racial Aspects of Media Coverage on the John Huang Matter," *Asian American Policy Review* 7 (spring 1997): 1–3. See also Helen Zia, "Can Asian Americans Turn the Media Tide?" *The Nation*, December 22, 1997, 10.

9. Wang, "Race, Class, Citizenship"; Ling-chi Wang, "Foreign Money Is No Friend of Ours," *AsianWeek*, November 8, 1996.

10. On the systemically repeated usage of key words and phrases such as "bad" and "disloyal," see Wu and Nicholson, "Have You No Decency?"

11. Wang, "Campaign Finance Scandal." One could, of course, argue that Wang overstates his point in calling it the worst setback for Asian Americans in the past 150 years. Japanese Americans placed in concentration camps during World War II might have something to say about this, as might Chinese immigrants to California in the 1850s and 1860s, who endured terrorizing white mobs, at worst, and rampant state-sponsored racism, at best. There is hardly a need to compete with narratives of victimization here. One need only acknowledge that this was an extraordinarily difficult period for Asian American interests in the United States.

12. Locke quoted in K. Connie Kang, "Asian American Needs Are Focus of New Group," *Los Angeles Times*, August 24, 1997, A1.

13. Political scientists' support of the two-party system as inclusive and as generative of democratic values extends throughout rational-choice, behavioralist, and new-institutionalist approaches. See, for example, Kenneth Benoit and Kenneth A. Shepsle, "Electoral Systems and Minority Representation," in *Classifying by Race*, ed. Paul E. Peterson (Princeton: Princeton University Press, 1995); John F. Bibby, "In Defense of the Two-Party System," in *Multiparty Politics in America*, ed. Paul S. Herrnson and John C. Green (Lanham, Md.: Rowman & Littlefield, 1997), 45–58; Bruce Cain, "Party Autonomy and Two-Party Electoral Competition," *University of Pennsylvania Law Review* 149 (2001); Sidney M. Milkis, *Political Parties and Constitutional Government: Remaking American Democracy* (Baltimore: Johns Hopkins University Press, 1999); James A. Reichley, *The Life of the Parties: A History of American Political Parties* (Lanham, Md.: Rowman & Littlefield, 1992); David W. Rhode, "Something's Happening Here, What It Is Ain't Exactly Clear: Southern Democrats in the House of Representatives," in *Home Style and Washington Work*, ed. Morris P. Fiorina and David W. Rhode (Ann Arbor: University of Michigan Press, 1991); Larry J. Sabato and Bruce A. Larson, *The Party's Just Begun: Shaping Political Parties for America's Future* (New York: Pearson Education, 2001); Martin Shefter, *Political Parties and the State: The American Historical Experience* (Princeton: Princeton University Press, 1994); and Benjamin Wattenberg, *The Decline of American Political Parties: 1952–1988* (Cambridge: Harvard University Press, 1990). On the positive values of the two-party system for racial, ethnic, and immigrant minority groups, see, for example, V. O. Key Jr., *Southern Politics in State and Nation*, new ed. (Knoxville: University of Tennessee Press, 1984); Robert A. Dahl, *Who Governs?* (New Haven: Yale University Press, 1961); and Michael Jones-Correa, "Bringing Outsiders In: Questions of Immigrant Incorporation," in *The Politics of Democratic Inclusion*, ed. Christina Wolbrecht

and Rodney E. Hero, with Peri E. Arnold and Alvin B. Tillery (Philadelphia: Temple University Press, 2002).

14. Moshei Ostrogorski and Herbert Croly were two turn-of-the-century critics of the two-party system in the political science literature. See Ostrogorski, *Democracy and the Party System in the United States* (New York: Macmillan, 1910), and Croly, *Progressive Democracy* (New York: Macmillan, 1915). More recently, see Theodore J. Lowi, "Political Parties and the Future State of the Union," in *American Political Parties: Decline or Resurgence?* ed. Jeffrey E. Cohen, Richard Fleisher, and Paul Kantor (Washington, D.C.: Congressional Quarterly Press, 2001); Douglas J. Amy, *Real Choices/New Voices* (New York: Columbia University Press, 1993); Lisa Jane Disch, *The Tyranny of the Two-Party System* (New York: Columbia University Press, 2002); Robert A. Dahl, *Democracy and Its Critics* (New Haven: Yale University Press, 1989); and Robert A. Dahl, *How Democratic Is the American Constitution?* (New Haven: Yale University Press, 2001). On how the party system hinders the advance of particular racial and ethnic minorities, see Paul Frymer, *Uneasy Alliances: Race and Party Competition in America* (Princeton: Princeton University Press, 1999); Claire Jean Kim, "Managing the Racial Breach: Clinton, Black-White Polarization, and the Race Initiative," *Political Science Quarterly* 117, no. 1 (2001): 55; and Luis Ricardo Fraga and David L. Leal, "Playing the 'Latino Card': Race, Ethnicity, and National Party Politics," *DuBois Review* 1, no. 2 (2004): 297–317.

15. Austin Ranney and Willmoore Kendall, *Democracy and the American Party System* (New York: Harcourt Brace, 1956), 508.

16. E. E. Schattschneider, *Party Government* (New York: Holt, Rinehart and Winston, 1942); William J. Keefe, *Parties, Politics and Public Policy in America* (New York: Holt, Rinehart and Winston, 1972); and Frank J. Sorauf, *Political Parties in the American System* (Boston: Little, Brown, 1964).

17. That political parties will fail Asian Americans should not be taken to mean that this racial formation should not pursue political power within the dominant political institutions that govern public life in the United States. Indeed, I argue in Chapter 4 that Asian American political interests have a better chance of being successfully represented in Congress given that institution's formal rules.

18. Edward S. Greenberg and Benjamin I. Page, *The Struggle for Democracy* (New York: HarperCollins, 1995), 268.

19. Benoit and Shepsle, "Electoral Systems and Minority Representation"; Key, *Southern Politics in State and Nation;* and Shefter, *Political Parties and the State.*

20. Dahl, *Who Governs?;* Alexis de Tocqueville, *Democracy in America,* ed. J. P. Mayer, trans. George Lawrence (New York: Harper & Row, 1966); and Gunnar Myrdal, *An American Dilemma: The Negro Problem and Modern Democracy,* vol. 1 (Brunswick, N.J.: Transaction Publishers, 1996).

21. See, for example, Donald R. Kinder and Lynn M. Sanders, *Divided by Color: Racial Politics and Democratic Ideals* (Chicago: University of Chicago Press, 1996); David O. Sears, Jim Sidanius, and Lawrence Bobo, eds., *Racialized Politics: The Debate about Racism in America* (Chicago: University of Chicago Press, 2000); and Paul M. Sniderman and Thomas Piazza, *The Scar of Race* (Cambridge: Harvard University Press, 1994).

22. For example, in two recent edited volumes on the state of American political parties, discussion of race and racism is almost entirely absent. See John C. Green and Daniel M. Shea, eds., *The State of the Parties: The Changing Role of Contemporary American Parties* (Lanham, Md.: Rowman & Littlefield, 1999), and L. Sandy Maisel, ed., *The Parties Respond: Changes in American Parties and Campaigns* (Boulder: Westview Press, 2002).

23. Frymer, *Uneasy Alliances,* chaps. 1–2.

24. Ibid.

25. Ibid., 15.

26. In not addressing the First Reconstruction, I am assuming that blacks could not effectively enjoin the cultural battle over the representation of their bodies as they were able to do in the post—World War II period.

27. On the dominant axis of the black-white paradigm, see, e.g., Claire Jean Kim, "The Racial Triangulation of Asian Americans," *Politics and Society* 27 (March 1999): 105–38.

28. Thomas Borstelmann, *The Cold War and the Color Line: American Race Relations in the Global Arena* (Cambridge: Harvard University Press, 2003); and Mary Dudziak, *Cold War, Civil Rights: Race and the Image of American Democracy* (Princeton: Princeton University Press, 2002).

29. Frymer does this himself in a later article on the role of court adjudication of labor law. Paul Frymer, "Racism Revised: Courts, Labor Law, and the Institutional Construction of Racial Animus," *American Political Science Review* 99 (August 2005): 373–88.

30. Michael Omi and Howard Winant, *Racial Formation in the United States from the 1960s to the 1990s* (New York: Routledge, 1994), 2.

31. For instance, Robert Lee's book, *Orientals: Asian Americans in Popular Culture* (Philadelphia: Temple University Press, 1999), demonstrates how different historical situations in American history (e.g., the consolidation of European immigrant working-class identity, World War II, the cold war, etc.) generate different racial meanings that are attached to the bodies of Asians in the United States.

32. Michael C. Dawson and Cathy Cohen, "Problems in the Study of the Politics of Race," in *Political Science: The State of the Discipline*, ed. Ira Katznelson and Helen Milner (New York: W. W. Norton, 2002).

33. Elaine Kim, *Asian American Literature: An Introduction to the Writings and Their Social Context* (Philadelphia: Temple University Press, 1982), chap. 1; Lisa Lowe, *Immigrant Acts: On Asian American Cultural Politics* (Durham: Duke University Press, 1996); Omi and Winant, *Racial Formation in the United States*; David Palumbo-Liu, *Asian/American: Historical Crossings of a Racial Frontier* (Stanford: Stanford University Press, 1999); Claire Jean Kim, *Bitter Fruit: The Politics of Black-Korean Conflict in New York City* (New Haven: Yale University Press, 2003); and Lee, *Orientals*. Of course, a great deal of excellent theory not specific to Asian Americans has also been generated; see, e.g., David Theo Goldberg, *Anatomy of Racism* (Minneapolis: University of Minnesota Press, 1990); Stuart Hall, "Gramsci's Relevance for the Study of Race and Ethnicity," *Journal of Communication Inquiry* 10, no. 2 (1986): 5–27; George Lipsitz, *The Possessive Investment in Whiteness: How White People Profit from Identity Politics* (Philadelphia: Temple University Press, 2006); and David Roediger, *Wages of Whiteness: Race and the Making of the American Working Class* (New York: Verso, 1999).

34. Although Kim is not specific about this, I would presume she means white Anglo, or white non-Hispanic, Americans.

35. Kim, *Bitter Fruit.*

36. Kim, "Racial Triangulation of Asian Americans."

37. Chang, *Racial Politics in an Era of Transnational Citizenship*, 7.

38. See, for instance, Earl Black and Merle Black, *Politics and Society in the South* (Cambridge: Harvard University Press, 1987).

39. See Steven J. Rosenstone and John Mark Hansen, *Mobilization, Participation, and Democracy in America* (New York: Macmillan, 1993).

40. For instance, Frymer, in *Uneasy Alliances*, argues that party elites, responding to the political necessity of building majority-based coalitions in order to win elections, consistently shortchange black Americans out of fear that the party will turn off white voters. See also John H. Aldrich, *Why Parties? The Origin and Transformation of Party Politics in America* (Chicago: University of Chicago Press, 1995); Amy Bridges, *Morning Glories: Municipal Reform in the Southwest* (Princeton: Princeton University Press, 1997); Scott C. James, *Presidents, Parties,*

and the State: A Party System Perspective on Democratic Regulatory Choice, 1884–1936 (New York: Cambridge University Press, 2000); Richard M. Valelly, "National Parties and Racial Disenfranchisement," in Peterson, *Classifying by Race*; and Christina Wolbrecht, *The Politics of Women's Rights: Parties, Positions, and Change* (Princeton: Princeton University Press, 2000).

41. See, for example, John Horton, *The Politics of Diversity: Immigration, Resistance, and Change in Monterey Park, California* (Philadelphia: Temple University Press, 1995); and Leland Saito, *Race and Politics: Asian Americans, Latinos, and Whites in a Los Angeles Suburb* (Urbana: University of Illinois Press, 1998).

42. Indeed, I will argue later that Asian Americans would be better served through greater investment in building political power through local structures.

43. For a discussion of the distinction between substantive and descriptive representation, see Hanna F. Pitkin, *The Concept of Representation* (Berkeley and Los Angeles: University of California Press, 1967).

44. Louis Hartz, *The Liberal Tradition in America* (New York: Harcourt Brace Jovanovich, 1955), and J. David Greenstone, *The Lincoln Persuasion: Remaking American Liberalism* (Princeton: Princeton University Press, 1993).

CHAPTER 2

1. There are three generally recognized approaches to two-party scholarship: pluralist theories of parties as diverse coalitions, a "responsible party" doctrine, and rational-choice theories emphasizing electoral competition. The distinctions between these approaches are not always clear. For instance, pluralist Robert Dahl's insight that parties "enable the many to pool their resources and offset the advantages of the few" is one shared by the responsible-party theorist E. E. Schattschneider. See Robert A. Dahl, *Pluralist Democracy in the United States* (Chicago: Rand McNally, 1967), and Schattschneider, *Party Government*.

2. Prominent turn-of-the-century political scientists did argue against the utility and normative functions of the American party system, even as a broad consensus around responsible parties developed at around the same time. See, e.g., Leon D. Epstein, *Political Parties in the American Mold* (Madison: University of Wisconsin Press, 1986), and Austin Ranney, *Curing the Mischiefs of Faction: Party Reform in America* (Berkeley and Los Angeles: University of California Press, 1975). Croly, in *Progressive Democracy*, argued that the United States could do without parties, but his position was rejected by most mainstream party scholars, as were the claims of prominent European scholars Moshei Ostrogorski (*Democracy and the Party System in the United States*) and Robert Michels (*Political Parties*, trans. Eden and Cedar Paul [New York: Free Press, 1959]), who saw parties as pathological agents working to disrupt democracy. Ostrogorski was exceptional in his advocacy of the abolition of political parties, while Michels saw them as permanent and unavoidable—and distinctly unfortunate—fixtures of modern politics. For a contemporary critic of the two-party system, see Theodore J. Lowi, "Toward a Responsible Three-Party System," in Green and Shea, *State of the Parties*, 45–60. The near universal absence of party literature invoking alternatives to the two-party system can be linked in part to the discipline's acceptance of Maurice Duverger's analysis of party competition given a winner-take-all elected office. See Duverger, *Political Parties: Their Organization and Activities in the Modern State* (New York: Wiley, 1954). Aldrich is typical in this regard, writing, "since American democracy chooses winner-take-all offices by plurality or majority rule, election to office therefore requires broad-based support wherever and from whomever it can be found. So strong are the resulting incentives for a two-party system to emerge that the effect is called Duverger's law." Aldrich, *Why Parties?* 25.

3. This report was generated by the Committee on Political Parties, an internal committee of the American Political Science Association. The report generated a great deal of scholarly debate about the normative roles and empirical functions of the American two-party system. American party scholars have brought forth insights on a significant range of substantive areas concerning the two-party system in the United States. They have posited an influential tripartite set of party arrangements by which to understand political parties and how they aggregate and then articulate interests through elections and governance; see V. O. Key Jr., *Politics, Parties, and Pressure Groups*, 5th ed. (New York: Crowell, 1964); Sorauf, *Political Parties in the American System*; and Paul Allen Beck and Frank J. Sorauf, *Party Politics in America*, 7th ed. (New York: HarperCollins, 1991). They have furthered our understanding of parties as organizations, debating the strength of national party organizations; see Paul S. Herrnson, "The Revitalization of National Party Organization," in Maisel, *Parties Respond*; Paul S. Herrnson, *Party Campaigning in the 1980s* (Cambridge: Harvard University Press, 1988); and Nelson Polsby, *Consequences of Party Reform* (Oxford: Oxford University Press, 1983). On the role of party activists, see Alan Abramowitz and Walter J. Stone, *Nomination Politics: Party Activists and Presidential Choice* (New York: Praeger, 1984), and Aldrich, *Why Parties?* 163–93. On the significance of changes to party rules, see Polsby, *Consequences of Party Reform*, and Byron E. Shafer, *Quiet Revolution: The Struggle for the Democratic Party and the Shaping of Post-Reform Politics* (New York: Russell Sage Foundation, 1983). And on party adaptation to campaign finance laws, see Herrnson, *Party Campaigning in the 1980s*, and Beck and Sorauf, *Party Politics in America*. They have discussed the central role of party in the electorate; see Angus Campbell, Philip E. Converse, Warren E. Miller, and Donald E. Stokes, *The American Voter* (New York: Willey, 1960); on the decline of partisan identification, see Wattenberg, *Decline of American Political Parties*; and on the role of party ideologies in electoral competition, see Anthony Downs, *An Economic Theory of Democracy* (New York: Harper & Row, 1957). They have furthered our understanding of parties in government; see Gary W. Cox and Mat McCubbins, *Legislative Leviathan: Party Government in the House* (Berkeley and Los Angeles: University of California Press, 1993); Keith Krehbiel, *Information and Legislative Systems* (Ann Arbor: University of Michigan Press, 1991); and David Rohde, *Parties and Leaders in the Postreform House* (Chicago: University of Chicago Press, 1991). They have reexamined the founding of political parties (see Aldrich, *Why Parties?*; Frymer, *Uneasy Alliances*), as well as the historical development of national parties; see Greenstone, *Lincoln Persuasion*; Milkis, *Political Parties and Constitutional Government*; and Joel H. Silbey, *The Partisan Imperative: The Dynamics of American Politics before the Civil War* (New York: Oxford University Press, 1985). And they have dissected the relationship between parties and the collective responsibility of national political institutions; see Morris Fiorina, "The Decline of Collective Responsibility in American Politics," *Daedalus* 109 (summer 1980), 25–45, and David Broder, *The Party's Over: The Failure of Politics in America* (New York: Harper & Row, 1972).

4. For instance, congressional scholar Gary Jacobson, in *The Politics of Congressional Elections*, 4th ed. (New York: Longman, 1997), 208, argues that electoral incentives lead members of Congress to pursue individual responsiveness to their constituents without encouraging collective responsibility by Congress, and points to the "home truth" that "the only instruments we have managed to develop for imposing collective responsibility on legislators are political parties." Presidential scholar Sam Kernell, in *Going Public: New Strategies of Presidential Leadership*, 3d ed. (Washington, D.C.: Congressional Quarterly Press, 1997), argues that the rise of going public—marshaling public opinion rather than the power of presidential persuasion—is in part a direct result of the fragmentation of parties inside the "bargaining community" of Washington, D.C. Moreover, Kernell argues, "outsider" presidents who succeed because of weaker party control over the nomination process are less capable of recognizing opportunities to bargain successfully with other political elites (38–46). In discussing

interest groups, Grant McConnell, *Private Power and American Democracy* (New York: Knopf, 1966), and Theodore J. Lowi, *The End of Liberalism: The Second Republic of the United States* (New York: W. W. Norton, 1979), argue that stronger parties are necessary to combat unelected and undemocratic interest groups who "capture" bureaucracies within the unwieldy and porous modern governmental administration. Samuel J. Eldersveld, in *Political Parties: A Behavioral Analysis* (Chicago: Rand McNally, 1964), remarks that "intellectually, [political scientists] have become committed to the position in the twentieth century that parties are central to our system" (20–21), and this commitment has endured into the twenty-first century.

5. Duverger, *Political Parties*.

6. Schattschneider, *Party Government*; Ranney, *Curing the Mischiefs of Faction*, 43; Arthur Lupia and Mat McCubbins, *The Democratic Dilemma: Can Citizens Learn What They Really Need to Know?* (Cambridge: Cambridge University Press, 1998); Dahl, *Pluralist Democracy in the United States*; Milkis, *Political Parties and Constitutional Government*; Richard Hofstadter, *The Idea of a Party System: The Rise of Legitimate Opposition in the United States* (Berkeley and Los Angeles: University of California Press, 1969).

7. Dahl, *Pluralist Democracy in the United States*; Downs, *Economic Theory of Democracy*; Key, *Southern Politics in State and Nation*; Sigmund Neumann, *Modern Political Parties* (Chicago: University of Chicago Press, 1956); Schattschneider, *Party Government*.

8. Dahl, *Pluralist Democracy in the United States*.

9. Sorauf, *Political Parties in the American System*; Ranney and Kendall, *Democracy and the American Party System*.

10. Downs, *Economic Theory of Democracy*.

11. Fiorina, "Decline of Collective Responsibility in American Politics," 26.

12. Gerald Pomper, ed., *Party Renewal in America* (New York: Praeger, 1980), 5.

13. Aldrich, *Why Parties?* 18.

14. Downs, *Economic Theory of Democracy*; Joseph A. Schlesinger, *Political Parties and the Winning of Office* (Chicago: University of Chicago Press, 1991).

15. Aldrich, *Why Parties?* 296.

16. All three approaches to party scholarship implicitly or explicitly assume uncertain voters, though they arrive at this assumption in different ways. For instance, while rational-choice theorists focus on the individual incentives for voters to be "rationally ignorant," Schattschneider, in *Party Government*, lays the blame for voter uncertainty at the feet of parties that look and act like two sides of the same coin. More recently, Arthur Lupia and Mat McCubbins, in *Democratic Dilemma*, have formalized an argument about how uncertain voters make political decisions via informational heuristics

17. Downs, *Economic Theory of Democracy*, 102.

18. For exceptions, see Keith Poole and Howard Rosenthal, "Patterns in Congressional Voting," *American Journal of Political Science* 35 (February 1991): 228–78, and Frymer, *Uneasy Alliances*.

19. Downs, *Economic Theory of Democracy*, 139. There is also a body of comparative literature demonstrating that two-party systems rely on a normal distribution to promote a stable democracy. See, e.g., Arend Lijphart, *Democracy in Plural Societies: A Comparative Exploration* (New Haven: Yale University Press, 1977), chap. 1; Arend Lijphart, *Power-Sharing in South Africa* (Berkley, Calif.: Institute of International Studies, 1985); Downs, *Economic Theory of Democracy*, 120; and Donald L. Horowitz, "Ethnic Conflict Management for Policymakers," in *Conflict and Peacemaking in Multiethnic Societies*, ed. Joseph V. Montville (Lanham, Md.: Lexington Books, 1991).

20. Frymer, *Uneasy Alliances*, 20.

21. On whether a similar dynamic occurs with Latino efforts to engage the two-party system, see Fraga and Leal, "Playing the 'Latino Card.'"

22. Greenberg and Page, *Struggle for Democracy*; Schattschneider, *Party Government*; Judson L. James, *American Political Parties in Transition* (New York: Harper & Row, 1974).

23. Party scholars do not address how a normal distribution comes to exist in a society. Downs, for instance, treats the question of its origin as unanswerable, "because the determinants are historic, cultural, and psychological, as well as economic; to attempt to analyze them would be to undertake a study vast beyond our scope" (*Economic Theory of Democracy*, 140). However, rich historical and theoretical accounts of the origins of ideological consensus have been offered. See, e.g., Hartz, *Liberal Tradition in America*, and Tocqueville, *Democracy in America*.

24. Hartz, *Liberal Tradition in America*.

25. Michael Rogin, *Ronald Reagan, the Movie, and Other Episodes in Political Demonology* (Berkeley and Los Angeles: University of California Press, 1993), 135.

26. Amy Gutmann, "Multiculturalism," in *Multiculturalism: Examining the Politics of Recognition*, ed. Amy Gutmann (Princeton: Princeton University Press, 2001), 10; Rogin, *Ronald Reagan, the Movie*, 134–68.

27. John Locke, *Two Treatises of Government*, ed. Thomas Cook (Simon & Schuster, 1947); John Stuart Mill, "Considerations on Representative Government," in John Stuart Mill, *On Liberty and Other Essays*, ed. John M. Gray (Oxford: Oxford University Press, 1998); John Rawls, *Political Liberalism* (New York: Columbia University Press, 1995).

28. In calling America a liberal society, I do not mean to suggest that the United States is a nation in which "progressive" values have continuously dominated—this is clearly not true. Indeed, even the meaning of the word "progressive" has changed so much over time that it would be hard to list examples of progressive policies without locating them in a historically specific context. Nor am I suggesting that there is no variation in party platforms or policy positions between the major parties at any historical moment—one need only see where today's Republican Party stands vis-à-vis the Democratic Party on issues such as abortion, the estate tax, and U.S. unilateralism to see the differences.

29. The standard spatial voter model posited by Downs, *Economic Theory of Democracy*, distributes voter preferences visually presented as a single dimensional issue axis, often explicitly or implicitly understood as measuring ideology. In stating that the ideological consensus around liberalism exists on a countless number of axes, I mean to suggest that within American society voters and politicians can take up positions on real or potential issues that may very well differ markedly from each other, yet these differences will still be bounded by liberal hegemony. Conceptualizing liberalism as a boundary condition thus allows us to imagine how there can be a (theoretically) infinite number of issues within a single dimensional axis—that of liberal ideology.

30. Two important challenges have been posed against the claim that liberalism has always dominated American political thought. The first comes from a historical debate over the role of a republican tradition in the founding of the American state. Beginning with J. G. A. Pocock's, *The Machiavellian Moment: Florentine Political Thought and the Atlantic Republican Tradition* (Princeton: Princeton University Press, 2003), civic republican revisionists have argued that the American colonies were more civic republican than they were liberal. See also Gordon Wood, *The Radicalism of the American Revolution* (New York: Vintage, 1993); Bernard Bailyn, *The Ideological Origins of the American Revolution* (Cambridge, Mass.: Belknap Press, 1992); and Michael Schudson, *The Good Citizen: A History of American Civic Life* (Cambridge: Harvard University Press, 1999). The second challenge emerged as the "liberal versus communitarian" debates of the 1980s and 1990s, enjoined by communitarian critics of liberalism such as Michael Sandel, *Democracy's Discontent: America in Search of a Public Philosophy* (Cambridge, Mass.: Belknap Press, 1998), Amitai Etzioni, *The Essential Communitarian Reader* (New York: Rowman & Littlefield, 1998), and Alistair MacIntyre, *After Virtue: A Study in Moral Theory* (Notre Dame: University of Notre Dame Press, 1984), among

others. For a review of this debate, see Stephen Mulhall and Adam Swift, *Liberals and Communitarians* (Malden, Mass.: Blackwell, 1996), and Michael Sandel, ed., *Liberalism and Its Critics* (New York: New York University Press, 1984). Important critiques of the consensus theory of liberal dominance have also been made by Greenstone, *Lincoln Persuasion*; Rogin, *Ronald Reagan, the Movie*, and Rogers Smith, *Civic Ideals: Conflicting Visions of Citizenship in U.S. History* (New Haven: Yale University Press, 1999). Smith's book builds on his earlier seminal article entitled "Beyond Tocqueville, Myrdal, and Hartz: The Multiple Traditions in America," *American Political Science Review* 87 (1993): 549–66. He presents a tripartite description of American national identity as consisting of liberalism, civic republicanism, and an ascriptive tradition that is produced by and productive of, among other things, racism and ethnoculturalism. Significantly, Smith does not place liberal norms at one end and the ascriptive tradition at the other, but instead shows how the three traditions are interrelated, and that establishing civic membership in the American polity is dependent on establishing that certain people fall outside this polity. The relevant point for my argument, of course, is that one need not agree that liberalism is completely hegemonic in the United States to recognize the enduring presence and political significance of bodies culturally positioned outside the American polity. Indeed, Smith demonstrates that the building of (white American) collective civic membership, marking who could and could not become a citizen, proceeded by ascribing identities and their attendant cultural characteristics to particular racialized bodies, a process not unlike that of racial formation. Smith's argument is consistent with the claims of contemporary cultural theorists such as Lisa Lowe, who points out in *Immigrant Acts* that the construction of the Asian immigrant in the United States has always been linked in binary opposition to the construction of the American citizen.

31. Kirsten Gronbjerg, David Street, and Gerald D. Suttles, *Poverty and Social Change* (Chicago: University of Chicago Press, 1978); Gaston Rimlinger, *Welfare Policy and Industrialization in Europe, America, and Russia* (New York: Wiley, 1971).

32. To take another example, consider constituent support for incumbents in predominantly African American districts versus predominantly white districts. Assume that over a series of elections, equal proportions of black and white American voters support the incumbent. Further assume that when the economy is healthy, African American districts are more likely than white districts to support the incumbent, but that they are less likely to do so when the economy is poor. Because economic fluctuation translates into greater or less support for the incumbent, it acts as the independent variable. On the other hand, the African American–white American distinction is a stable feature of the equation, and no "causal" inference can be made, yet this stable feature affects the causal relationship (support for the incumbent as a function of the strength of the economy) within the example.

33. Greenstone, *Lincoln Persuasion*, 44.

34. Ibid., 45.

35. See Key, *Politics, Parties, and Pressure Groups*, 232.

36. See Downs, *Economic Theory of Democracy*, 136.

37. Ibid., 136.

38. Ibid., 135.

39. There are, of course, a number of variables involved in becoming a coalitional partner in a major party, not just the ideological or policy positions of a given constituency or organized group.

40. Lowe, *Immigrant Acts*, 4.

41. For a discussion of these various cultural representations of Asian bodies in the United States, see Lee, *Orientals*.

42. See, e.g., Angelo N. Ancheta, *Race, Rights, and the Asian American Experience* (New Brunswick: Rutgers University Press, 1998); Robert Chang, *Disoriented: Asian Americans, the*

Law, and the Nation-State (New York: New York University Press, 1999); Neil Gotanda, "Exclusion and Inclusion: Immigration and American Orientalism," in *Across the Pacific: Asian Americans and Globalization,* ed. Evelyn Hu-DeHart (Philadelphia: Temple University Press, 1999), 129–51; Ian Haney López, *White by Law: The Legal Construction of Race* (New York: New York University Press, 1998); John S. Park, *Elusive Citizenship: Immigration, Asian Americans, and the Paradox of Civil Rights* (New York: New York University Press, 2004); and John Skrentny, *The Minority Rights Revolution* (Cambridge: Harvard University Press, 2004).

43. See, e.g., Sucheng Chan, *Asian Americans: An Interpretive History* (Boston: Twayne, 1991); George E. Mowry, *The California Progressives* (Berkeley and Los Angeles: University of California Press, 1993); Tomás Almaguer, *Racial Fault Lines: The Historical Origins of White Supremacy in California* (Berkeley and Los Angeles: University of California Press, 1994), 153–204; Lowe, *Immigrant Acts*; Gary Okihiro, *Margins and Mainstreams: Asians in American History and Culture* (Seattle: University of Washington Press, 1994); Lee, *Orientals*; Ancheta, *Race, Rights, and the Asian American Experience*; Robert Chang, *Disoriented*; Gotanda, "Exclusion and Inclusion"; and Haney López, *White by Law*.

44. Befitting the very real diversity that exists in Asian American communities, surveys of Asian Americans routinely pick up differences in partisanship and public opinion, over both issue priorities and opinions. This is not to say that some policy and attitudinal consistency does not exist. For further discussion, see Bok-Lim Kim, "Problems and Service Needs of Asian Americans in Chicago: An Empirical Study," *Amerasia Journal* 5 (1978): 23–44; U.S. Commission on Civil Rights, *Civil Rights Issues of Asian and Pacific Americans: Myths and Realities* (Washington, D.C.: U.S. Commission on Civil Rights, 1979); Ki-Taek Chun, "The Myth of Asian American Success and Its Educational Ramifications," *IRCD Bulletin* 15 (1980): 1–12; Russell Endo, Stanley Sue, and Nathaniel Wagner, eds., *Asian Americans: Social and Psychological Perspectives,* vol. 2 (Palo Alto: Science & Behavior Books, 1980); Robert Gardner, Bryant Robey, and Peter Smith, "Asian Americans: Growth, Change, Diversity," in *Population Bulletin* 4, no. 4 (1985): 1–43; United Way, Asian Pacific Research and Development Council, *Pacific Profiles: A Demographic Study of the Asian Pacific Population in Los Angeles County* (Los Angeles: United Way, 1985); James T. Fawcett and Benjamin Carino, eds., *Pacific Bridges* (Staten Island, N.Y.: Center for Migration Studies, 1987); Wendy Tam, "Asians—A Monolithic Voting Bloc?" *Political Behavior* 17, no. 2 (1995): 223–49; Lien, *Making of Asian America*; Pei-te Lien, Margaret Conway, and Janelle Wong, *The Politics of Asian Americans: Diversity and Community* (New York: Routledge, 2004); and "The Asian American Vote 2004: A Report on the Multilingual Exit Poll in the 2004 Presidential Election" (New York: Asian American Legal Defense and Education Fund, 2005).

45. Surveys also suggest that Asian Americans see themselves as victims of racial discrimination and stereotyping at levels comparable to African Americans and Latinos. In a 1995 *Washington Post*/Kaiser Foundation/Harvard University poll and a 1993 *Los Angeles Times* poll, Asian Pacific American respondents ranked behind only African Americans in reporting personal experience of racial discrimination. Taeku Lee, "Racial Attitudes and the Color Line(s) at the Close of the Twentieth Century," in *The State of Asian Pacific America: Transforming Race Relations,* ed. Paul Ong (Los Angeles: LEAP Asian Pacific American Public Policy Institute and UCLA Asian American Studies Center, 2000), 103–58. A 1998 University of Massachusetts poll that asked whether the respondent had experienced racial discrimination in the last three months reported that 25 percent of Asian Pacific American respondents answered in the affirmative. The same poll reported that 57 percent of Asian Pacific American respondents said they had experienced racial discrimination "very" or "fairly" often. By comparison, 33 percent of African Americans and 31 percent of Latinos reported such experiences in the last three months, and 60 percent of African Americans and 52 percent of Lati-

nos reported that they happened "very" or "fairly" often. Paul Watanabe and C. Hardy-Fanta, "Conflict and Convergence: Race, Public Opinion, and Political Behavior in Massachusetts" (Boston: University of Massachusetts, Institute for Asian American Studies, 1998), cited in Lee, "Racial Attitudes and the Color Line(s)."

46. See, e.g., Darrell Hamamoto, *Monitored Peril: Asian Americans and the Politics of TV Representation* (Minneapolis: University of Minnesota Press, 1994); Gina Marchetti, *Romance and the 'Yellow Peril': Race, Sex, and Discursive Strategies in Hollywood Fiction* (Berkeley and Los Angeles: University of California Press, 1994); John Huey-Long Song and John Dombrink, "'Good Guys' and Bad Guys: Media, Asians, and the Framing of a Criminal Event," *Amerasia Journal* 22, no. 3 (1996): 25–45; Zia, *Asian American Dreams*; Don T. Nakanishi, "Driveby Victims of DNC Greed," *1998–99 National Asian Pacific American Political Almanac* (Los Angeles: UCLA Asian American Studies Center, 1998); Setsuko Matsunaga Nishi, "Asian Americans at the Intersection of International and Domestic Tensions," in Hu-DeHart, *Across the Pacific*, 152–90; and Wu and Nicholson, "Have You No Decency?"

47. Nishi, in "Asian Americans at the Intersection," examined the presentation of Asian Americans in the press in four major areas: U.S.-Asian country tensions, the Pearl Harbor anniversary, the treatment of Asian Americans in the news, and, finally, Asian Americans and race relations from July 1991 through June 1992. This period included both the L.A. disturbances after the Rodney King verdict and the fiftieth anniversary of the bombing of Pearl Harbor by Japan. The data came from the titles, subject descriptors, and abstracts of articles from twenty-eight newspapers, including five African American weeklies, covering the seven years from January 1989 to December 1995. For a case study of the coverage of the fiftieth anniversary of Pearl Harbor, Nishi also accessed the entire text of the articles. Data analysis looked at the most frequent subjects of articles about Asian Americans by number of articles, a ratio of subject emphasis, and an index of attention.

48. Ibid., 182–83.

49. The insufficiency of formal-legal citizenship has led Leti Volpp to argue that Asian Americans potentially acquire four different types of "citizenship," only one of which is formal-legal, while the other three—citizenship as rights, citizenship as political activity, and citizenship as identity/solidarity—are discursively negotiated. Leti Volpp, "Obnoxious to Their Very Nature: Asian Americans and Constitutional Citizenship," *Citizenship Studies* vol. 5, no. 1, (2001): 71–87. See also Park, *Elusive Citizenship*.

50. Neil Gotanda, "Citizenship Nullification: The Impossibility of Asian American Politics," in *Asian Americans and Politics: Perspectives, Experiences, Prospects*, ed. Gordon H. Chang (Stanford: Stanford University Press, 2000), 79–102.

51. *United States v. Bhagat Singh Thind*, 261 U.S. 204 (1923). For a discussion of this case, see Haney López, *White by Law*.

52. The lack of empirical studies analyzing whether a connection exists between attitudes and political behavior stems largely from the inability to find data with which to employ quantitative analyses. However, a growing number of surveys that place racial attitudes in an explicitly multiracial, multiethnic context have recently been conducted, and political scientists have in the last few years begun to address the gaps in the literature on political attitudes toward Asian Americans. See especially Lee, "Racial Attitudes and the Color Line(s)." Lee took advantage of a number of polls that looked specifically at anti-Asian stereotypes and sentiments to analyze whether they existed and, if so, what the policy impact might be. His analysis revealed that the level of anti-Asian attitudes (sentiments and stereotypes) was quite high. "Across all respondent groups there is widespread acceptance of the stereotype of Asian Pacific Americans as inscrutable [whites 44%, blacks 59%, Latinos 56%, Asians 53%] and as perpetual foreigners [32%, 42%, 37%, 31%] and feelings of hostility towards Asian neighbors [43%, 42%, 34%, 24%] and towards Japan [44%, 42%, 33%, 24%].... For whites, anti-Asian stereotypes and

sentiments are the single strongest influence on anti-Asian policy preferences. Anti-Asian attitudes also strongly shape the policy preferences of Latinos and African Americans, but they no longer predominate over other factors" (128). Lee also employed multivariate analyses to link anti-Asian attitudes with positions on policies affecting Asian Americans. Asian Pacific Americans took the strongest position across all respondent groups in opposing a moratorium on legal immigration, supporting reparations to Japanese Americans interned in concentration camps during World War II, opposing returning Chinese refugees seeking asylum without a hearing, and supporting a "meritocratic" admissions policy at the University of California.

53. This analysis is agnostic on the specific interests represented by these Asian American political organizations.

54. For example, outside of their immediate constituencies, leading Asian American groups like the National Asian Pacific American Legal Council and the Organization of Chinese Americans, leading Asian American political interest group leaders like Karen Narasaki and Daphne Kwok, and even Asian American elected officials like former Washington State governor Gary Locke and Oregon congressman David Wu, fly completely under the public radar.

55. See, for example, Paul Frymer's discussion of the interplay between Democratic presidential nominees and Jesse Jackson in *Uneasy Alliances*. Consistent with the argument posed here, Frymer emphasizes the key role played by strategic party elites who incorporate race into their party strategies, not necessarily because they are racist but because to do otherwise would be politically foolish.

56. Kim, *Bitter Fruit*.

57. See Dana Takagi, *The Retreat from Race: Asian American Admissions and Racial Politics* (New Brunswick: Rutgers University Press, 1993).

58. On the ongoing production and productive consequences of the "brown peril," see David Cole, *Enemy Aliens* (New York: New Press, 2003); Tram Nguyen, *We Are All Suspects Now* (Boston: Beacon Press, 2005); and Leti Volpp, "The Citizen and the Terrorist," *UCLA Law Review* 49 (2002): 1575–99.

59. For recent assessments of the diversity of Asian American policy positions and political attitudes, see Tam, "Asians—A Monolithic Voting Bloc?"; Lien, *Making of Asian America*; and Lien, Conway, and Wong, *Politics of Asian Americans*. Note also that the Asian American Legal Defense and Education Fund determined that a good majority of Asian Americans in major urban areas voted Democratic in the 2004 presidential election. This is not to say, of course, that a partisan alignment has taken place in Asian American communities. See, e.g., "Asian American Vote 2004."

60. See, e.g., Kinder and Sanders, *Divided by Color*; and Carol Swain, *Black Faces, Black Interests* (Cambridge: Harvard University Press, 1995).

61. Dianna Pinderhughes, "Political Choices: A Realignment in Partisanship among Black Voters?" in *The State of Black America*, ed. James D. Williams (New York: National Urban League, 1984), 85–113; Ronald Walters, *Black Presidential Politics in America: A Strategic Approach* (Albany: State University of New York Press, 1988).

62. Ibid.

63. For an analysis of Irish immigrant sociopolitical incorporation into America, see Steven P. Erie, *Rainbow's End: Irish-Americans and the Dilemmas of Urban Machine Politics, 1840–1985* (Berkeley and Los Angeles: University of California Press, 1990).

64. On the processes and consequences of white racialization for different racial and ethnic communities, see, e.g., Noel Ignatiev, *How the Irish Became White* (New York: Routledge, 1996), Roediger, *Wages of Whiteness*; Karen Brodkin, *How Jews Became White Folks and What That Says about Race in America* (New Brunswick: Rutgers University Press, 1998); Michael Rogin, *Blackface, White Noise: Jewish Immigrants in the Hollywood Melting Pot* (Berkeley and Los Angeles: University of California Press, 1996); and Thomas A. Guglielmo, *White on*

Arrival: Italians, Race, Color, and Power in Chicago, 1890–1945 (Oxford: Oxford University Press, 2003). Consistent among these texts is the theme of how white supremacist cultural practices were a primary mechanism by which this "whitening" occurred.

65. For an elaboration of this argument as it relates to the acquisition of citizenship, see Volpp, "Obnoxious to Their Very Nature."

66. Lowe, *Immigrant Acts.*

CHAPTER 3

1. CAPACI later became the Asian Pacific American Institute for Congressional Studies (APAICS).

2. "Clout in the Capital," *AsianWeek*, May 24–30, 1996.

3. CAPACI declined a last-minute offer from the White House to send a high-ranking, non-cabinet level official to speak at the fund-raiser. "Guilt by Association? The Asian American Connection," PBS Online NewsHour Report, http://www.pbs.org/newshour/campaign/issues/asian_8-3.html.

4. Associated Press, "Chronological Overview of the Campaign Finance Scandal," December 24, 1997.

5. Wang, "Campaign Finance Scandal."

6. "Washington Governor Received Money from China-Linked Donor: Report," *Agence France-Presse*, August 5, 1998; Eric Bailey, "Films with State Pacts Are Fertile Donors to Fong," *Los Angeles Times*, May 25, 1998; Cathleen Decker, "Republican Fong Confronts Role of Race in Senate Drive," *Los Angeles Times*, August 13, 1997, A3; Paul Jacobs and Alan C. Miller, "State Treasurer Linked to Asian Funds, Reports Show," *Los Angeles Times*, February 25 1998, A1; Paul Jacobs and Dan Morain, "Fong Returns $100,000 in Gifts," *Los Angeles Times*, April 23, 1997, A3; Michelle Malkin, "More Than Money Troubles at Harmony Place," *Seattle Times*, August 5, 1997; Michelle Malkin, "Locke's Money Trail Leads to Buddhist Temple's Door," *Seattle Times*, September 23, 1997; Marc Sandalow, "State Treasurer in Election Probe: House Panel Wants to Ask Matt Fong about Donation," *San Francisco Chronicle*, March 6, 1998, A1; "The Gary Locke File: The Trouble with Cash," *Seattle Times*, August 5, 1997.

7. Seth Rosenfeld, "Tien Ties to Asia Money May Have Cost Him Job," *San Francisco Chronicle*, December 22, 1996; "Riady Helped Kin Enter UC—Berkeley; Indonesian Magnate Wrote to Chancellor," *Washington Post*, December 14, 1996; Marc Lacey, "Parties Exchange Charges at Hearing on Anti-Asian Bias," *Los Angeles Times*, December 6, 1997, A20; Mark Gladstone, "Nothing Sinister in Calls to Huang, Activists Say," *Los Angeles Times*, July 19, 1997, A15.

8. Lacey, "Parties Exchange Charges at Hearing."

9. Glenn R. Simpson, David Rogers, and Jeffrey Taylor, "Asian-American Institute Becomes Latest Victim of Controversy over Democratic Fund Raising," *Wall Street Journal*, March 5, 1997, A20; "Glass Houses," Inside Politics column, *Washington Times*, July 16, 1997.

10. In describing Asian bodies in America as being racialized as illiberal, I mean to suggest that individuals in the United States that racially "perform" as being from Asia are politically and socially constructed as invariably and perpetually lacking the fundamental qualities prized by classic liberal ideology. Briefly, those values are understood as individualism, a separation between the public and private spheres, government by consent, belief in the economic system of capitalism, and belief in liberal institutions and a concomitant suspicion of institutions and societies not deemed liberal.

11. The analysis in this chapter relies predominantly on government documents and news articles. In particular, I use the U.S. Senate *Hearings before the Committee on Governmental Affairs of the United States Senate on the Investigation of Illegal or Improper Activities in Con-*

nection with the 1996 Federal Election Campaign, parts I—X (Washington, D.C.: U.S. Government Printing Office, 1997) (hereafter *Hearings before the Senate Committee on Governmental Affairs*), conducted during the 105th Congress from July 8 to October 30, 1997, and the *Final Report of the Committee on Governmental Affairs of the United States Senate on the Investigation of Illegal or Improper Activities in Connection with the 1996 Federal Election Campaign* (Washington, D.C.: U.S. Government Printing Office, 1998), published in March 1998 (hereafter *Final Report*). I also use several publicly released documents, such as correspondence between party officials, which have emerged in the investigation into the campaign finance controversy, as well as press releases of the national party committees and Asian American political organizations. Because my argument necessitates an evaluation of the tremendous publicity and press coverage generated by the controversy, and because other data on the campaign finance controversy are lacking, I examine reports from newspapers, news magazines, and visual media (internet and television) on the subject of the campaign finance controversy. In general, the accounts are taken from the period between the first report of alleged improprieties in October 1996 and the Senate committee's *Final Report* in March 1998. A few news articles from outside this period are used to provide necessary historical background or to discuss the organized Asian American response to the campaign finance controversy.

It should be noted that the House Government Reform and Oversight Committee, chaired by Representative Dan Burton (R-IN), also held hearings on the campaign finance controversy in both the 105th and 106th Congresses. I generally do not include the House hearings in my analysis, for several reasons. First of all, the House committee issued no comprehensive report similar to the Senate committee's. Second, while the Senate hearings ended before the Cox Commission was established, the House hearings began before the Cox Commission and continued after the Cox Commission released its report; thus the House hearings overlapped with the controversy over technological advances allegedly being given to China and the alleged attempt by the Chinese government to influence U.S. presidential and congressional elections. I do not mean to imply that the controversies do not share much in common, but the overlap between public hearings and a secretive commission that relied on classified information means that an unbroken line of relevant data is unavailable. Third, because the Senate hearings occurred before the House hearings got under way, press accounts of the Senate hearings are far more detailed and readily available than are accounts of the House hearings. Fourth, because the Senate hearings took place relatively soon after the campaign finance controversy, again, press accounts are much more detailed and readily available. Fifth, Chairman Burton was widely criticized for conducting a deeply partisan exercise rather than a meaningful investigation. In contrast, the chair of the Senate Governmental Affairs Committee, Fred Thompson (R-TN), was widely respected for his actions and experience as a prosecutor in the events surrounding Watergate. Perhaps because of Burton's partisanship, the Senate hearings were widely seen by both the national press and national politicians as more important than the House hearings. As should be evident by now, I do not use the Cox Commission report.

I have not included several news items that came out after the *Final Report* was published. For instance, some of the Asian American individuals I discuss below have now been indicted and have pled guilty or negotiated settlements with the government. However, my argument neither requires that I show nor attempts to show the guilt or innocence of any of these individuals, nor am I interested in whether politicians predicted badly or well any future connections in the investigation. Rather, my focus is on how leading figures in the Republican and Democratic Parties dealt with Asian Americans as the process played out, since the individuals under analysis could neither have predicted future political events nor controlled the release of important information.

12. Paul Pringle, "Los Angeles Asians Seeking Political Clout," *Dallas Morning News,* June 11, 1987; Richard T. Cooper et al., "How DNC Got Caught in a Donor Dilemma," *Los Angeles Times,* December 23, 1996; Michael Kranish, "Clinton Policy Shift Followed Asian-American Fund-Raiser," *Boston Globe,* January 16, 1997; David Rogers, "Battle over Immigration Bill Taught Washington's Ropes to Huang and Hsia," *Wall Street Journal,* May 15 1997, A24.

13. Quoted in Thomas Massey, "The Wrong Way to Court Ethnics," *Washington Monthly,* May 1986, 21–26.

14. C. N. Lee, "A View from the Campaign Headquarters," *Bridge* 4, no. 5 (1976): 18–21; Robin Wu, "Profile: Joji Konoshima, Asian Americans in the Democratic National Committee," *Bridge* 6, no. 1 (1978): 61–63.

15. William Wei, *The Asian American Movement* (Philadelphia: Temple University Press, 1993).

16. Bill Chong, "Letter to National Asian American Coordinator of Jesse Jackson for President Committee," January 12, 1984, cited in Wei, *Asian American Movement,* 224.

17. Democratic Party activist Thomas Hsieh remarked upon the political disappointment that increased dollars were not translating into aid. See "First National Convention of the National Democratic Council of Asian Pacific Americans," *AsianWeek,* October 16, 1987. This is not the ad hoc group of the same name that participated in the Democratic Party's 1976 national convention.

18. Quoted in East/West Institute, "Caucus Warns Democratic Party Leaders to Pay Heed to Asian Pacific Issues," July 1984, cited in Wei, *Asian American Movement,* 130.

19. David Takami, "Can Asian Americans Influence the Election?" *AsiAm,* January 1988.

20. James R. Dickenson, "Democrats Seek Identity after Loss," *Washington Post,* December 17, 1984, A6; John Herbers, "Party Looks Inward for Ways to Regain Majority," *New York Times,* November 8, 1984, A24; "Asians Appointed to DNC; Caucus Status in Doubt," *Pacific Citizen,* July 12, 1985, cited in Wei, *Asian American Movement,* 261; Ernestine Tayabas, "Demo Drops Asian Caucus," *East/West* May 22, 1985, cited in Wei, *Asian American Movement,* 180; Frymer, *Uneasy Alliances.*

21. Quoted in Phil Gailey, "Political Memo: Slouching toward the Center (Post-Reagan)," *New York Times,* September 18, 1985, B8; see also Philip A. Klinkner, *The Losing Parties: Out-Party National Committees, 1956–1993* (New Haven: Yale University Press, 1994), 180–83.

22. National Broadcasting Company, *Meet the Press,* February 3, 1985; J. K. Yamamoto, "Democratic National Chair Questions Need for Asian/Pacific Caucus," *Pacific Citizen,* March 8, 1985, cited in Wei, *Asian American Movement,* 262.

23. It should be noted that although the African American and Hispanic caucuses were not eliminated in 1984, this was largely due to their charter status in the by-laws of the DNC. Indeed, the DNC made extra efforts to distance itself from African Americans in the 1980s. See Frymer, *Uneasy Alliances,* 112–18.

24. "Asians Appointed to DNC," cited in Wei, *Asian American Movement,* 261.

25. Anze Maitland, "Asian Leaders Accuse Democratic Party of Racism," *San Francisco Chronicle,* May 22, 1985; Tayabas, "Demo Drops Asian Caucus."

26. Edward Iwata, "Asian Americans Host Democratic Hopefuls," *San Francisco Chronicle,* October 20, 1987.

27. Quoted in "First National Convention of the National Democratic Council of Asian Pacific Americans," *AsianWeek,* October 16, 1987.

28. Iwata, "Asian Americans Host Democratic Hopefuls." Progressive Asian Americans found sympathy and made headway in the presidential campaigns of 1984 and 1988 with party outsider Jesse Jackson. Jackson's decentralized campaigns meant that Asian Americans often found themselves in positions of responsibility. His appeal to left-leaning Asian Americans apparently stemmed in part from his status as a symbolic outsider from the Democratic Party,

even as he was running a campaign for the party's presidential nomination. Wei, *Asian American Movement*, 251–57.

29. Robert Suro, "Gore's Ties to Hsia Cast Shadow on 2000 Race," *Washington Post*, February 23, 1998, A1.

30. Cooper et al., "How DNC Got Caught in a Donor Dilemma."

31. Suro, "Gore's Ties to Hsia Cast Shadow." Hsia's circumvention of campaign finance law was hardly unique; as Senator Durbin (D-IL) noted during the committee hearings, "There is not a Member up here who doesn't deal with tally as a reality in a campaign." Francis X. Clines, "Donor-Checking Plan Failed, Ex-Democratic Official Says," *New York Times*, July 11, 1997, A1; *Hearings before the Senate Committee on Governmental Affairs*, part I, 197.

32. Cooper et al., "How DNC Got Caught in a Donor Dilemma"; Hsia interview in Yen Le Espiritu, *Asian American Panethnicity* (Philadelphia: Temple University Press, 1992), 62.

33. Quoted in "Chennault Tells OCA of Frustrations in Dallas," *AsianWeek*, August 31, 1984.

34. Interim Coordinating Committee for Chinese Americans, "The Chinese American Declaration Concerning the 1998 Presidential Election," (n.p., n.d.); see Wei, *Asian American Movement*, 245.

35. 80-20 Initiative, http://www.80-20.net/longfaq.htm (accessed September 15, 1999). The 80-20 Initiative is a nonpartisan organization dedicated to forming an Asian American swing voting bloc in presidential and other elections.

36. Ibid. The list included the first Chinese American deputy secretary in the federal government, the first Chinese American ambassador, the first Asian American vice chair of the Civil Rights Commission, the first Asian American member of the National Science Board, an assistant commissioner of the Immigrant and Naturalization Service, a number of federal judges, and a voice in the Small Business Administration. The ICCCA disbanded in 1989.

37. Nakanishi, "When Numbers Do Not Add Up," 47. This figure includes donations to all candidates and parties, not just those to national parties or candidates for national office. All other figures refer to donations to national party organizations or national candidates. On the Democratic side, Dukakis raised record amounts of money from Asian Americans. Scott Armstrong and John Dillin, "Ethnic Votes Are Vital in California Primary," *Christian Science Monitor*, May 24, 1988. Nakanishi's estimates do not distinguish between Asian Americans and Pacific Islanders—thus the term "Asian Pacific Americans."

38. Wei, *Asian American Movement*, 244. Yen Le Espiritu and Don T. Nakanishi have been more cautious about judging the effect of campaign contributions on national politics, holding out the possibility that meaningful political returns have accrued. Espiritu, *Asian American Panethnicity*, 61–63; Nakanishi, "When Numbers Do Not Add Up"; Nakanishi, "Next Swing Vote?"

39. Tim Weiner and David E. Sanger, "Democrats Hoped to Raise $7 Million from Asians in U.S.," *New York Times*, December 28, 1996, A1.

40. Cooper et al., "How DNC Got Caught in a Donor Dilemma"; James Sterngold, "Political Tangle of a Taiwan Immigrant," *New York Times*, June 9, 1997; see *Final Report*, 1653–69, 4811–5269.

41. Cooper et al., "How DNC Got Caught in a Donor Dilemma."

42. *Final Report*, 4813; Don Van Natta Jr., "President Is Linked to Urgent Enlisting of Top Fund-Raiser," *New York Times*, July 7, 1997, A1.

43. *Hearings before the Senate Committee on Governmental Affairs*, part I, 95.

44. ABC *Nightline* (aired June 28, 1999). Additionally, even if the DNC had really contacted only individuals solicited by Huang—a claim that cannot be sustained against the evidence—this does not mean that DNC elites were really acting in a "color-blind" fashion, since they may have assumed, because of Huang's professional role as a fund-raiser in the Asian

American community and his racialized identity, that they were going to investigate only Asian American–based contributions.

45. Democratic National Committee, "DNC Refunds Contributions," Democratic News press release, June 27, 1997; Alan Miller, "DNC Raises $19 Million But Is Still in Debt, Report Says," *Los Angeles Times*, August 1, 1997, A18.

46. Miller, "DNC Raises $19 Million But Is Still in Debt."

47. Organization of Chinese Americans, "Asian Pacific American Groups Pleased with DNC Reversal of Immigrant Donations Policy," press release, January 13, 1998.

48. Ibid.

49. Democratic National Committee, "DNC In-Depth Contribution Review" (n.d.).

50. *Hearings before the Senate Committee on Governmental Affairs*, part I, 96. Sullivan believed that the DNC investigation had upset Asian American citizens, who then declined to respond to personal questions about their private lives or to respond to threats. This was not exactly news to Asian American political leaders like Michael Woo, who spoke for their political establishment when he stated that "Asian Pacific American Democrats [have] been very disturbed that the DNC would mount a guilt-by-association investigation of contributors simply because they have Asian last names." Organization of Chinese Americans, "National Asian American Groups File Unprecedented Civil Rights Petition Against Congress and Others for Scapegoating," press release, September 11, 1997, http://www.ocanatl.org/pr91197.htm (accessed June 27, 1999).

51. DNC, "DNC In-Depth Contribution Review"; ABC *Nightline* (aired June 28, 1999). Noncitizen legal permanent residents (LPRs), a category in which Asian immigrants have long been overrepresented, are not barred by U.S. law from donating campaign money. This suggests that the DNC wanted to distinguish between legal donations from Asian American citizens and legal donations from LPRs.

52. Stephen Holmes, "Asian-American Groups Complain of Bias in Inquiries and Coverage," *New York Times*, September 12, 1997; Terry Neal, "Asian American Voters Feel Stigmatized," *Washington Post*, September 8, 1997.

53. *Final Report*, 9562.

54. DNC, "DNC In-Depth Contribution Review"; *Hearings before the Senate Committee*, Part I, 96.

55. This figure is from mid-1997. There is no evidence that the DNC publicized the fact that it had returned a large sum of legal money to Asian Americans.

56. Neal, "Asian American Voters Feel Stigmatized."

57. Robert L. Jackson, "German Given Record Fine in Campaign Donation Case," *Los Angeles Times*, July 19, 1997, A16.

58. DNC, "DNC Refunds Contributions."

59. It is worth pointing out that if every accusation about illegal or inappropriate donations had proved valid, the cash involved would still amount to a tiny fraction of the hard and soft dollars collected and spent during the 1995–96 election cycle.

60. See, e.g., PBS Online *NewsHour* Forum, "Unfair Scrutiny? The Asian American Community and the U.S. Political System," http://www.pbs.org/newshour/forum/march97/asian1.html.

61. *Hearings before the Senate Committee on Governmental Affairs*, part I, 1; Francis X. Clines, "Partisan Maneuvering for Hearing's Spotlight," *New York Times*, July 9 1997, B7; David E. Rosenbaum, "Huang May Yet Testify to Senate Panel: As Hearings Open, Chairman Alleges a Chinese Plot," *New York Times*, July 9, 1997, A1; Michael Kelly, "The China Syndrome," *New Republic*, July 28, 1997.

62. *Hearings before the Senate Committee on Governmental Affairs*, part I, 33; David E. Rosenbaum, "Smoke, But No Gun," *New York Times*, July 19, 1997, A1.

63. *Hearings before the Senate Committee on Governmental Affairs*, part I, 11; Kelly, "China Syndrome."

64. *Hearings before the Senate Committee on Governmental Affairs*, part I, 59; Kelly, "China Syndrome."

65. *Hearings before the Senate Committee on Governmental Affairs*, part I, 45.

66. *Final Report*, 9561.

67. Ibid., 9570.

68. *Hearings before the Senate Committee on Governmental Affairs*, part I, 188; Norman Y. Mineta, "The Scandal within the Scandal," *San Francisco Chronicle*, August 25, 1997.

69. *Hearings before the Senate Committee on Governmental Affairs*, part IV, 141.

70. Ibid., 143.

71. Organization of Chinese Americans, "Red Peril and Chinese Laundry," http://www.ocanatl.org/aa61297.htm (1997) (accessed September 15, 1999).

72. See generally coverage in the *New York Times* and the *Washington Post* during the month of July 1997.

73. The term "scandal control specialist" was used by Clines to describe Davis. Davis quoted in Francis X. Clines, "Partisan Fencing, But Little Bloodshed," *New York Times*, July 10, 1997, B9.

74. Ibid.

75. Eric Schmitt, "Few Leads to Show Chinese Money in `96 Race," *New York Times*, July 9, 1997.

76. Rosenbaum, "Smoke, But No Gun."

77. Reuters, "Limits to China Influence Peddling Probe Recognized," *Washington Post*, August 3, 1997.

78. John B. Judis, "Bull in a China Scandal," *New Republic*, September 22, 1997, 18–23.

79. Ibid.

80. Eric Schmitt, "Kinetic Energy from a Senator's Words," *New York Times*, July 18, 1997, A16.

81. Eric Schmitt, "Parties Debate Joint Strategy for Hearings on China's Gifts," *New York Times*, July 15, 1997, A16; Schmitt, "Kinetic Energy from a Senator's Words."

82. Rosenbaum, "Smoke, But No Gun." The same article led with the claim that it had been established as fact that the "Chinese Government had a plan to try to influence the American election last year."

83. *Final Report*, 9562.

84. Roger Tamraz, an international financier and naturalized citizen of Arab descent, was also investigated (see *Final Report*, 2905–3070, 8095–249); Jackson, "German Given Record Fine." By entering into the settlement, Kramer made it unlikely that the Justice Department would pursue a criminal case against him. Leslie Wayne, "F.E.C. Fines German Citizen for U.S. Campaign Donations," *New York Times*, July 19, 1997, A8.

85. Sources on the Governmental Affairs Committee staff confirmed that Madigan said this on background to a group of reporters. Shelia Kaplan, *Analysis*, MSNBC broadcast, July 28, 1997.

86. See also Gregg Birnbaum, "Gov Has Own Fund-Raising Scandal," *New York Post*, January 22, 1998; Robert Parry, "The GOP's Own Asian Connection: Reverend Moon," *Los Angeles Times*, November 16, 1997, M2.

87. Quoted in Leslie Wayne, "G.O.P., for First Time, Admits It Accepted Foreign Donations," *New York Times*, May 9, 1997, A1.

88. Christopher Drew, "Ex-G.O.P. Chairman Sought Overseas Aid, Memo Says," *New York Times*, July 24, 1997, B9; *Hearings before the Senate Committee on Governmental Affairs*, part III, 15–16.

89. Guy Gugliotta, "Taipei Office Was Intermediary for Gift to GOP Tank, Papers Show," *Washington Post*, July 22, 1997; *Hearings before the Senate Committee on Governmental Affairs*, part III, 31–33, and generally part III; Leslie Wayne, "Democrats Get to Scrutinize G.O.P. Ties to Asian Connection," *New York Times*, July 22, 1997, A13; and Leslie Wayne, "Senate Committee Focuses on G.O.P.'s Ties to Foreign Money," *New York Times*, July 27, 1997, A18; David E. Rosenbaum, "Ex-G.O.P. Chairman Strongly Defends His Fund-Raising," *New York Times*, July 25, 1997, A1.

90. *Final Report*, 5683–91; see also 5573–84. Kim and his wife agreed to plead guilty on July 31, 1997, to misdemeanor and felony charges that they had accepted more than $230,000 in illegal campaign funds. Associated Press, "Lawmaker to Plead Guilty in Campaign Case," July 31, 1997. An investigation had started four years earlier, well before the campaign finance controversy began. Kim's settlement with the local U.S. Attorney's Office came after top officials in the Justice Department refused to allow the local office to seek felony indictments against the couple. Conveniently for the Democratic Party and unhappily for Asian American political advocates, Kim and his wife pled guilty during the first month of the Senate hearings. See David Rosenzweig, "Rep. Kim, Wife to Plead Guilty to Misdemeanors," *Los Angeles Times*, August 1, 1997, A1.

91. See generally the minority report in the *Final Report*, 4559–9574.

92. Committee chairman Burton was so widely perceived to be conducting a highly partisan investigation of the campaign finance controversy that he became a burden to the Republican Party. See, for instance, Alison Mitchell, "Gingrich Plans Panel on China and Clinton Tie," *New York Times*, May 20, 1998, A1; and David Johnston and Don Van Natta Jr., "Two Top Officials Quit Inquiry on Campaign Finance," *New York Times*, April 24, 1998, A22. Democratic representatives complained throughout the hearings that Chairman Burton was selectively issuing subpoenas to Democrats or their allies in order to gain partisan advantage.

93. Sandalow, "State Treasurer in Election Probe."

94. Ibid.

95. U.S. Congress, House Committee on Government Reform and Oversight, *Interim Report of the House Committee on Government Reform and Oversight: Campaign Finance Report and Related Matters*, chap. IV, "Unprecedented Infusion of Foreign Money into the American Political System" (1999), www.house.gov/reform/reports/fundraising/4d_sioeng.htm.

96. On the other hand, one could argue that given the majority's power to issue subpoenas and dictate the committee's agenda, it could have chosen never to raise the issue of Sioeng's contributions to Fong's campaign.

97. *Final Report*, 972, 977.

98. Ibid., 966, 971.

99. Jacobs and Morain, "Fong Returns $100,000 in Gifts."

100. Mark J. MacDougall and Steven R. Ross to William R. Turner, May 27, 1997, *Final Report*, vol. 4.

101. *Final Report*, 972; see also 977–78.

102. The House Committee's eventual portrayal of Fong was less speculative but also made clear that any contact Sioeng had with Gingrich had been facilitated by Fong. "In July 1995, the Speaker sponsored a reception for Asian-American leaders at the Peninsula Beverly Hills Hotel. Prior to the event, Kinney asked Matt Fong for the names of some community, business and elected leaders who should be invited. Among the names supplied by Fong were those of Sioeng and his family." House Committee on Government Reform and Oversight,

Interim Report of the House Committee on Government Reform and Oversight: Campaign Finance Report and Related Matters, chap. IV: "Unprecedented Infusion of Foreign Money into the American Political System," 972.

103. Ibid., 972–73; see also 978–79.

104. Ibid., 972.

105. See, e.g., Judi Hasson and Judy Keen, "Glenn Cites 'Bipartisan Abuses,'" *USA Today*, July 9, 1997, 4A.

106. Haley Barbour to Jason Hu, August 22, 1996, printed in the minority report in the *Final Report*, 4772.

107. John R. Bolton to Michael Hsu, August 7, 1996, "Investigation of Illegal or Improper Activities in Connection with 1996 Federal Election Campaigns," *Final Report*.

108. House Report 105-829, part 4, 105th Cong., 2d sess., 105 H. Rpt. 829, vol. 4 of 4, note 16.

109. Francis X. Clines, "Barbour Called Loan 'Urgent,' a Witness Says," *New York Times*, July 26, 1997; *Hearings before the Senate Committee on Governmental Affairs*, part III, 31–33, 267; Richard Richards to Haley Barbour, September 17, 1996, *Final Report*.

110. Steven S. Walker Jr., comptroller of the National Policy Forum, to Kevin Killoren, Signet Bank, October 13, 1994, *Final Report*; Wayne, "Senate Committee Focuses on G.O.P.'s Ties to Foreign Money."

111. Michael Baroody, Memorandum for Chairman Barbour from Michael Baroody, June 28, 1994, *Final Report*.

112. Ibid.

113. Edward K. Karcher, Chief of Exempt Organizations of the Internal Revenue Service, to the National Policy Forum, February 21, 1997, ibid.; Wayne, "Senate Committee Focuses on G.O.P.'s Ties to Foreign Money."

114. Baroody, Memorandum for Chairman Barbour; Drew, "Ex-G.O.P. Chairman Sought Overseas Aid."

115. Haley Barbour to Benton Becker, August 30, 1994, *Final Report*; Wayne, "Senate Committee Focuses on G.O.P.'s Ties to Foreign Money."

116. Clines, "Barbour Called Loan 'Urgent.'"

117. *Hearings before the Senate Committee on Governmental Affairs*, part III; Wayne, "G.O.P., for First Time, Admits It Accepted Foreign Donations."

118. Rosenbaum, "Huang May Yet Testify."

119. David E. Rosenbaum, "A Day of Spin Follows a Month of Hearings," *New York Times*, July 31, 1997, A8.

120. Adam Clymer, "A Senator Finds Himself in Conflicting Roles Again," *New York Times*, July 15, 1997.

121. ACLU statistics provided in Lena Sun, "Asian Americans Seen as Foreign, Stopped," *Washington Post*, September 11, 1997.

122. Organization of Chinese Americans, "National Asian American Groups File Unprecedented Civil Rights Petition."

123. Organization of Chinese Americans, "Asian Americans Outraged with US House of Reps' Overwhelming Disrespect for Legal Permanent Residents," press release, March 31, 1998, http://www.ocanatl.org/pr33198.htm (accessed June 27, 1999).

124. Quoted in "What Does John Huang Have to Do with Me?" *Filipinas*, May 1997, 27–30.

125. Organization of Chinese Americans, "National Asian American Groups File Unprecedented Civil Rights Petition."

126. Both chambers of Congress must pass an identical bill before it can be signed into law by the president.

127. The list included Daphne Kwok (executive director of the Organization of Chinese Americans), Susan Au Allen (president of the U.S. Pan Asian American Chamber of Commerce), Suzanne Ahn, M.D., Michael Woo (president of Independent Fiber Network), L. Ling-chi Wang (chair of Asian Americans for Campaign Finance Reform and a professor at the University of California, Berkeley), Frank Wu (professor at the Howard University School of Law), Helen Zia (freelance writer), Virginia Mansfield-Richardson (professor at Pennsylvania State University), William Woo (professor at Stanford University), and Joann Lee (professor at Queens College, CUNY).

128. Executive Summary of the Statement before the U.S. Commission on Civil Rights, 1997.

129. Quoted in Neal, "Asian American Donors Feel Stigmatized."

130. Ibid.

131. Quoted in Kang, "Asian American Needs Are Focus of New Group."

132. Omi and Winant, *Racial Formation in the United States.*

133. If Asian Americans cannot control the spin resulting from the actions of a few Asian American individuals, perhaps more stringent vetting mechanisms within party organizations and national campaign committees would ensure the end of illegal foreign donations stemming from Asian or Asian American fund-raisers. But this seems perhaps even more unlikely than a major party coming to the rescue of Asian Americans, given the cost of national campaigns, the thirst for campaign contributions, and the porous nature of the campaign finance system. Even when one firewall against illegal contributions holds, another one may buckle elsewhere. For instance, then White House Deputy Chief of Staff Harold Ickes learned about the questionable propriety of donations brought in by Trie as early as April 1996, but he failed to inform Democratic Party officials of the problem. Don Van Natta Jr. and Christopher Drew, "Fundraisers' Moment of Triumph Seems Part of Pattern of Suspicious Gifts," *New York Times,* July 2, 1997, A16. After Ickes refused to let Trie donate to the president's legal defense fund, Trie went on to contribute large sums to the DNC.

134. "Thirty-four Took Taiwan Trips," *The Hill,* June 8, 2005. http://www.thehill.com/thehill/export/TheHill/News/Frontpage/060805/taiwan.html (accessed June 8, 2005).

135. See the following papers in Hu-Dehart, *Across the Pacific:* Evelyn Hu-Dehart, "Asian American Foundations in the Age of Globalization," 1–28; Lucie Cheng, "Chinese Americans in the Formation of the Pacific Regional Economy," 61–78; Arif Dirlik, "Asians on the Rim: Transitional Capital and Local Community in the Making of Contemporary Asian America," 29–60; Le Ahn Tu Packard, "Asian American Economic Engagement: Vietnam Case Study," 79–108; and Paul Watanabe, "Asian American Activism and U.S. Foreign Policy," 109–28.

136. Nakanishi, "Drive-by Victims of DNC Greed." See also Paul Watanabe, "Dismissed and Discredited: The Media's Response to Asian American Criticism," *Asian American Policy Review* 7 (1998).

137. Watanabe, "Dismissed and Discredited"; Wang, "Race, Class, Citizenship"; Wu and Nicholson, "Have You No Decency?"; Zia, "Can Asian Americans Turn the Media Tide?"; Helen Zia, presentation at the conference of Asian Americans for Campaign Finance Reform, San Francisco, November 4, 1997.

138. Zia, presentation at the conference of Asian Americans for Campaign Finance Reform; see also Zia, "Can Asian Americans Turn the Media Tide?"

139. "The 'Asian Bashing' Defense," editorial, *Washington Post,* July 10, 1997, A18.

140. Bob Woodward, "FBI Had Overlooked Key Files in Probe of Chinese Influence," *Washington Post,* November 14, 1997.

141. Brooks Jackson, "Judge Dismisses Five Counts against Fund-raiser Maria Hsia," CNN news broadcast, September 10, 1998, http://japan.cnn.com/ALLPOLITICS/stories/1998/09/10/hsia/ (accessed January 10, 1999); Suro, "Gore's Ties to Hsia Cast Shadow."

142. Woodward devoted one paragraph to quoting Hsia's attorney as saying the charges were simply untrue. Woodward, "FBI Had Overlooked Key Files." Hsia was indicted on February 18, 1998, on charges of disguising illegal campaign contributions from a Buddhist temple to the DNC, the Clinton-Gore 1996 campaign, and other campaigns. Ronald J. Ostrow and William C. Rempel, "Hsia Indicted over Temple Fund-Raiser," *Los Angeles Times*, February 19, 1998, A1; Robert Suro, "Democratic Fund-Raiser Hsia Indicted: Temple Is Named Co-Conspirator," *Washington Post*, February 19, 1998. On September 10, 1998, a federal judge dismissed five counts of a six-count indictment against Hsia. A single conspiracy count of orchestrating illegal donations to the DNC was left standing. Jackson, "Judge Dismisses Five Counts against Maria Hsia."

143. Cooper et al., "How DNC Got Caught in a Donor Dilemma"; Jeff Gerth and Stephen Labaton, "Wealthy Indonesian Businessman Has Strong Ties to Clinton," *New York Times*, October 11, 1996, A20; Rich Lowry, "Selling Out? China Syndrome," *National Review*, March 10, 1997; David Sanger, "'Asian Money,' American Fears," *New York Times*, January 4, 1997, A1; Lena Sun and John Pomfret, "Some Sought Access to Clinton, Others' Motives Remain Murky," *Washington Post*, January 27, 1997, A1; William C. Rumpel, "Buddhist Temple May Be Indicated in Donor Probe," *Los Angeles Times*, January 30, 1998.

144. Freelancers Johnny Chung ($366,000), Charlie Trie ($645,000 to the DNC and $600,000 to the Presidential Legal Defense Trust), Ted Sioeng ($250,000), and Pauline Kanchanalak ($253,000) delivered large sums to, among others, the DNC, the Clinton-Gore 1996 campaign, the RNC, and the Presidential Legal Defense Fund.

145. Wang, "Campaign Finance Scandal." For instance, Wang's own testimony before the U.S. Commission on Civil Rights reads, "I do not condone [Huang's] contribution to political corruption, nor do I feel obligated to defend him and other Asian Americans implicated in the scandal."

146. "The 'Asian Bashing' Defense," editorial.

147. Terry Frieden, "Maria Hsia Indicated in Campaign Finance Probe: Gore Tries to Put Some Distance between Himself and a Longtime Friend," CNN, http://japan.cnn.com/ALLPOLITICS/1998/02/18/hsia.indict/index.html (accessed March 23, 1998); David Johnston, "Democratic Fund-Raiser Indicted in Campaign Finance Abuses," *New York Times*, February 19, 1998, A18. From her office at the Pacific Leadership Council, Hsia had begun to raise money for Senator Gore as early as his 1990 reelection campaign.

148. Robert Suro and Peter Baker, "Clinton Aides Split over Next Step on Lee Nomination to Civil Rights Post," *Washington Post*, November 21, 1997, A13.

149. They wanted Clinton to appoint Lee acting chief of the Justice Department's Civil Rights Division.

150. Julie Chao, "Coalition Backs Lee Nomination," *San Francisco Examiner*, December 10, 1997; Frank Wu, "Clinton's 'Honorable Decision,'" *AsianWeek*, December 18, 1997, 11–12.

151. John M. Broder, "Clinton, Softening Slap at Senate, Names 'Acting' Civil Rights Chief," *New York Times*, December 16, 1997; John M. Broder, "While Congress Is Away, Clinton Toys with Idea of an End Run," *New York Times*, November 24, 1997, A17; Jonathan Peterson, "Clinton Defies GOP, Names Lee Rights Chief," *Los Angeles Times*, December 16, 1997, A1. Lee was finally given a recess appointment in August 2000.

152. On the Lee nomination, Baker reported that "the fight over Lee has evolved into a larger partisan wrestling match in which both sides are positioning for next year's mid-term congressional elections." Peter Baker, "Clinton to Put Lee in Civil Rights Post: President Prepared to Bypass Senate, Uses Recess Appointment," *Washington Post*, December 13, 1997, A1. From an institutional standpoint, the battle over Lee also implicated the constitutional tension between the president's prerogative to make appointments and the Senate's power to confirm them. Consequently, opposition to Clinton's effort to defy the Senate ran into Democratic

opposition as well; Senate Democratic leader Robert C. Byrd (D-WV) urged Clinton to drop Lee's nomination and warned against the "desire to circumvent the regular nomination process." Broder, "Clinton, Softening Slap at Senate, Names 'Acting' Civil Rights Chief"; John M. Broder, "Problems Vowed on Rights Appointment," *New York Times*, December 13, 1997, A9.

153. Some examples of common interests include hate crimes motivated by race or ancestry, language rights, racial profiling, media invisibility, and policy program eligibility. Asian Americans have consistently recognized that building coalitions with other racial and ethnic groups often means their greatest chance of at least partial success.

154. Chao, "Coalition Backs Lee Nomination."

155. Stephen Holmes, "Senator Wants Deal to Support Rights Nominee," *New York Times*, November 1, 1997. Holmes reported that Senate Judiciary Committee chair Orrin Hatch sought to broker a deal whereby his support for Lee would be tied to the Clinton administration's promise not to file a "friend of the court" brief with the Supreme Court in a challenge to California's Proposition 209. Extending this, *Los Angeles Times* political writer Ronald Brownstein wrote that the battle over Lee was "more aptly understood as an escalation of the ideological struggle between the civil rights establishment that built the modern structure of affirmative action and a conservative counter-establishment intent on dismantling it." Ronald Brownstein, "Fight over Civil Rights Nominee Is Latest Battle in Capital's 'Tong War,'" *Los Angeles Times*, November 10, 1997, A5.

156. The three preceding nominees supplied by the NAACP were Drew Days, Lani Guinier, and Deval Patrick.

157. Roger Clegg, "The Quota King," *Weekly Standard*, November 3, 1997, 15–16.

158. See, e.g., Peterson, "Clinton Defies GOP, Names Lee Rights Chief."

159. Perla Ni, "Bill Lann Lee under Attack Again," *AsianWeek*, February 25, 1999, 10.

160. Quoted in "Are Politicians Discounting the Asian-American Vote?" CNN newscast, August 2, 1999.

161. In July 2000 President Clinton appointed former Democratic congressman Norman Mineta to the post of secretary of commerce. He served in that post for all of six months. When the first Bush administration came to power, in an interesting twist, Republican president George W. Bush appointed Mineta secretary of transportation.

162. This analysis is agnostic on whether party elites are, in fact, prejudiced.

CHAPTER 4

1. "Representatives and direct Taxes shall be apportioned among the several States which may be included within this Union, according to their respective Numbers, which shall be determined by adding to the whole Number of free Persons, including those bound to Service for a Term of Years, and excluding Indians not taxed, three fifths of all other Persons. The actual Enumeration shall be made within three Years after the first Meeting of the Congress of the United States, and within every subsequent Term of ten Years, in such Manner as they shall by Law direct." U.S. Constitution, art. 1, sec. 2, cl. 3.

2. The official categories of the 1790 census were (1) free white males sixteen and older, (2) free white males under age sixteen, (3) free white females, (4) all other free persons, and (5) slaves.

3. Those who checked "American Indian or Alaska native," "Other Asian," "Other Pacific Islander," or "Some other race" were asked to write in the race or tribe with which they identified. The U.S. government considers the categories "Latino," "Hispanic," and "Spanish" ethnic rather than racial categories.

4. Throughout the book, I have not made distinctions between various ethnic communities within the Asian American racial formation because this was unnecessary to my argument, which does not depend on acknowledging the tensions within what is a constantly shift-

ing and negotiated racial formation. In this chapter I use the categories of Asian American, Asian American and Pacific Islander, and Asian and Pacific Islander interchangeably. I realize that each of these terms has its own scholarly and political inflection. When necessary to move the chapter's analysis forward, I distinguish between specific communities.

5. See, e.g., U.S. General Accounting Office, *Census Reform: Early Outreach and Decisions Needed on Race and Ethnic Questions*, report to the Chairman of the Subcommittee on Census, Statistics, and Postal Personnel, House of Representatives Committee on Post Office and Civil Service, January 28, 1993.

6. It should be noted that it is not always clear whether Arab Americans are part of the Asian American racial formation. For a discussion of the racial status of Arabs in the United States, see Moustafa Bayoumi, "After Words: Who Speaks on War, Justice, and Peace?" *Amerasia Journal* 27, no. 3, and 28, no. 1 (March 15, 2002).

7. Kathay Feng, panel presentation at the Conference on Legal Issues and California Redistricting, organized by the University of California at Berkeley, Institute for Governmental Studies, and the Brennan Center for Justice, March 20, 2000.

8. Juanita Tamayo Lott, *Asian Americans: From Racial Categories to Multiple Identities* (Walnut Creek, Calif.: Altamira Press, 1998), 81.

9. See, e.g., Tessie Guillermo, "Health Care Needs and Service Delivery for Asian and Pacific Islander Americans: Health Policy," in *The State of Asian Pacific America: Policy Issues to the Year 2020*, (Los Angeles: LEAP Asian Pacific American Public Policy Institute and UCLA Asian American Studies Center, 1993), 61–78; Stanley Sue, "The Changing Asian American Population: Mental Health Policy," ibid., 79–94; Ngoan Le, "The Case of Southeast Asian Refugees: Policy for a Community 'At-Risk,'" ibid., 167–88.

10. Race data derived from the census are used for so many policy programs at the national, state, and local levels, and in the private sector, that it is impossible to list them all here. For example, the Department of Commerce uses them for legislative redistricting; the Department of Education, for grants for basic skills of high-school dropouts; the Equal Employment and Opportunity Commission, for federal affirmative action programs; the Federal Reserve, for charting home mortgages and community investment; the Department of Housing and Urban Development, for various housing programs; the Department of Justice, for voting rights and civil rights; the Department of Labor, for employment practices; and the Veteran's Association, for veteran benefits—to name a few. See U.S. Bureau of the Census, "Planning for Census 2000: Federal Legislative and Program Uses" (March 1998). For additional discussion of the uses of racial and ethnic data from the census, see Espiritu, *Asian American Panethnicity*; Arthur J. Maurice and Richard P. Nathan, "The Census Undercount Effects on Federal Aid to Cities," *Urban Affairs Quarterly* 17, no. 3 (1982): 251–84; Constance F. Citro and Michael L. Cohen, eds., *The Bicentennial Census: New Directions for Methodology in 1990* (Washington, D.C.: National Academy Press, 1985); and Herman Belz, *Equality Transformed: A Quarter Century of Affirmative Action* (New Brunswick, N.J.: Transaction Publishers, 1991).

11. On how the structure of Congress deploys countermajoritarian rules to facilitate the reelection of members, see David Mayhew, *Congress: The Electoral Connection* (New Haven: Yale University Press, 1974); Morris Fiorina, *Divided Government* (New York: Macmillan, 1992); and Richard F. Fenno Jr., "The Institutionalization of the U.S. House of Representatives," *American Political Science Review* 62 (1968): 144–68. An alternative explanation for the organization of Congress emphasizes how the committee system enables a division of labor and specialization of expertise designed for efficiency, rather than to facilitate incumbent reelection. See Krehbiel, *Information and Legislative Systems*; and Keith Krehbiel, "Where's the Party?" *British Journal of Political Science* 23 (1993): 235–66.

12. The countermajoritarian tendency is greater in the Senate than in the House, and the average senator, regardless of her party's majority or minority status, has greater power than

the average representative. Briefly, the Senate rule of "unanimous consent" to bring existing bills to the floor for debate means that a single individual senator has disproportionate bargaining leverage with regard to setting the agenda and terms of floor debate. Because the Senate does not require floor amendments to be germane to the bill being discussed, any senator can—and often will—propose an amendment that is completely unrelated to the matter at hand. If the amendment is attached to the bill being discussed, then legislators determined to pass the bill will have to pass the unrelated amendment as well. The Senate also has the countermajoritarian rule of the filibuster, whereby a minority of senators can prevent a bill or a nominee from being voted upon by the full Senate. On the other hand, especially since the 1994 Republican takeover of the House, that chamber has seen a greater assertion of Republican majority power.

13. It should be noted that enforcement of the rule of seniority has declined in the House since the 1994 Republican takeover of that chamber of Congress, as the Republican congressional leadership has asserted authority to name committee chairs.

14. There is an extensive literature debating who holds the balance of power within the national administrative state. On bureaucrats holding great leverage, see McConnell, *Private Power and American Democracy*; William A. Niskanen, *Bureaucracy and Representative Government* (Chicago: University of Chicago Press, 1971); Lowi, *End of Liberalism*; and Mark Moran Calvert and Barry Weingast, "Congressional Influence over Policymaking: The Case of the FTC," in *Congress: Structure and Policy*, ed. Mat McCubbins and Terry Sullivan (Cambridge: Cambridge University Press, 1987), 493–522. On legislators having greater authority through a variety of mechanisms, see Mat McCubbins and Thomas Schwartz, "Congressional Oversight Overlooked: Policy Patrols Versus Fire Alarms," in McCubbins and Sullivan, *Congress: Structure and Policy*; and Rod Kiewiet and Mat McCubbins, *The Logic of Delegation: Congressional Parties and the Appropriations Process* (Chicago: University of Chicago Press, 1991). For a discussion of presidential control over bureaucrats, see Terry Moe, "The Politicized Presidency," in *New Directions in American Politics*, ed. John Chubb and Paul Peterson (Washington, D.C.: Brookings Institution Press, 1985), 235–71.

15. Jacobson, *Politics of Congressional Elections*.

16. Gary W. Cox and Jonathan N. Katz, "Why Did the Incumbency Advantage in U.S. House Elections Grow?" *American Journal of Political Science* 40 (1996): 478–97; Bruce Cain, John Ferejohn, and Morris P. Fiorina, *The Personal Vote: Constituency Service and Electoral Independence* (Cambridge: Harvard University Press, 1987), chaps. 5–7; Gary C. Jacobson, "The Marginals Never Vanished: Incumbency and Competition in Elections to the U.S. House of Representatives, 1952–82," *American Journal of Political Science* 31 (1987): 126–41; and Jacobson, *Politics of Congressional Elections*, 19–34.

17. Frymer, *Uneasy Alliances*, 145.

18. See, e.g., Mayhew, *Congress: The Electoral Connection*; Paul S. Herrnson, "Party Strategy and Campaign Activities in the 1992 Congressional Elections," in Green and Shea, *State of the Parties*, and Jacobson, *Politics of Congressional Elections*.

19. On the degree to which party leadership can institute party discipline, or "conditional party government," in Congress, see Cox and McCubbins, *Legislative Leviathan*; Rohde, *Parties and Leaders in the Postreform House*; Herrnson, "Revitalization of National Party Organizations"; and Jacobson, *Politics of Congressional Elections*.

20. "Responding to the social and political issues raised by the swelling tide of immigration, the census schedules from 1890 through 1930 increasingly attended to the complexities of ethnic identification.... In 1930, the list of categories for 'Race and Color' expanded to include 'White, Negro, Mexican, Indian, Chinese, Japanese, Filipino, Hindu, and Korean,' plus a space for other write-in choices. However, after the passage of the restrictive immigration laws of the 1920s, interest in ethnic composition waned." Espiritu, *Asian American Panethnicity*, 113.

See also Margo Anderson, *The American Census: A Social History* (New Haven: Yale University Press, 1988), and Yen Le Espiritu and Michael Omi, "'Who Are You Calling Asian?' Shifting Identity Claims, Racial Classifications, and the Census," in Ong, *State of Asian Pacific America*, 43–101.

21. Espiritu and Omi, "'Who Are You Calling Asian?'" On racial formation, see Omi and Winant, *Racial Formation in the United States*.

22. Anderson, *American Census*.

23. There are a number of reasons why the hegemonic consensus around race as a biological fact broke down. A key factor was the ability of black civil rights activists to take advantage of U.S. propaganda efforts during World War II that combated the Nazi rhetoric of Aryan supremacy by insisting on the inherent equality of all people. By emphasizing the hypocrisy of U.S. racism in light of its international pronouncements and its efforts to spread American influence throughout the world, these activists were able to force white American elites to repudiate the biological conception of race. See Dudziak, *Cold War, Civil Rights*, and Borstelmann, *Cold War and the Color Line*. This conception was also under attack in academic circles; see, e.g., Ashley Montague, *The Fallacy of Race: Man's Most Dangerous Myth*, 6th ed. (Lanham, Md.: Altamira Press, 1997).

24. David L. Kaplan, "Politics and the Census," *Asian and Pacific Census Forum* 6, no. 2 (1979): 4. Of particular importance for racial and ethnic groups at the time were the 1964 Civil Rights Act and the 1965 Voting Rights Act, the enforcement of which depended on racial population statistics.

25. Omi and Winant, *Racial Formation in the United States*.

26. U.S. Commission on Civil Rights, *To Know or Not to Know: Collection and Use of Racial and Ethnic Data in Federal Assistance Programs* (Washington, D.C.: U.S. Government Printing Office, 1973). In June 1974 the Federal Interagency Committee on Education (FICE), made up of some thirty federal agencies, created the Ad Hoc Committee on Racial and Ethnic Definitions. Through this committee, FICE completed its work on a draft set of categories in the spring of 1975, reaching agreement between and with the Office of Management and Budget, the General Accounting Office, the Department of Health Education and Welfare (later renamed Health and Human Services) Office for Civil Rights, and the Equal Employment Opportunity Commission to adopt these categories for a trial period of at least one year. The following year, OMB prepared revised racial and ethnic categories and definitions that became effective in September 1976 for all compliance record keeping and reporting required by the federal agencies represented on FICE.

27. Office of Management and Budget, Statistical Directive 15 (1977), http://www.whitehouse.gov/omb/fedreg/directive_15.html.

28. The high number of immigrants and refugees from Asia and the Pacific Islands who arrived after the 1965 Immigration Act was passed have complicated both the legal status and the cultural understanding of the term "Asian American." Many of these individuals had no affinity with the term, even as the national government was engaged in formally classifying them as such, and even as more established Asians in America were actively self-identifying with and promoting this moniker. See, e.g., Lott, *Asian Americans*.

29. Anderson, *American Census*, 221.

30. Michels, *Political Parties*.

31. Harvey M. Choldin, "Statistics and Politics: The 'Hispanic Issue' in the 1980 Census," *Demography* 23, no. 3 (1986): 410.

32. Espiritu, *Asian American Panethnicity*, 119.

33. Espiritu and Omi, "'Who Are You Calling Asian?'"; Lott, *Asian Americans*.

34. Manuel D. Plotkin, "Statement of Manuel D. Plotkin, U.S. Census Bureau, Accompanied by Leobardo F. Estrada, Special Assistant to Division Chief, Population Division;

Nampeo D. R. McKenney, Chief Ethnic and Racial Statistics Staff, Population Division; and Daniel B. Levine, Associate Director for Demographic Fields," in U.S. Congress, House Committee on Post Office and Civil Service, *1980 Census Hearing*, 95th Cong., 1st sess., 9–10, June 24, 1977, 158.

35. See also Espiritu, *Asian American Panethnicity.*

36. Steven Braun, "Simpler 1990 Census Form Upsets Asian-Americans," *Los Angeles Times*, April 12, 1988, A3; General Accounting Office, *Census Reform: Early Outreach and Decisions Needed on Race and Ethnic Questions*, 18–19. Results came from the 1986 national content test, the Mississippi test, and the Los Angeles test. Paula Schneider, then chief of the population division, argued that in several of the tests the write-in question had been more accurate than the checkoff from detailed listings. See Eugene Carlson, "Census Won't List Various Asian Groups," *Wall Street Journal*, May 23, 1988, 19. In addition, with the exception of Filipinos, the percentage of the population reporting in the detailed categories versus the write-in blank was statistically insignificant. In the 1986 national content test, a larger percentage of the population reported as Filipino when presented with the detailed list. See General Accounting Office, *Census Reform: Early Outreach and Decisions Needed on Race and Ethnic Questions*, 20. Bureau officials appeared to be simultaneously claiming that results from write-in responses were both "better than" and the "same as" the detailed checkoffs.

37. Government officials considered this the most controversial proposed change to the race and ethnic question for the 1990 census. See General Accounting Office, *Census Reform: Early Outreach and Decisions Needed on Race and Ethnic Questions.*

38. U.S. Congress, House Committee on Post Office and Civil Service, Subcommittee on Census and Population, *Hearings before the Subcommittee on Census and Population of the Committee on Post Office and Civil Service, Content of 1990 Census Questionnaire: Race, Ethnicity, and Ancestry* serial no. 100-13, May 19, 1987 (Washington, D.C.: U.S. Government Printing Office, 1987) (hereafter *Hearings before the House Subcommittee on Census and Population*).

39. General Accounting Office, *Census Reform: Early Outreach and Decisions Needed on Race and Ethnic Questions*, 30.

40. Braun, "Simpler 1990 Census Form Upsets Asian-Americans"; Carlson, "Census Won't List Various Asian Groups"; Spencer Rich, "Census Listing; Approval Far from 'Global,'" *Washington Post*, May 11, 1988, A23.

41. Braun, "Simpler 1990 Census Form Upsets Asian-Americans."

42. Matsui's statement quoted in Espiritu, *Asian American Panethnicity*, 126.

43. Ibid.

44. Ibid.; Sharon Lee, "Racial Classifications in the U.S. Census: 1890–1990," *Ethnic and Racial Studies* 16 (January 1993): 75–94.

45. A pocket veto is a failure by the president to return a bill passed by Congress during its last days in session, thereby preventing its being enacted.

46. General Accounting Office, *Census Reform: Early Outreach and Decisions Needed on Race and Ethnic Questions*, 21.

47. Ibid.

48. Ibid.

49. Indeed, Matsui never lost a reelection campaign, passing away while still in office in January 2005. His wife, Doris Matsui, was elected in his stead, thus keeping the seat in the family. See "2005 Elections; Matsui Wins Late Husband's Seat," *Los Angeles Times*, March 10, 2005.

50. See Espiritu and Omi, "'Who Are You Calling Asian?'" Partisan politicking over the issue of statistical sampling was clearly at the top of the bureau's political agenda in the run-

up to the 2000 census, potentially affecting its ability to tackle other census issues. Preparation for the 2000 census began in 1992 in an attempt to head off potential problems, and also involved an expensive and lengthy research and testing program. In 1993 OMB announced that it would undertake a comprehensive review of the current categories for data on race and ethnicity as specified by Directive 15; any new standards would automatically be applied to the 2000 census. The review was completed four years later, when the Interagency Committee for the Review of the Racial and Ethnic Standards submitted its final recommendations to OMB. Notwithstanding the bureau's efforts to run a tight ship, legislative aides in the Senate Governmental Affairs Committee with jurisdiction over the bureau believed that it was in some disarray. Esther Kiaaina (then legislative staff to Senator Daniel Akaka), phone interview by author, April 26, 1999.

51. U.S. Office of Management and Budget, "Recommendations from the Interagency Committee for the Review of the Racial and Ethnic Standards to the Office of Management and Budget Concerning Changes to the Standards for the Classification of Federal Data on Race and Ethnicity: Part II," *Federal Register*, July 9, 1997, http://www.whitehouse.gov/omb/fedreg/directive_15.html.

52. Kiaaina, interview.

53. *Hearings before the House Subcommittee on Census and Population.*

54. Neil Abercrombie, Daniel K. Akaka, and Patsy T. Mink to Katherine Wallman, September 8, 1997; Daniel Inouye to Franklin D. Raines, September 7, 1997, *Final Report*; Kiaaina, interview.

55. Kiaania, interview; Inouye to Raines, September 7, 1997, *Final Report*. Because Senator Inouye had served on the Senate Committee on Indian Affairs for nineteen years—eight as chair and three as vice-chair—he sent a separate letter to OMB responding specifically to American Indian concerns.

56. Kiaaina, interview.

57. Ibid.

58. U.S. Office of Management and Budget, "Revisions to the Standards for the Classification of Federal Data on Race and Ethnicity: Part II," *Federal Register* 62, no. 210 (October 30, 1997): 59781–90, http://www.census.gov/population/www/socdemo/race/Ombdir15.html.

59. The revised standards would now have five minimum categories for race: American Indian or Alaska Native; Asian; Black or African American; Native Hawaiian or Other Pacific Islander; and White. OMB, "Revisions to the Standards for the Classification of Federal Data." Other Pacific Islander groups include Carolinian, Fijian, Melanesian, Micronesian, Northern Mariana Islander, Palauan, Papua New Guinean, Ponapean (Pohnpelan), Polynesian, Solomon Islander, Tahitian, Tarawa Islander, Tokelauan, Tongan, Trukese (Chuukese), and Yapese.

60. Taiwanese American Citizens League, TACL-NR2-1998, "The US Census Bureau Should Disaggregate All APA Dada [*sic*]." See also the testimony of Wen-Yen Chen of the Formosan Association for Public Affairs, in "Census 2000 Updates: Subcommittee Hears Nearly Unanimous Support for Census 'Long Form' in 2000," in Jon Harrison, ed. *Red Tape: The Official Newsletter of the Government Documents Round Table of Michigan*, May 22, 1998.

61. *Hearings before the House Subcommittee on Census and Population.*

62. "Census 2000 Updates."

63. Peter Skerry, *Counting on the Census? Race, Group Identity, and the Evasion of Politics* (Washington, D.C.: Brookings Institution Press, 2000).

64. OMB, "Recommendations from the Interagency Committee for the Review of the Racial and Ethnic Standards."

65. As its name suggests, Project RACE tended to emphasize race rather than ethnicity.

66. U.S. Congress, House Committee on Post Office and Civil Service, Subcommittee on Census and Population, *Review of Federal Measurements of Race and Ethnicity,*

103rd Cong., 1st sess., serial no. 103-7, April 14, June 30, July 29, and November 3, 1993; and U.S. Congress, House Committee on Government Reform and Oversight, Subcommittee on Government Management, Information, and Technology, *Activities of the House Committee on Government Reform and Oversight, Subcommittee on Government Management, Information, and Technology*, 105th Cong., 1st sess. (Washington, D.C.: Library of Congress, 1997).

67. Internal divisions also apparently hampered the effectiveness of the multiracial and multiethnic organizations. The HAPA Issues Forum—an organization focused on multiracials with an Asian Pacific forebear—and AMEA had an uneasy relationship with Project RACE. According to Ramona Douglass, the head of AMEA, an outright split occurred between AMEA and Project RACE at the June 7, 1997, summit meeting of multiethnic/multiracial organizations. The head of Project RACE, Susan Graham, signed a joint statement, but "then went behind our backs" to denigrate the statement, after "making everyone else swear that no one would talk about the statement until the appropriate political moment." Ramona Douglass, phone interview by author, August 5, 1999.

68. The bipolar construction of mono- and multiraciality as a means of culturally signifying or formally categorizing people on the basis of race should not be taken to mean that individuals in nominally monoracial categories are somehow "racially pure," or that biologistic "racial mixing" has occurred in recent American society. Just as race is a social construct, so too are the concepts of monoraciality and multiraciality, and ultimately the movement of individuals from a nominally monoracial category to a multiracial category should not be seen as reflective of biologistic patterns but as social movements. If race were really a matter of biology, at least 70 percent of the nominally "racially pure" African American population identified through the census could identify as multiracial.

69. This point was echoed by Douglas Besharov, a scholar at the neoconservative American Enterprise Institute, who noted that the biggest impact of recognizing multiracials/multiethnics "may well be on affirmative action programs." See Stephen Barr and Michael A. Fletcher, "U.S. Proposes Multiple Racial Identification for 2000 Census," *Washington Post*, July 9, 1997.

70. Quoted in Michael A. Fletcher, "Census Change Could Have Little Effect," *Washington Post*, May 16, 1997.

71. Bureau of the Census, "Results of the 1996 Race and Ethnic Targeted Test," Population Division Working Paper No. 18 (Washington, D.C.: Government Printing Office, 1997).

72. Philip Tajitsu Nash, "Will the Census Go Multiracial?" *Amerasia Journal* 23, no. 1 (1997): 23; House Subcommittee on Government Management, Information, and Technology, *Activities of the House Committee on Government Reform and Oversight*, 414.

73. Quoted in Stephen Holmes, "People Can Claim One or More Races on Federal Forms," *New York Times*, October 30, 1997, A1.

74. House Subcommittee on Government Management, Information, and Technology, *Activities of the House Committee on Government Reform and Oversight*, 662.

75. House Subcommittee on Census and Population, *Review of Federal Measurements of Race and Ethnicity*, 96.

76. Barbara Vobejda, "Hill Reassured on Racial Checkoff Plan for Census," *Washington Post*, July 26, 1997; Eric Schmitt, "Experts Clash over Need for Changing Census Data by Race," *New York Times*, April 24, 1997; U.S. Bureau of the Census, Census Advisory Committees on the African American, American Indian and Alaska Native, Asian and Pacific Islander, and Hispanic Populations, *Minutes and Report of Committee Recommendations*, May 22–23 (Washington, D.C.: U.S. Government Printing Office, 1997).

77. OMB, "Revisions to the Standards for the Classifications of Federal Data on Race and Ethnicity: Part II." OMB's decision to allow multiple responses to the race question

touched off a second controversy. After the decision, the focus turned to which tabulation scheme would be used to allocate multiple responses and, not surprisingly, different racial groups pressed for whichever tabulation scheme would result in the highest number for their respective group. See Faye Fiore, "Multiple Race Choices to Be Allowed on 2000 Census," *Los Angeles Times*, October 30, 1997, A1; Holmes, "People Can Claim One or More Races."

78. Vobejda, "Hill Reassured on Racial Checkoff Plan."

79. Ibid.; Fiore, "Multiple Race Choices to Be Allowed."

80. Japanese Americans might have been more likely to support a multiracial/multiethnic category because of their greater rates of outmarriage and their resulting experiences with multiracial children. In addition to the JACL, the Asian American Donor Program later came out in support of officially recognizing multiracials/multiethnics.

81. The leader of the National Coalition, Henry Der, acknowledged that multiracial/multiethnic people existed and had the right to recognition, but suggested that more research was necessary before any major changes were recommended. Henry Der, phone interview by author, August 5, 1999. The AMEA's Ramona Douglass identified individuals like Der as "what we're up against." Douglass, interview.

82. Two major accounts have been written about the passage of the 1988 Civil Liberties Act. Former legislative aide Leslie T. Hatamiya, *Righting a Wrong: Japanese Americans and the Passage of the Civil Liberties Act of 1988* (Stanford: Stanford University Press, 1993), provides a detailed legislative history, focusing almost exclusively on the insider actions of important legislators and key strategic decisions within congressional circles. Mitchell T. Maki, Harry H. L. Kitano, and S. Megan Berthold, in *Achieving the Impossible Dream: How Japanese Americans Obtained Redress* (Urbana: University of Illinois Press, 1999), provide a more historical account of its passage, beginning with actions taken by Japanese Americans during the war and providing a narrative account of succeeding decades and events. They argue that a range of factors coalesced to make passage possible. Both books emphasize the key role played by individual legislators in creating the conditions for the passage of the CLA. In particular, they emphasize Spark Matsunaga's (D-HI) ceaseless efforts to muster support in the Senate, and Barney Frank's (D-MA) appointment as chair of the House Judiciary Subcommittee on Administrative Law and Governmental Relations. The CLA would have died without subcommittee approval, and Frank's support was instrumental in moving the bill forward, while the man he replaced, Dan Glickman (D-KS), had made no real effort in this direction.

Unfortunately, neither treatment of the CLA's passage addresses why and how reparations succeeded for Japanese Americans in the context of African American demands for reparations for slavery. It is worthwhile to note as well that the passage of the CLA followed eight years of spending cuts targeted disproportionately toward programs that benefited black communities. Inasmuch as passage of the CLA relied upon efforts by Japanese Americans and their allies to present themselves as model American minorities, the possibility that Japanese Americans were being valorized vis-à-vis an implicit denigration of African Americans cannot be discounted without further investigation.

83. Maki, Kitano, and Berthold, *Achieving the Impossible Dream*, 205.

84. To put this amount into perspective, consider that when Japanese Americans were interned in the 1940s, they lost not only their freedom but their businesses, homes, other property and possessions, and jobs.

85. Both also note the important role of Senator S. I. Hayakawa as a prominent Japanese American elected official who opposed redress.

86. Changes in racial classifications have sometimes moved bodies from one official category to another through shifting definitions and new counting policies. See, e.g., Michael Omi, "Racial Identity and the State: Contesting the Federal Standards for Classification," in

Race, Ethnicity, and Nationality in the United States: Toward the 21st Century, ed. Paul Wong (Boulder: Westview Press, 1997), 25–33; Espiritu and Omi, "'Who Are You Calling Asian?'"; and William Peterson, "Politics and the Measurement of Ethnicity," in *The Politics of Numbers*, ed. William Alonso and Paul Starr (New York: Russell Sage Foundation, 1983).

87. Robert Lee, "Fu Manchu Lives! Asian Pacific Americans as Permanent Aliens in American Culture," in Ong, *State of Asian Pacific America*, 159–90.

88. See, e.g., Leonard Freedman, *Power and Politics in America*, 7th ed. (Fort Worth, Texas: Harcourt Press, 2000).

89. See Larry Hajime Shinagawa, "The Impact on Immigration on the Demography of Asian Pacific Americans," in *The State of Asian Pacific America: Reframing the Immigration Debate*, ed. Bill Ong Hing and Ronald Lee (Los Angeles: LEAP Asian Pacific American Public Policy Institute and UCLA Asian American Studies Center, 1996); Robert M. Jiobu, "Recent Asian Pacific Immigrants: The Demographic Background," ibid., 35–57; Paul Ong and Suzanne J. Hee, "Economic Diversity," in *The State of Asian Pacific America: Economic Diversity, Issues, and Policies*, ed. Paul Ong (Los Angeles: LEAP Asian Pacific American Public Policy Institute and UCLA Asian American Studies Center, 1994), 31–56. Note that some geographically concentrated Asian American ethnic subgroups, such as Native Hawaiians, Hmong Americans, and Cambodian Americans, are disproportionately represented in the lower-income and less-educated brackets of American society. See Paul Ong and Evelyn Blumenberg, "Welfare and Work among Southeast Asians," in Ong, *State of Asian Pacific America: Economic Diversity, Issues, and Policies*, 113–38; Shinagawa, "Impact of Immigration"; Jiobu, "Recent Asian Pacific Immigrants"; and Le, "Case of the Southeast Asian Refugees." Even within a universe of more assimilated and wealthier Asian Americans, researchers using census data have attacked the model minority narrative by revealing the existence of a discriminatory "glass ceiling" that remains a significant barrier for white-collar professionals, who lag far behind other groups in acquiring government grants and make less even when they attain higher levels of education. Paul Ong and Evelyn Blumenberg, "Scientists and Engineers," in Ong, *State of Asian Pacific America: Economic Diversity, Issues, and Policies*, 165–92; Paul Ong, "The Affirmative Action Divide," in Ong, *State of Asian Pacific America: Transforming Race Relations*, 313–62.

CHAPTER 5

1. See, e.g., "Proposition 187 and the Law of Unintended Consequences: Anti-Immigrant Initiative Would Deny Medical Care, Roil Schools and Make Snoops Out of Teachers," *Los Angeles Times*, October 2, 1994, M4; Tammerlin Drummond, "Experts Weigh Ballot Measure's Possible Impact Series: Prop. 187," *Los Angeles Times*, September 4, 1994, A24; and "Perspective on Immigration: Why Damn a Great State Resource?" *Los Angeles Times*, September 28, 1994.

2. Paul Feldman, "The Times News Poll: 62% Would Bar Services to Illegal Immigrants," *Los Angeles Times*, September 14, 1994, A1.

3. See, e.g., Mark Fineman, "Mexico Assails State's Passage of Prop. 187 Immigration," *Los Angeles Times*, November 10, 1994, A28; and "Platform Prop. 187: 'Racist Initiative' or a 'Step in the Right Direction?'" op-ed, *Los Angeles Times*, August 29, 1994, B4.

4. See, e.g., Cathleen Decker and Amy Wallace, "Wilson and Brown Cap Long, Grueling Race Politics: Confident Governor Campaigns for Fellow Republicans," *Los Angeles Times*, November 8, 1994, A1.

5. Bill Stall and Amy Wallace, "Brown Runs on Empty; Leader Wilson Coasts," *Los Angeles Times*, November 5, 1994.

6. See, e.g., Patrick J. McDonnell and Chip Johnson, "70,000 March through L.A. against Prop. 187 Immigration," *Los Angeles Times*, October 17, 1994, A1.

7. See, e.g., Sandy Banks, "Unflagging Controversy: Why Did Some Protesters against Proposition 187 Carry the Red, White and Green Instead of the Red, White and Blue?" *Los Angeles Times*, November 10, 1994, A1.

8. For accounts of the battle over Proposition 187, see Kent A. Ono and John M. Sloop, *Shifting Borders: Rhetoric, Immigration, and California's Proposition 187* (Philadelphia: Temple University Press, 2002); and Hector Tobar, "New Tide of Latino Activism Stung by Props. 187 and 209," *Los Angeles Times*, April 13, 1998, A1.

9. On the mass demonstrations, see Banks, "Unflagging Controversy"; Robert J. Lopez, "California Elections: 7,000 Attend Protest Denouncing Proposition 187," *Los Angeles Times*, October 31, 1994, A16; Patrick J. McDonnell and Robert J. Lopez, "Some See New Activism in Huge March Protest: Leaders of Sunday's Demonstration against Prop. 187 Predict Surge of Political Energy among Latinos," *Los Angeles Times*, October 18, 1994, B1.

10. See, e.g., Feldman, "Times News Poll"; and Stall and Wallace, "Brown Runs on Empty."

11. See Herman Schwartz, "The Constitutional Issue behind Proposition 187," *Los Angeles Times*, October 9, 1994, M1; Paul Feldman and Patrick J. McDonnell, "U.S. Judge Blocks Most Sections of Prop. 187 Courts: Jurist Cites Significant Constitutional Questions," *Los Angeles Times*, December 15, 1994, A1; and Patrick J. McDonnell, "Clinton, Feinstein Declare Opposition to Prop. 187 Immigration," *Los Angeles Times*, October 22, 1994, A1.

12. See Tobar, "New Tide of Latino Activism Stung by Props. 187 and 209."

13. See David E. Hayes-Bautista and Gregory Rodriguez, "A Rude Awakening for Latinos: Prop. 187 Proved the Power of the Vote to Those Reluctant to Become U.S. Citizens," *Los Angeles Times*, November 11, 1994, B7.

14. On Proposition 187 as a watershed event, see, e.g., Tobar, "New Tide of Latino Activism Stung by Props. 187 and 209."

15. On the explosion of Latino voters, political action committees, and legislative power after Proposition 187, see ibid.; Southwest Voter Registration Education Project, *Latino Vote Reporter* 9, no. 3 (fall/winter 2004); and Latino Legislative Caucus, "Historical Overview of the Latino Caucus," http://democrats.assembly.ca.gov/LatinoCaucus/history_purpose.htm (accessed August 1, 2005).

16. See, e.g., McDonnell and Johnson, "70,000 March through L.A."

17. See, respectively, David Lang, "The Fixers," PBS *Frontline*, aired April 14, 1997, http://www.pbs.org/wgbh/pages/frontline/shows/fixers/interviews/lang.html; Henry Der, "Don't Play the Money Game to Be Heard: Asian Americans," *Los Angeles Times*, September 17, 1997; and Wang, "Campaign Finance Scandal."

18. Scholarship explaining the political silence of Asian Americans is extensive. On how Asian immigrants were denied political rights and prevented from participating in American political life, see, e.g., Bill Ong Hing, *Making and Remaking Asian America through Immigration Policy, 1850–1990* (Stanford: Stanford University Press, 1993); Gotanda, "Exclusion and Inclusion"; Haney López, *White by Law*; and Ancheta, *Race, Rights, and the Asian American Experience*. For explanations focusing on internal diversity, see, e.g., Michael Haas, "Comparing Paradigms of Ethnic Politics in the United States: The Case of Hawaii," *Western Political Quarterly* 40, no. 4 (1987): 647–72; Cain, "Asian American Electoral Power: Imminent or Illusory?"; Bruce Cain, D. Roderick Kiewiet, and Carole J. Uhlaner, "The Acquisition of Partisanship by Latinos and Asian Americans," *American Journal of Political Science* 35 (May 1991): 390–422; Don T. Nakanishi, *The UCLA Asian Pacific American Voter Registration Study* (Los Angeles: Asian Pacific American Studies Center, 1986); Tam, "Asians—A Monolithic Voting Bloc?"; and David Lee, presentation at the University of California at Berkeley Asian Pacific Islander Issues Forum, Berkeley, May 6, 2000.

19. On social-structural factors, see, e.g., Nakanishi, "Next Swing Vote?"; and Jiobu, "Recent Asian Pacific Immigrants." On differences in political participation and voting behavior, see, e.g., Cain, Kiewiet, and Uhlaner, "Acquisition of Partisanship"; Tam, "Asians—A Monolithic Voting Bloc?"; Pei-te Lien, *The Political Participation of Asian Americans: Voting Behavior in Southern California* (New York: Garland, 1997); Lien, Conway, and Wong, *Politics of Asian Americans*; Nakanishi, *UCLA Asian Pacific American Voter Registration Study*; Stephen S. Fujita and David J. O'Brien, *Japanese American Ethnicity: The Persistence of Community* (Seattle: University of Washington Press, 1991); Paul Ong and Don T. Nakanishi, "Becoming Citizens, Becoming Voters: The Naturalization and Political Participation of Asian Pacific Americans," in Hing and Lee, *Reframing the Immigration Debate*, 275–305; Field Institute, "A Digest on California's Political Demography," November 6, 1992, 6; and Steven P. Erie and Harold Brackman, *Paths to Political Incorporation for Latinos and Asian Pacifics in California* (Berkeley: University of California, California Policy Seminar, 1993). On age and generations, see David Lopez and Yen Le Espiritu, "Panethnicity in the United States: A Theoretical Framework," *Ethnic and Racial Studies* 13, no. 2 (1990): 198–224; and Carol Uhlaner, Bruce Cain, and Roderick Kiewiet, "Political Participation of Ethnic Minorities in the 1980s," *Political Behavior* 11 (September 1989): 195–231. On public opinion, see, e.g., Cain, Kiewiet, and Uhlaner, "Acquisition of Partisanship"; Madge Bellow and Vincent Reyes, "Filipino Americans and the Marcos Overthrow: The Transformation of Political Consciousness," *Amerasia Journal* 13, no. 1 (1986–87): 73–83; Cain, "Asian American Electoral Power"; Lien, Conway, and Wong, *Politics of Asian Americans*; and Tam, "Asians—A Monolithic Voting Bloc?" On legal status, see, e.g., Alejandro Portes and Ruben G. Rumbaut, *Immigrant America: A Portrait* (Berkeley and Los Angeles: University of California Press, 1990); Hing, *Making and Remaking Asian America*; and Ong and Nakanishi, "Becoming Citizens, Becoming Voters." On language, see, e.g., Jiobu, "Recent Asian Pacific Immigrants." On population figures and geographic concentration, see, e.g., Shinagawa, "Impact of Immigration"; Jiobu, "Recent Asian Pacific Immigrants"; Gardner, Robey, and Smith, "Asian Americans"; William P. O'Hare and Judy C. Felt, *Asian Americans: America's Fastest Growing Minority Group* (Washington, D.C.: Population Reference Bureau, 1991); and U.S. Bureau of the Census, *1990 Census of the Population, Asians and Pacific Islanders in the United States* (Washington, D.C.: U.S. Government Printing Office, 1993). On country of ancestry, see, e.g., Shinagawa, "Impact of Immigration"; and Jiobu, "Recent Asian Pacific Immigrants." On partisanship, see, e.g., Haas, "Comparing Paradigms of Ethnic Politics"; Cain, "Asian American Electoral Power"; Cain, Kiewiet, and Uhlaner, "Acquisition of Partisanship"; Grant Din, "An Analysis of Asian/Pacific American Registration and Voting Patterns in San Francisco" (master's thesis, Claremont Graduate University, 1984); Nakanishi, *UCLA Asian Pacific American Voter Registration Study*; Tam, "Asians—A Monolithic Voting Bloc?"; and Lee, presentation at the U.C. Berkeley Asian Pacific Islander Issues Forum. On ideology and issues, see, e.g., Bellow and Reyes, "Filipino Americans and the Marcos Overthrow"; Lopez and Espiritu, "Panethnicity in the United States"; Cain, "Asian American Electoral Power"; and Tam, "Asians—A Monolithic Voting Bloc?" On education, see Timothy P. Fong, *The Contemporary Asian American Experience: Beyond the Model Minority* (Upper Saddle River, N.J.: Prentice-Hall, 1998), 72–107. On socioeconomic status, see Fong, *Contemporary Asian American Experience*, 65–67; Bureau of the Census, *1990 Census of the Population, Asians and Pacific Islanders*; Yen Le Espiritu and Paul Ong, "Class Constraints on Racial Solidarity among Asian Americans," in *The New Asian Immigration in Los Angeles and Global Restructuring*, ed. Paul Ong, Edna Bonacich, and Lucie Cheng (Philadelphia: Temple University Press, 1994), 295–321; and Ong and Hee, "Economic Diversity."

20. For studies on consistency across Asian American ethnic subgroups, see Lee, "Racial Attitudes and the Color Line(s)"; Alethea Yip, "Dueling Data," *AsianWeek*, November 15, 1996;

and Feng, presentation at the Conference on Legal Issues and California Redistricting. On disidentification between Asian American ethnic groups, see, e.g., David Hayano, "Ethnic Identification and Disidentification: Japanese-American Views of Chinese-Americans," *Ethnic Groups* 3, no. 2 (1981): 157–71; Roger Daniels, *Asian America: Chinese and Japanese in the United States since 1850* (Seattle: University of Washington Press, 1988); Yuji Ichioka, *The Issei: The World of the First Generation of Japanese Immigrants, 1885–1924* (New York: Free Press, 1988); and Ronald Takaki, *Strangers from a Different Shore* (Boston: Little, Brown, 1989).

21. On the construction of racial and ethnic classifications through ascriptive practices, see Mary Waters, *Ethnic Options: Choosing Identities in America* (Berkeley and Los Angeles: University of California Press, 1990); Robert Blauner, *Racial Oppression in America* (New York: Harper & Row, 1972); Stephen Cornell and Douglass Hartmann, *Ethnicity and Race: Making Identities in a Changing World* (Thousand Oaks, Calif.: Pine Forge Press, 1997); Charles F. Keyes, "The Dialects of Ethnic Change," in *Ethnic Change*, ed. Charles F. Keyes (Seattle: University of Washington Press, 1981), 4–30; Joane Nagel, "The Political Mobilization of Native Americans," *Social Science Journal* 19 (1982): 37–45; Joan Moore and Harry Pachon, *Hispanics in the United States* (Englewood Cliffs, N.J.: Prentice-Hall, 1985); and Lowe, *Immigrant Acts*.

22. See Zia, *Asian American Dreams*. There is some dispute over whether the two white attackers actually mistook Chin as Japanese. See Chang, *Disoriented*, chap. 1. What is not in dispute is that the attack was animated by some form of anti-Asian sentiment.

23. See, e.g., Espiritu, *Asian American Panethnicity*; and Espiritu and Omi, "'Who Are You Calling Asian?'"

24. On the ability to shift in and out of panethnic and ethnic identities, see, e.g., Joane Nagel, "The Political Construction of Ethnicity," in *Competitive Ethnic Relations*, ed. Susan Olzak and Joane Nagel (San Diego: Academic Press, 1986), 93–112; Espiritu, *Asian American Panethnicity*; Lowe, *Immigrant Acts*; Pierre L. van den Berghe, *The Ethnic Phenomenon* (New York: Elsvier Raiser, 1981); Omi and Winant, *Racial Formation in the United States*; Lopez and Espiritu, "Panethnicity in the United States"; and Cornell and Hartmann, *Ethnicity and Race*.

25. Lizbeth Cohen, *Making a New Deal: Industrial Workers in Chicago, 1919–1939* (New York: Cambridge University Press, 1990); Daniel Czitrom, "Underworlds and Underdogs: Big Tim Sullivan and Metropolitan Politics in New York, 1889–1913," *Journal of American History* 78, no. 2 (1991): 536–58; Erie, *Rainbow's End*; Espiritu, *Asian American Panethnicity*; Aldon Morris, *The Origins of the Civil Rights Movement* (New York: Free Press, 1984); and Raphael Sonenshein, *Politics in Black and White: Race and Power in Los Angeles* (Princeton: Princeton University Press, 1995).

26. Espiritu discusses how a "go-it-alone" strategy in the politics of social service funding succeeded when external decision makers only had to deal with a single, dominant organized ethnic group. However, when faced with multiple Asian ethnic communities, decision makers made clear their preference for these communities to come together and present a single, unified proposal for social service funds. Espiritu, *Asian American Panethnicity*, 93.

27. See Raymond E. Wolfinger, *The Politics of Progress* (Englewood Cliffs, N.J.: Prentice-Hall, 1974). Broadly speaking, politicians can dole out wholesale or retail benefits to interest groups. Wholesale benefits apply to an entire group of people and are indivisible and nonexcludable to that group, whereas retail benefits give something only to a specific subgroup or individual within a larger group. Wholesale benefits are often, though not necessarily, symbolic, and can be given in a variety of ways. Symbolic wholesale benefits might include token appointments to public office, attendance at cultural events, the use of signifying cultural markers such as language, or the conspicuous consumption of ethnic food. Such recognition is geared toward communicating the political elite's "recognition" of the validity of that ethnic group's cultural heritage and values. Wholesale benefits that are not symbolic

might include laws providing collective benefits to the group in question, such as the labor and social welfare legislation passed by the Irish machines in the early part of the twentieth century to satisfy newly arrived non-Irish immigrants. See Erie, *Rainbow's End*, 103. A classic example of retail benefits, on the other hand, would be patronage—a divisible and excludable benefit. Winning over constituents or gaining campaign contributions can be a function of "'retail" tactics whereby the political actor bestows individual gifts, or this can be accomplished via "wholesale" tactics, such as "'recognizing' the merits of a particular group."

28. "Asian Pacific Americans have been increasingly recognized as a major new source of campaign funds, a veritable mountain of gold for Democratic and Republican prospectors in California and across the nation." Nakanishi, "Next Swing Vote?" Asian Americans have been giving millions of dollars to the major political parties and their candidates since 1976, with sums increasing up to the 1996 election cycle. See Chapter 3 for additional information.

29. See Wendy K. Tam-Cho, "Foreshadowing Asian American Pan-Ethnic Politics: Asian American Campaign Finance Activity in Varying Multicultural Contexts," *State Politics and Policy Quarterly* 1 (September 2001): 273–94; Wendy K. Tam-Cho, "Tapping Motives and Dynamics behind Campaign Contributions: Insights from the Asian American Case," *American Politics Research* 30 (July 2002): 347–83; Wendy K. Tam-Cho, "Contagion Effects and Ethnic Contribution Networks," *American Journal of Political Science* 47 (April 2003): 368–87; and James S. Lai et al., "Asian Pacific-American Campaigns, Elections, and Elected Officials," *PS: Political Science and Politics* 34 (September 2001): 611–17.

30. Clinton's reelection in 1996 led Asian American elites to bandy about the possibility that either Chang-lin Tien or Norman Mineta, or both, would be appointed to cabinet positions in the second Clinton administration.

31. Political scientists have argued with little opposition and much empirical evidence that a single-minded reliance on elite networks based on money and influence is generally insufficient for an interest group to maintain political power beyond a single election. See, e.g., Frank J. Sorauf, *Money in American Elections* (Boston: Addison-Wesley Educational Publishers, 1988).

32. I was introduced to the term "gatekeeper" by Theodore Wang of the San Francisco-based Chinese for Affirmative Action in an interview I conducted in 1999.

33. On the economic conflict between Asian American capital and Asian American labor, see, e.g., Peter Kwong, *Forbidden Workers: Illegal Immigrants and American Labor* (New York: New Press, 1997), and Peter Kwong, *The New Chinatown* (New York: Hill & Wang, 1987). See also Wang, "Race, Class, Citizenship."

34. See Wang, "Race, Class, Citizenship," 8. Wang observes that "the class background of the big Asian donors ... represent the interests of a very small class of people within the Asian American communities: A handful of the rich business entrepreneurs and professionals and above all, persons with extensive connections to transnational Asian capital and multinational corporations based in places like Indonesia, Thailand, Hong Kong, Taiwan, South Korea, and Japan." See also Kang, "Asian American Needs Are Focus of New Group"; Chang, *Racial Politics in an Era of Transnational Citizenship*; and Hu-Dehart, "Asian American Foundations in the Age of Globalization."

35. See, e.g., Der, "Don't Play the Money Game"; Chang, *Racial Politics in an Era of Transnational Citizenship*; and Paul Van Slambrouck, "Asian Americans Forge Larger Political Role," *Christian Science Monitor*, February 24, 1998.

36. Of course, Asian Americans have been quite active in what Nakanishi has termed "politics by other means," or nonelectoral politics that covers a range of activities. See Nakanishi, "Next Swing Vote?"

37. On the general importance of immigration laws to the political development of Asian Americans, see Nakanishi, "When Numbers Do Not Add Up"; Hing, *Making and Remaking Asian America*; Jere Takahashi, "Changing Responses to Racial Subordination: An Exploratory

Study of Japanese American Political Styles," (Ph.D. diss., University of California, Berkeley, Department of Sociology, 1980); Vincent Parillo, "Asian Americans in American Politics," in *America's Ethnic Politics*, ed. Joseph S. Roucek and Bernard Eisenberg (Westport, Conn.: Greenwood Press, 1982), 89–112; M. H. Jo, "The Putative Political Complacency of Asian Americans" *Political Psychology* 5, no. 4 (1984): 583–605; Uhlaner, Cain, and Kiewiet, "Political Participation of Ethnic Minorities in the 1980s"; A. Uyematsu, "The Emergence of Yellow Power in America," in *Roots: An Asian American Reader*, ed. Amy Tachiki, Eddie Wong, Franklin Odo, and Buck Wong (Los Angeles: Continental Graphics, 1971), 9–13; Massey, "Wrong Way to Court Ethnics"; Daniels, *Asian America*; Lowe, *Immigrant Acts*; Gotanda, "Exclusion and Inclusion"; and Charles J. McClain, *In Search of Equality* (Berkeley and Los Angeles: University of California Press, 1994). Whether or not Asian Americans continue to be formally discriminated against is a matter of much debate. Neoconservatives argue that affirmative action programs targeting non–Asian American communities of color often have the effect of benefiting these groups at the expense of Asian Americans. Alternatively, some legal scholars argue that because antidiscrimination laws today function within a "black-white" bipolar paradigm, the laws contain significant limitations in accommodating the full array of Asian American experiences. See Ancheta, *Race, Rights, and the Asian American Experience*, and Shinagawa, "Impact of Immigration."

38. On the discriminatory laws and events that prevented Asians from entering the country beginning in the mid- to late 1800s, see Chan, *Asian Americans: An Interpretive History*; Harry Kitano and Roger Daniels, *Asian Americans: Emerging Minorities*, 2d ed. (Englewood Cliffs, N.J.: Prentice-Hall, 1995); Hing, *Making and Remaking Asian America*; and E. P. Hutchinson, *Legislative History of Immigration Policy, 1798–1965* (Philadelphia: University of Pennsylvania Press, 1981). The most restrictive immigration laws against Asians were significantly eased in 1965, leading to an unpredicted wave of immigrants and refugees from Asia. Key groups included skilled immigrant Chinese, refugee Chinese, educated urban Filipinos, educated Koreans and Asian Indians, and refugees from the Southeast Asian countries of Vietnam, Cambodia, and Laos. The new immigrants came into an environment where Japanese Americans and Chinese Americans dominated and Filipino Americans and Korean Americans played somewhat lesser roles, and differences had begun to blur. On the politics surrounding the 1965 Immigration Act, see Skrentny, *Minority Rights Revolution*. On migration after the 1965 Immigration Act, see Hing, *Making and Remaking Asian America*; Kitano and Daniels, *Asian Americans*; Chan, *Asian Americans: An Interpretive History*; Takaki, *Strangers from a Different Shore*; Brett Melendy, *Asians in America: Filipinos, Koreans, and East Indians* (Boston: Twayne, 1977); and Fujita and O'Brien, *Japanese American Ethnicity*. In the late 1960s, at a time when Asian America was uniting in political activism and building shared organizations, the post-1965 immigration made it increasingly difficult for collective panethnic action. Few subgroups of post-1965 arrivals had much in common with those who claimed an Asian American identity, and, not surprisingly, most of them initially declined to identify as such. See Wei, *Asian American Movement*; Blauner, *Racial Oppression in America*; Uyematsu, "Emergence of Yellow Power in America," 9–13; Susie Ling, "The Mountain Movers: Asian American Women's Movement in Los Angeles," *Amerasia Journal* 15, no. 1 (1989): 51–67; Karen Umemoto, "'On Strike!' San Francisco State College Strike, 1968–69: The Role of Asian American Students," *Amerasia Journal* 15, no. 1 (1989): 3–41; and Wen H. Kuo, "On the Study of Asian-Americans: Its Current State and Agenda," *Sociological Quarterly* 20 (spring 1979): 279–90.

39. See Gotanda, "Exclusion and Inclusion"; Haney López, *White by Law*; Ancheta, *Race, Rights, and the Asian American Experience*; John H. Torok, "Asians and the Reconstruction Era Constitutional Amendments and Civil Rights Laws," in *Asian Americans and Congress*, ed. Hyung-Chan Kim (Westport, Conn.: Greenwood Press, 1996), 13–70; and Jeffrey

Lesser, "Always Outsiders: Asians, Naturalization, and the Supreme Court," *Amerasia Journal* 12, no. 1 (1985): 83–100. It was not until 1952 and the passage of the McCarran-Walter Immigration Act that Asian Americans were allowed to become naturalized as citizens. See Chan, *Asian Americans: An Interpretive History*, 40. Asian immigrants were held ineligible to own property, legally prevented from testifying in courts of law, and officially segregated from white institutions and neighborhoods. See *People v. Hall* 4 Cal. 399 (1854); and *Gong Lum v. Rice* 275 U.S. 78 (1927).

41. Scholars of Asian American politics have emphasized the historical legacy of discrimination and exclusion to dispute the putative political apathy of Asian Americans, arguing that cultural explanations for Asian American political nonparticipation ignore how state actions retarded certain kinds of Asian American political development. See, e.g., Harold Brackman and Steven P. Erie, "At Rainbow's End: Empowerment Prospects for Latinos and Asian Pacific Americans in Los Angeles," in Preston, Cain, and Bass, *Racial and Ethnic Politics in California*, 1:73–111; Jo, "Putative Political Complacency of Asian Americans"; Takahashi, "Changing Responses to Racial Subordination"; Parillo, "Asian Americans in American Politics"; Uyematsu, "Emergence of Yellow Power in America," 9–13; and John Modell, *The Economics and Politics of Racial Accommodation: The Japanese in Los Angeles, 1900–1942* (Urbana: University of Illinois Press, 1977). A critique from the opposite perspective might argue that state-sponsored discrimination and internal heterogeneity do not demonstrate that Asian Americans would be politically active in conventional politics if these internally generated centrifugal forces and externally imposed hurdles did not exist. After all, there are countless potential and unorganized interests that do not become players in American politics, for whatever reasons. Finally, it should also be noted that Americans of Asian descent who were born in the United States and therefore have U.S. citizenship obviously faced a good deal of societal discrimination that influenced their social, political, and economic prospects.

42. The Electoral College, whose "electors" are chosen by a state-by-state popular vote, decides the presidency. In the absence of a majority Electoral College vote, the decision is thrown to the U.S. House of Representatives.

43. Mobilization efforts would have had an important impact on offices below that of the president, since voters rarely vote only for that office when they cast a ballot.

44. See, e.g., 80-20 Initative, http://www.80-20.net/longfaq.htm; and Nakanishi, "Next Swing Vote?"

45. This is particularly clear when we see how parties have historically not rewarded African Americans even when their votes have been decisive in national two-party elections. See Frymer, *Uneasy Alliances*, and Walters, *Black Presidential Politics in America*.

46. Lang, "The Fixers."

47. Lang's responses raise the question of how he and other Asian American political elites responded to the news in July 2000 that former congressman Norman Mineta had been appointed the first-ever Asian American cabinet member, serving as secretary of commerce for all of six months. Marc Lacey, "First Asian-American Named for Cabinet," *New York Times*, June 30, 2000. In 2001 President George W. Bush appointed Mineta to the position of secretary of transportation. President Bush also appointed Chinese American Elaine Chao secretary of labor.

SELECTED BIBLIOGRAPHY

"2005 Elections; Matsui Wins Late Husband's Seat." *Los Angeles Times*, March 10, 2005, B8.

Abramowitz, Alan, and Walter J. Stone. *Nomination Politics: Party Activists and Presidential Choice*. New York: Praeger, 1984.

Aguilar, Delia D. "Lost in Translation: Western Feminism and Asian Women." In *Dragon Ladies: Asian American Feminists Breathe Fire*, ed. Sonia Shah, 153–68. Boston: South End Press, 1997.

Aldrich, John. *Why Parties? The Origin and Transformation of Political Parties in America*. Chicago: University of Chicago Press, 1995.

Almaguer, Tomás. *Racial Fault Lines: The Historical Origins of White Supremacy in California*. Berkeley and Los Angeles: University of California Press, 1994.

Ancheta, Angelo N. *Race, Rights, and the Asian American Experience*. New Brunswick: Rutgers University Press, 1998.

Anderson, Margo. *The American Census: A Social History*. New Haven: Yale University Press, 1988.

Arax, Mark. "Group Seeks to Reverse Voter Apathy by Asians." *Los Angeles Times*, March 3, 1986, 1.

Armstrong, Scott, and John Dillin. "Ethnic Votes Are Vital in California Primary." *Christian Science Monitor*, May 24, 1988, 1–4.

Arnold, R. Douglas. *The Logic of Congressional Action*. New Haven: Yale University Press, 1990.

"The Asian American Vote 2004: A Report on the Multilingual Exit Poll in the 2004 Presidential Election." New York: Asian American Legal Defense and Education Fund, 2005.

"The 'Asian Bashing' Defense." Editorial. *Washington Post*, July 10, 1997, A18.

"Asians Called a 'Major National Force' in Political Fund-Raising." *AsianWeek*, June 1, 1984.

Associated Press. "Lawmaker to Plead Guilty in Campaign Case." July 31, 1997.

———. "Chronological Overview of the Campaign Finance Scandal." December 3, 1997.

Bailey, Eric. "Firms with State Pacts Are Fertile Donors to Fong." *Los Angeles Times*, May 25, 1998, 1.

Bailyn, Bernard. *The Ideological Origins of the American Revolution*. Cambridge, Mass.: Belknap Press, 1992.

Baker, Peter. "Clinton to Put Lee in Civil Rights Post: President Prepared to Bypass Senate, Use Recess Appointment." *Washington Post*, December 13, 1997, A1.

Banks, Sandy. "Unflagging Controversy: Why Did Some Protesters against Proposition 187 Carry the Red, White and Green Instead of the Red, White and Blue?" *Los Angeles Times*, November 10, 1994, A1.

Barr, Stephen, and Michael A. Fletcher. "U.S. Proposes Multiple Racial Identification for 2000 Census." *Washington Post*, July 9, 1997, A14.

Bayoumi, Moustafa. "After Words: Who Speaks on War, Justice, and Peace?" *Amerasia Journal* 27, no. 3, and 28, no. 1 (March 15, 2002).

Beck, Paul Allen, and Frank J. Sorauf. *Party Politics in America*. 7th ed. New York: HarperCollins, 1991.

Bell, Daniel. "Interpretations of American Politics." In *The Radical Right: The New American Right*, ed. Daniel Bell, 25–28. New York: Criterion Books, 1964.

Bellow, Madge, and Vincent Reyes. "Filipino Americans and the Marcos Overthrow: The Transformation of Political Consciousness." *Amerasia Journal* 13, no. 1 (1986–87): 73–83.

Belz, Herman. *Equality Transformed: A Quarter Century of Affirmative Action*. New Brunswick, N.J.: Transaction Publishers, 1991.

Bennet, James, and Don Van Natta Jr. "Democrats Win First Round of Fund-Raising Inquiry." *New York Times*, July 13, 1997, 14.

Benoit, Kenneth, and Kenneth A. Shepsle. "Electoral Systems and Minority Representation." In *Classifying by Race*, ed. Paul E. Peterson. Princeton: Princeton University Press, 1995.

Bentley, Arthur F. *The Process of Government: A Study of Social Pressures*. 4th ed. Evanston: Principia Press of Illinois, 1955.

Bhattacharjee, Anannya. "A Slippery Path: Organizing Resistance to Violence against Women." In *Dragon Ladies: Asian American Feminists Breathe Fire*, ed. Sonia Shah, 29–45. Boston: South End Press, 1997.

Bibby, John F. "In Defense of the Two-Party System." In *Multiparty Politics in America*, ed. Paul S. Herrnson and John C. Green, 45–58. Lanham, Md.: Rowman & Littlefield, 1997.

Birnbaum, Gregg. "Gov Has Own Fund-Raising Scandal." *New York Post*, January 22, 1998.

Black, Earl, and Merle Black. *Politics and Society in the South*. Cambridge: Harvard University Press, 1987.

Blauner, Robert. *Racial Oppression in America*. New York: Harper & Row, 1972.

Borstelmann, Thomas. *The Cold War and the Color Line: American Race Relations in the Global Arena*. Cambridge: Harvard University Press, 2003.

Brackman, Harold, and Steven P. Erie. "At Rainbow's End: Empowerment Prospects for Latinos and Asian Pacific Americans in Los Angeles." In *Racial and Ethnic Politics in California*, vol. 2, ed. Michael B. Preston, Bruce E. Cain, and Sandra Bass, 73–111. Berkeley: Institute of Governmental Studies Press, 1999.

Braun, Stephen. "Simpler 1990 Census Form Upsets Asian-Americans." *Los Angeles Times*, April 12, 1988, A3.

Broder, David. *The Party's Over: The Failure of Politics in America*. New York: Harper & Row, 1972.

Broder, John M. "While Congress Is Away, Clinton Toys with Idea of an End Run." *New York Times*, November 24, 1997, A17.

———. "Problems Vowed on Rights Appointment." *New York Times*, December 13, 1997, A9.

———. "Clinton, Softening Slap at Senate, Names 'Acting' Civil Rights Chief." *New York Times*, December 16, 1997, A1.

Brodkin, Karen. *How Jews Became White Folks and What That Says about Race in America.* New Brunswick: Rutgers University Press, 1998.

Brownstein, Ronald. "Fight over Civil Rights Nominee Is Latest Battle in Capital's 'Tong War.'" *Los Angeles Times,* November 10, 1997, A5.

Cable News Network. "Are Politicians Discounting the Asian-American Vote?" Newscast, August 2, 1999.

Cain, Bruce. "Asian American Electoral Power: Imminent or Illusory?" *Election Politics* 5 (1988): 27–30.

———. "The Contemporary Context of Ethnic and Racial Politics in California." In *Racial and Ethnic Politics in California*, vol. 2, ed. Michael B. Preston, Bruce E. Cain, and Sandra Bass, 9–24. Berkeley: Institute of Governmental Studies Press, 1999.

Cain, Bruce, John Ferejohn, and Morris P. Fiorina. *The Personal Vote: Constituency Service and Electoral Independence.* Cambridge: Harvard University Press, 1987.

Cain, Bruce, D. Roderick Kiewiet, and Carole J. Uhlaner. "The Acquisition of Partisanship by Latinos and Asian Americans." *American Journal of Political Science* 35 (May 1991): 390–422.

Calvert, Mark Moran, and Barry Weingast. "Congressional Influence over Policymaking: The Case of the FTC." In *Congress: Structure and Policy*, ed. Mat McCubbins and Terry Sullivan, 493–522. Cambridge: Cambridge University Press, 1987.

Campbell, Angus, Philip E. Converse, Warren E. Miller, and Donald E. Stokes. *The American Voter.* New York: Wiley, 1960.

Carlson, Eugene. "Census Won't List Various Asian Groups." *Wall Street Journal,* May 23, 1988, 19.

Chan, Sucheng. *Asian Americans: An Interpretive History.* Boston: Twayne, 1991.

Chang, Grace. "The Global Trade in Filipina Workers." In *Dragon Ladies: Asian American Feminists Breathe Fire*, ed. Sonia Shah, 132–52. Boston: South End Press, 1997.

Chang, Michael. *Racial Politics in an Era of Transnational Citizenship: The 1996 "Asian Donorgate" Controversy in Perspective.* Lanham, Md.: Rowman & Littlefield, 2004.

Chang, Robert. *Disoriented: Asian Americans, the Law, and the Nation-State.* New York: New York University Press, 1999.

Chao, Julie. "Coalition Backs Lee Nomination." *San Francisco Examiner,* December 10, 1997.

Cheng, Lucie. "Chinese Americans in the Formation of the Pacific Regional Economy." In *Across the Pacific: Asian Americans and Globalization*, ed. Evelyn Hu-DeHart, 61–78. Philadelphia: Temple University Press, 1999.

"Chennault Tells OCA of Frustrations in Dallas." *AsianWeek,* August 31, 1984.

Choldin, Harvey M. "Statistics and Politics: The 'Hispanic Issue' in the 1980 Census." *Demography* 23, no. 3 (1986): 403–18.

Chow, Esther Ngan-Ling. "The Feminist Movement: Where Are All the Asian American Women?" In *Making Waves: An Anthology of Writing by and about Asian American Women*, ed. Asian Women United, 362–77. Boston: Beacon Press, 1989.

Chun, Ki-Taek. "The Myth of Asian American Success and Its Educational Ramifications." *IRCD Bulletin* 15 (1980): 1–12.

Citro, Constance F., and Michael L. Cohen, eds. *The Bicentennial Census: New Directions for Methodology in 1990.* Washington, D.C.: National Academy Press, 1985.

Clegg, Roger. "The Quota King." *Weekly Standard,* November 3, 1997, 15–16.

Clifford, Frank. "Contributors to Mayoral Race Seek a Friendly Ear." *Los Angeles Times,* March 11, 1985, 1, 3, 14.

———. "Election Money—The New, the Old, the Bid to Limit It." *Los Angeles Times,* March 27, 1985, 1, 3.

Clines, Francis X. "Partisan Maneuvering for Hearing's Spotlight." *New York Times*, July 9, 1997, B7.

———. "Partisan Fencing, But Little Bloodshed." *New York Times*, July 10, 1997, B9.

———. "Donor-Checking Plan Failed, Ex-Democratic Official Says." *New York Times*, July 11, 1997, A1.

———. "Republican Shows Flair for Lead Role in Inquiry." *New York Times*, July 21, 1997, A14.

———. "Barbour Called Loan 'Urgent,' a Witness Says." *New York Times*, July 26, 1997.

"Clinton Views on Hearings." *New York Times*, July 10, 1997, B8.

"Clout in the Capital." *AsianWeek*, May 24, 1996.

Clymer, Adam. "A Senator Finds Himself in Conflicting Roles Again." *New York Times*, July 15, 1997.

Cohen, Lizabeth. *Making a New Deal: Industrial Workers in Chicago, 1919–1939*. New York: Cambridge University Press, 1990.

Cole, David. *Enemy Aliens*. New York: New Press, 2003.

Cooper, Richard T., with Glenn F. Bunting, Sara Fritz, Alan Miller, Rich Connell, Evelyn Iritani, K. Connie Kang, David Rosenzweig, and Maggie Farley. "How DNC Got Caught in a Donor Dilemma." *Los Angeles Times*, December 23, 1996.

Cornell, Stephen, and Douglass Hartmann. *Ethnicity and Race: Making Identities in a Changing World*. Thousand Oaks, Calif.: Pine Forge Press, 1997.

Cox, Gary W., and Jonathan N. Katz. "Why Did the Incumbency Advantage in U.S. House Elections Grow?" *American Journal of Political Science* 40, no. 2 (1996): 478–97.

Cox, Gary W., and Mat McCubbins. *Legislative Leviathan: Party Government in the House*. Berkeley and Los Angeles: University of California Press, 1993.

Croly, Herbert. *Progressive Democracy*. New York: Macmillan, 1915.

Czitrom, Daniel. "Underworlds and Underdogs: Big Tim Sullivan and Metropolitan Politics in New York, 1889–1913. *Journal of American History* 78, no. 2 (1991): 536–58.

Dahl, Robert A. *Who Governs?* New Haven: Yale University Press, 1961.

———. "The American Oppositions: Affirmation and Denial." In *Political Oppositions in Western Democracies*, ed. Robert A. Dahl, 34–69. New Haven: Yale University Press, 1966.

———. *Pluralist Democracy in the United States*. Chicago: Rand McNally, 1967.

———. *Democracy and Its Critics*. New Haven: Yale University Press, 1989.

———. *How Democratic Is the American Constitution?* New Haven: Yale University Press, 2001.

Daniels, Roger. *Asian America: Chinese and Japanese in the United States since 1850*. Seattle: University of Washington Press, 1988.

Dawson, Michael C., and Cathy Cohen. "Problems in the Study of the Politics of Race." In *Political Science: The State of the Discipline*, ed. Ira Katznelson and Helen Milner. New York: W. W. Norton, 2002.

Decker, Cathleen. "Republican Fong Confronts Role of Race in Senate Drive." *Los Angeles Times*, August 13, 1997, A3.

Decker, Cathleen, and Amy Wallace. "Wilson and Brown Cap Long, Grueling Race Politics: Confident Governor Campaigns for Fellow Republicans." *Los Angeles Times*, November 8, 1994, A1.

Del Pinal, Jorge (assistant division chief of special population statistics, U.S. Bureau of the Census, Population Division). Phone interview by author.

Democratic National Committee. "DNC Refunds Contributions" Press release. June 27, 1997.

———. "DNC In-Depth Contribution Review." N.d.

Der, Henry. "Asian Pacific Islanders and the 'Glass Ceiling'—New Era of Civil Rights Activism? Affirmative Action Policy." In *The State of Asian Pacific America: Policy Issues to the Year 2020*, 215–32. Los Angeles: LEAP Asian Pacific American Public Policy Institute and UCLA Asian American Studies Center, 1993.

———. "Don't Play the Money Game to Be Heard: Asian Americans." *Los Angeles Times*, September 17, 1997.

———. (director of the National Coalition for an Accurate Count of Asians and Pacific Americans). Phone interview by author, August 5, 1999.

Dickenson, James R. "Democrats Seek Identity after Loss." *Washington Post*, December 17, 1984, A6.

Din, Grant. "An Analysis of Asian/Pacific American Registration and Voting Patterns in San Francisco." Master's thesis, Claremont Graduate University, 1984.

Dirlik, Arif. "Asians on the Rim: Transnational Capital and Local Community in the Making of Contemporary Asian America." In *Across the Pacific: Asian Americans and Globalization*, ed. Evelyn Hu-DeHart, 29–60. Philadelphia: Temple University Press, 1999.

Douglass, Ramona (director of media and public relations, Association of MultiEthnic Americans). Phone interview by author, August 5, 1999.

Downs, Anthony. *An Economic Theory of Democracy*. New York: Harper & Row, 1957.

Drew, Christopher. "Ex-G.O.P. Chairman Sought Overseas Aid, Memo Says." *New York Times*, July 24, 1997, B9.

Drummond, Tammerlin. "Experts Weigh Ballot Measure's Possible Impact Series: Prop. 187." *Los Angeles Times*, September 4, 1994, A24.

Dudziak, Mary. *Cold War, Civil Rights: Race and the Image of American Democracy*. Princeton: Princeton University Press, 2002.

Duverger, Maurice. *Political Parties: Their Organization and Activities in the Modern State*. New York: Wiley, 1954.

East/West Institute. "Caucus Warns Democratic Party Leaders to Pay Heed to Asian Pacific Issues." July 1984.

Edmonston, Barry, Joshua Goldstein, and Juanita Tamayo Lott, eds. *Spotlight on Heterogeneity: The Federal Standards for Racial and Ethnic Classification; Summary of a Workshop*. Washington, D.C.: National Academy Press, 1996.

Edmonston, Barry, and Charles Schultze, eds. *Modernizing the U.S. Census*. Panel on Census Requirements in the Year 2000 and Beyond, Committee on National Statistics, National Research Council. Washington, D.C.: National Academy Press, 1995.

Eldersveld, Samuel J. *Political Parties: A Behavioral Analysis*. Chicago: Rand McNally, 1964.

Endo, Russell, Stanley Sue, and Nathaniel Wagner, eds. *Asian Americans: Social and Psychological Perspectives*. Vol. 2. Palo Alto: Science & Behavior Books, 1980.

Epstein, Leon D. *Political Parties in the American Mold*. Madison: University of Wisconsin Press, 1986.

Erie, Steven P. *Rainbow's End: Irish-Americans and the Dilemmas of Urban Machine Politics, 1840–1985*. Berkeley and Los Angeles: University of California Press, 1990.

Erie, Steven P., and Harold Brackman. *Paths to Political Incorporation for Latinos and Asian Pacifics in California*. Berkeley: University of California, California Policy Seminar, 1993.

Espiritu, Yen Le. *Asian American Panethnicity*. Philadelphia: Temple University Press, 1992.

Espiritu, Yen Le, and Michael Omi. "'Who Are You Calling Asian?' Shifting Identity Claims, Racial Classifications, and the Census." In *The State of Asian Pacific America: Transforming Race Relations*, ed. Paul Ong, 43–101. Los Angeles: LEAP Asian Pacific American Public Policy Institute and UCLA Asian American Studies Center, 2000.

Espiritu, Yen Le, and Paul Ong. "Class Constraints on Racial Solidarity among Asian Americans." In *The New Asian Immigration in Los Angeles and Global Restructuring*, ed. Paul Ong, Edna Bonacich, and Lucie Cheng, 295–321. Philadelphia: Temple University Press, 1994.

Etzioni, Amitai. *The Essential Communitarian Reader*. New York: Rowman & Littlefield, 1998.

Fawcett, James T., and Benjamin Carino, eds. *Pacific Bridges*. Staten Island, N.Y.: Center for Migration Studies, 1987.

Feldman, Paul. "The Times News Poll: 62% Would Bar Services to Illegal Immigrants." *Los Angeles Times*, September 14, 1994, A1.

Feldman, Paul, and Patrick J. McDonnell. "U.S. Judge Blocks Most Sections of Prop. 187 Courts: Jurist Cites Significant Constitutional Questions." *Los Angeles Times*, December 15, 1994, A1.

Feng, Kathay. Panel presentation at the Conference on Legal Issues and California Redistricting, organized by the University of California at Berkeley, Institute for Governmental Studies, and the Brennan Center for Justice, March 20, 2000.

Fenno, Richard F., Jr. *Home Style: House Members in Their Districts*. Boston: Little, Brown, 1978.

Field Institute. "A Digest on California's Political Demography." November 6, 1992.

Fineman, Mark. "Mexico Assails State's Passage of Prop. 187 Immigration." *Los Angeles Times*, November 10, 1994, A28.

Fiore, Faye. "Multiple Race Choices to Be Allowed on 2000 Census." *Los Angeles Times*, October 30, 1997, A1.

———. "Kim Loses to Miller in Bid to Keep Seat." *Los Angeles Times*, June 3, 1998, A3.

Fiorina, Morris. "The Decline of Collective Responsibility in American Politics." *Daedalus, Journal of the Academy of Arts and Sciences* 109 (summer 1980): 25–45.

———. *Congress: Keystone of the Washington Establishment*. 2d ed. New Haven: Yale University Press, 1989.

———. *Divided Government*. New York: Macmillan, 1992.

"First National Convention of the National Democratic Council of Asian Pacific Americans." *AsianWeek*, October 16, 1987.

Fletcher, Michael A. "Census Change Could Have Little Effect." *Washington Post*, May 16, 1997.

Fong, Timothy P. *The Contemporary Asian American Experience: Beyond the Model Minority*. Upper Saddle River, N.J.: Prentice-Hall, 1998.

Fraga, Luis Ricardo, and David L. Leal. "Playing the 'Latino Card': Race, Ethnicity, and National Party Politics." *DuBois Review* 1, no. 2 (2004): 297–317.

Freedman, Leonard. *Power and Politics in America*. 7th ed. Fort Worth, Texas: Harcourt Brace, 2000.

Frieden, Terry. "Maria Hsia Indicted in Campaign Finance Probe: Gore Tries to Put Some Distance between Himself and a Longtime Friend." CNN. http://japan.cnn.com/ALLPOLITICS/1998/02/18/hsia.indict/index.html (accessed March 23, 1998).

Frymer, Paul. *Uneasy Alliances: Race and Party Competition in America*. Princeton: Princeton University Press, 1999.

———. "Racism Revised: Courts, Labor Law, and the Institutional Construction of Racial Animus." *American Political Science Review* 99 (August 2005): 373–88.

Fujita, Stephen S., and David J. O'Brien. "Economics, Ideology, and Ethnicity: The Struggle between the United Farm Workers and the Nisei Farmers League." *Social Problems* 25, no. 2 (1991): 146–56.

———. *Japanese American Ethnicity: The Persistence of Community*. Seattle: University of Washington Press, 1991.

Gailey, Phil. "Political Memo: Slouching toward the Center (Post-Reagan)." *New York Times*, September 18, 1985, B8.

Gardner, Robert, Bryant Robey, and Peter Smith. "Asian Americans: Growth, Change, Diversity." *Population Bulletin* 4, no. 4 (1985): 1–43.

"The Gary Locke File: The Trouble with Cash." Editorial. *Seattle Times*, August 5, 1997.

Gerth, Jeff, and Stephen Labaton. "Wealthy Indonesian Businessman Has Strong Ties to Clinton." *New York Times*, October 11, 1996, A20.

Gladstone, Mark. "Nothing Sinister in Calls to Huang, Activist Says." *Los Angeles Times*, July 19, 1997, A15.

"Glass Houses." Inside Politics column. *Washington Times*, July 16, 1997.

Glazer, Nathan, and Daniel Patrick Moynihan. *Beyond the Melting Pot: The Negroes, Puerto Ricans, Jews, Italians, and Irish of New York City*. Cambridge: MIT Press, 1963.

Goldberg, David Theo. *Anatomy of Racism*. Minneapolis: University of Minnesota Press, 1990.

Gotanda, Neil. "Exclusion and Inclusion: Immigration and American Orientalism." In *Across the Pacific: Asian Americans and Globalization*, ed. Evelyn Hu-DeHart, 129–51. Philadelphia: Temple University Press, 1999.

———. "Citizenship Nullification: The Impossibility of Asian American Politics." In *Asian Americans and Politics: Perspectives, Experiences, Prospects*, ed. Gordon H. Chang, 79–102. Stanford: Stanford University Press, 2000.

Green, John C., and Danial M. Shea, eds. *The State of the Parties: The Changing Role of Contemporary American Parties*. Lanham, Md.: Rowman & Littlefield, 1999.

Greenberg, Edward S., and Benjamin I. Page. *The Struggle for Democracy*. New York: Harper-Collins, 1995.

Greenstone, J. David. *The Lincoln Persuasion: Remaking American Liberalism*. Princeton: Princeton University Press, 1993.

Gronbjerg, Kirsten, David Street, and Gerald D. Suttles. *Poverty and Social Change*. Chicago: University of Chicago Press, 1978.

Guglielmo, Thomas A. *White on Arrival: Italians, Race, Color, and Power in Chicago, 1890–1945*. Oxford: Oxford University Press, 2003.

Gugliotta, Guy. "Taipei Office Was Intermediary for Gift to GOP Think Tank, Papers Show." *Washington Post*, July 22, 1997.

Guillermo, Tessie. "Health Care Needs and Service Delivery for Asian and Pacific Islander Americans: Health Policy." In *The State of Asian Pacific America: Policy Issues to the Year 2020*, 61–78. Los Angeles: LEAP Asian Pacific American Public Policy Institute and UCLA Asian American Studies Center, 1993.

———. (president and CEO, Community Technology Foundation of California). Interview by author, 1999.

Guinier, Lani. *The Tyranny of the Majority: Fundamental Fairness in Representative Democracy*. New York: Free Press, 1994.

Gurwitt, Rob. "Have Asian Americans Arrived Politically? Not Quite." *Governing* (November 1990): 32–38.

Gutmann, Amy. "Multiculturalism." In *Multiculturalism: Examining the Politics of Recognition*, ed. Amy Gutmann, 3–24. Princeton: Princeton University Press, 2001.

Haas, Michael. "Comparing Paradigms of Ethnic Politics in the United States: The Case of Hawaii." *Western Political Quarterly* 40, no. 4 (1987): 647–72.

Hall, Stuart. "Gramsci's Relevance for the Study of Race and Ethnicity." *Journal of Communication Inquiry* 10, no. 2 (1986): 5–27.

Hamamoto, Darrell. *Monitored Peril: Asian Americans and the Politics of TV Representation*. Minneapolis: University of Minnesota Press, 1994.

Haney López, Ian. *White by Law: The Legal Construction of Race*. New York: New York University Press, 1998.

Hardin, Russell. *Collective Action*. Baltimore: Johns Hopkins University Press, 1982.

Harris, John. "White House Unswayed by China Allegations." *Washington Post*, July 20, 1997, A1.

Harrison, Jon. "Census 2000 Updates: Subcommittee Hears Nearly Unanimous Support for Census 'Long Form' in 2000." *Red Tape: The Official Newsletter of the Government Documents Round Table of Michigan*, May 22, 1998.

Harrison, Roderick (director of DataBank of the Joint Center for Political and Economic Studies in Washington, D.C.). Interview by author.

Hartz, Louis. *The Liberal Tradition in America*. New York: Harcourt Brace Jovanovich, 1955.

Hasson, Judi, and Judy Keen. "Glenn Cites 'Bipartisan Abuses.'" *USA Today*, July 9, 1997, 4A.

Hatamiya, Leslie T. *Righting a Wrong: Japanese Americans and the Passage of the Civil Liberties Act of 1988*. Stanford: Stanford University Press, 1993.

Hayano, David. "Ethnic Identification and Disidentification: Japanese-American Views of Chinese-Americans." *Ethnic Groups* 3, no. 2 (1981): 157–71.

Hayes-Bautista, David E., and Gregory Rodriguez. "A Rude Awakening for Latinos: Prop. 187 Proved the Power of the Vote to Those Reluctant to Become U.S. Citizens." *Los Angeles Times*, November 11, 1994, B7.

Herbers, John. "Party Looks Inward for Ways to Regain Majority." *New York Times*, November 8, 1984, A24.

Hero, Rodney E., and Caroline J. Tolbert. "Latinos and Substantive Representation in the U.S. House of Representatives: Direct, Indirect, or Nonexistent?" *American Journal of Political Science* 39, no. 3 (1995): 640–52.

Herrnson, Paul S. *Party Campaigning in the 1980s*. Cambridge: Harvard University Press, 1988.

———. "Party Strategy and Campaign Activities in the 1992 Congressional Elections." In *The State of the Parties: The Changing Role of Contemporary American Parties*, ed. John C. Green and Daniel M. Shea. Lanham, Md.: Rowman & Littlefield, 1999.

———. "The Revitalization of National Party Organizations." In *The Parties Respond: Changes in American Parties and Campaigns*, ed. L. Sandy Maisel, 45–68. Boulder: Westview Press, 2002.

Hing, Bill Ong. *Making and Remaking Asian America through Immigration Policy, 1850–1990*. Stanford: Stanford University Press, 1993.

Hofstadter, Richard. *The Idea of a Party System: The Rise of Legitimate Opposition in the United States*. Berkeley and Los Angeles: University of California Press, 1969.

Holmes, Stephen. "U.S. Urged to Reflect Wider Diversity in Racial and Ethnic Classifications." *New York Times*, July 8, 1994, A18.

———. "Asian-American Groups Complain of Bias in Inquiries and Coverage." *New York Times*, September 12, 1997.

———. "People Can Claim One or More Races on Federal Forms." *New York Times*, October 30, 1997, A1.

———. "Senator Wants Deal to Support Rights Nominee." *New York Times*, November 1, 1997.

Horowitz, Donald L. "Ethnic Conflict Management for Policymakers." In *Conflict and Peacemaking in Multiethnic Societies*, ed. Joseph V. Montville, 115–30. Lanham, Md.: Lexington Books, 1991.

Horton, John. *The Politics of Diversity: Immigration, Resistance, and Change in Monterey Park, California*. Philadelphia: Temple University Press, 1995.

Hu-Dehart, Evelyn. "Asian American Formations in the Age of Globalization." In *Across the Pacific: Asian Americans and Globalization*, ed. Evelyn Hu-Dehart, 1–28. Philadelphia: Temple University Press, 1999.

Huey-Long Song, John, and John Dombrink. "'Good Guys' and Bad Guys: Media, Asians, and the Framing of a Criminal Event." *Amerasia Journal* 22, no. 3 (1996): 25–45.

Hutchinson, E. P. *Legislative History of Immigration Policy, 1798–1965*. Philadelphia: University of Pennsylvania Press, 1981.

Ichioka, Yuji. *The Issei: The World of the First Generation of Japanese Immigrants, 1885–1924*. New York: Free Press, 1988.

Ignatiev, Noel. *How the Irish Became White*. New York: Routledge, 1996.

Imahara, Kathryn K. "Language Rights Issues to the Year 2020 and Beyond: Language Rights Policy." In *The State of Asian Pacific America: Policy Issues to the Year 2020*, 233–52. Los Angeles: LEAP Asian Pacific American Public Policy Institute and UCLA Asian American Studies Center, 1993.

Interim Coordinating Committee for Chinese Americans. "The Chinese American Declaration Concerning the 1988 Presidential Election." N.p., n.d.

Iwata, Edward. "Asian Americans Host Democratic Hopefuls." *San Francisco Chronicle*, October 20, 1987.

Jackson, Brooks. "Judge Dismisses Five Counts against Fund-Raiser Maria Hsia." CNN, news broadcast, September 10, 1998. http://japan.cnn.com/ALLPOLITICS/stories/1998/09/10/hsia/ (accessed January 10, 1999).

Jackson, Robert L. "German Given Record Fine in Campaign Donation Case." *Los Angeles Times*, July 19, 1997, A16.

Jacobs, Paul, and Alan C. Miller. "State Treasurer Linked to Asian Funds, Records Show." *Los Angeles Times*, February 25, 1998, A1.

Jacobs, Paul, and Dan Morain. "Fong Returns $100,000 in Gifts." *Los Angeles Times*, April 23, 1997, A3.

Jacobson, Gary C. "The Marginals Never Vanished: Incumbency and Competition in Elections to the U.S. House of Representatives, 1952–82." *American Journal of Political Science* 31 (1987): 126–41.

———. *The Politics of Congressional Elections*. 4th ed. New York: Longman, 1997.

James, Judson L. *American Political Parties in Transition*. New York: Harper & Row, 1974.

Jiobu, Robert M. "Recent Asian Pacific Immigrants: The Demographic Background." In *The State of Asian Pacific America: Reframing the Immigration Debate*, ed. Bill Ong Hing and Ronald Lee, 35–57. Los Angeles: LEAP Asian Pacific American Public Policy Institute and UCLA Asian American Studies Center, 1996.

Jo, M. H. "The Putative Political Complacency of Asian Americans." *Political Psychology* 5, no. 4 (1984): 583–605.

Jo, Yung-Hwan, ed. *Political Participation of Asian Americans: Problems and Strategies*. Chicago: Pacific/Asian American Mental Health Research, 1980.

Johnson, James Weldon. "The Gentlemen's Agreement and the Negro Vote." *Crisis* 28 (October 1924).

Johnston, David. "Democratic Fund-Raiser Indicted in Campaign Finance Abuses." *New York Times*, February 19, 1998, A18.

Johnston, David, and Don Van Natta Jr. "Two Officials Quit Inquiry on Campaign Finance." *New York Times*, April 24, 1998, A22.

Jones, Mack H. "Black Office Holding and Political Development in the Rural South." *Review of Black Political Economy* 6 (summer 1976): 375–407.

Judis, John B. "Bull in a China Scandal." *New Republic*, September 22, 1997, 18–23.

Kang, K. Connie. "Asian American Needs Are Focus of New Group." *Los Angeles Times*, August 24, 1997, A1.

Kaplan, David L. "Politics and the Census." *Asian and Pacific Census Forum* 6, no. 2 (1979).

Kaplan, Sheila. *Analysis*. MSNBC news broadcast, aired July 28, 1997.

Keefe, William J. *Parties, Politics and Public Policy in America*. New York: Holt, Rinehart and Winston, 1972.

Kelly, Michael. "The China Syndrome." *New Republic*, July 28, 1997.

Kernell, Samuel. *Going Public: New Strategies of Presidential Leadership*. 3d ed. Washington, D.C.: Congressional Quarterly Press, 1997.

Key, V. O., Jr. *Politics, Parties, and Pressure Groups*. 5th ed. New York: Crowell, 1964.

———. *Southern Politics in State and Nation*. New ed. Knoxville: University of Tennessee Press, 1984.

Keyes, Charles F. "The Dialectics of Ethnic Change." In *Ethnic Change*, ed. Charles F. Keyes, 4–30. Seattle: University of Washington Press, 1981.

Kiaaina, Esther (chief of staff for Congressman Ed Case [D-HI]). Phone interview by author, April 26, 1999.

Kiang, Peter N., and Vivian Wai-Fun Lee. "Exclusion or Contribution: Education K–12 Policy." In *The State of Asian Pacific America: Policy Issues to the Year 2020*, 25–48. Los Angeles: LEAP Asian Pacific American Public Policy Institute and UCLA Asian American Studies Center, 1993.

Kiewiet, Rod, and Mat McCubbins. *The Logic of Delegation: Congressional Parties and the Appropriations Process*. Chicago: University of Chicago Press, 1991.

Kikimura, Akemi, and Harry Kitano. "Interracial Marriages." *Journal of Social Sciences* 29 (1973): 570–82.

Kim, Bok-Lim. "Problems and Service Needs of Asian Americans in Chicago: An Empirical Study." *Amerasia Journal* 5 (1978): 23–44.

Kim, Clair Jean. "The Racial Triangulation of Asian Americans." *Politics and Society* 27 (March 1999): 105–38

———. "Managing the Racial Breach: Clinton, Black-White Polarization, and the Race Initiative." *Political Science Quarterly* 117, no. 1 (2001).

———. *Bitter Fruit: The Politics of Black-Korean Conflict in New York City*. New Haven: Yale University Press, 2003.

Kinder, Donald R. "The Continuing American Dilemma: White Resistance to Racial Change 40 Years after Myrdal." *Journal of Social Issues* 42 (1986): 151–72.

Kinder, Donald R., and Lynn M. Sanders. *Divided by Color: Racial Politics and Democratic Ideals*. Chicago: University of Chicago Press, 1996.

Kinder, Donald, and David O. Sears. "Prejudice and Politics: Symbolic Racism versus Racial Threats to the Good Life." *Journal of Personality and Social Psychology* 3 (1981): 414–31.

Kitano, Harry, and Roger Daniels. *Asian Americans: Emerging Minorities*. 2d ed. Englewood Cliffs, N.J.: Prentice-Hall, 1995.

Klinkner, Philip A. *The Losing Parties: Out-Party National Committees, 1956–1993*. New Haven: Yale University Press, 1994.

Kornhauser, William. *The Politics of Mass Society*. New York: Free Press, 1959.

Kranish, Michael. "Clinton Policy Shift Followed Asian-American Fund-Raiser." *Boston Globe*, January 16, 1997.

Krehbiel, Keith. *Information and Legislative Systems*. Ann Arbor: University of Michigan Press, 1991.

———. "Where's the Party?" *British Journal of Political Science* 23 (1993): 235–66.

Kuo, Wen H. "On the Study of Asian-Americans: Its Current State and Agenda." *Sociological Quarterly* 20 (spring 1979): 279–90.

Kwong, Peter. *The New Chinatown*. New York: Hill & Wang, 1987.

———. *Forbidden Workers: Illegal Chinese Immigrants and American Labor*. New York: New Press, 1997.

Kwong, Peter, and JoAnn Lum. "A Silent Minority Tests Its Clout." *The Nation*, January 16, 1988, 50–52.

Lacey, Marc. "Parties Exchange Charges at Hearing on Anti-Asian Bias." *Los Angeles Times*, December 6, 1997, A20.

———. "First Asian-American Named for Cabinet." *New York Times*, June 30, 2000.

Lai, James S., Wendy K. Tam-Cho, Thomas P. Kim, and Okiyoshi Takeda. "Asian Pacific-American Campaigns, Elections, and Elected Officials." *PS: Political Science and Politics* 34 (September 2001): 611–17.

Lang, David. "The Fixers." PBS *Frontline*, aired April 14, 1997.

Latino Legislative Caucus. "Historical Overview of the Latino Caucus." http://democrats. assembly.ca.gov/LatinoCaucus/history_purpose.htm.

Le, Ngoan. "The Case of the Southeast Asian Refugees: Policy for a Community 'At-Risk.'" In *The State of Asian Pacific America: Policy Issues to the Year 2020*, 167–88. Los Angeles: LEAP Asian Pacific American Public Policy Institute and UCLA Asian American Studies Center, 1993.

Lee, C. N. "A View from the Campaign Headquarters." *Bridge* 4, no. 5 (1976): 18–21.

Lee, David. Presentation at the University of California at Berkeley Asian Pacific Islander Issues Forum, Berkeley, California, May 6, 2000.

Lee, Robert. *Orientals: Asian Americans in Popular Culture*. Philadelphia: Temple University Press, 1999.

———. "Fu Manchu Lives! Asian Pacific Americans as Permanent Aliens in American Culture." In *The State of Asian Pacific America: Transforming Race Relations*, ed. Paul Ong, 159–90. Los Angeles: LEAP Asian Pacific American Public Policy Institute and UCLA Asian American Studies Center, 2000.

Lee, Sharon. "Racial Classifications in the U.S. Census: 1890–1990." *Ethnic and Racial Studies* 16 (January 1993): 75–94.

Lee, Taeku. "Racial Attitudes and the Color Line(s) at the Close of the Twentieth Century." In *The State of Asian Pacific America: Transforming Race Relations*, ed. Paul Ong, 103–58. Los Angeles: LEAP Asian Pacific American Public Policy Institute and UCLA Asian American Studies Center, 2000.

Leong, Russell, ed. *Moving the Image: Independent Asian Pacific American Media Arts*. Los Angeles: UCLA Asian American Studies Center and Visual Communications, 1991.

Lesser, Jeffrey. "Always Outsiders: Asians, Naturalization, and the Supreme Court." *Amerasia Journal* 12, no. 1 (1985): 83–100.

Lien, Pei-te. "Ethnicity and Political Participation: A Comparison between Asian and Mexican Americans." *Political Behavior* 16, no. 2 (1994): 237–64.

———. *The Political Participation of Asian Americans: Voting Behavior in Southern California*. New York: Garland, 1997.

———. "What Ties That Bind? Comparing Patterns of Political Opinion across Major Asian American Groups." Paper presented at the annual meeting of the American Political Science Association, Atlanta, Georgia, September 2–5, 1999.

———. *The Making of Asian America through Political Participation*. Philadelphia: Temple University Press, 2001.

Lien, Pei-te, Margaret Conway, and Janelle Wong. *The Politics of Asian Americans: Diversity and Community*. New York: Routledge, 2004.

Lijphart, Arend. *Democracy in Plural Societies: A Comparative Exploration*. New Haven: Yale University Press, 1977.

———. *Power-Sharing in South Africa*. Berkeley: Institute of International Studies, 1985.

Lin, Sam Chu. "Optimism on Both Sides: Campaigns Look to APAs as Swing Votes in 10 States." *AsianWeek*, October 11–17, 1996. http://www.asianweek.com/101196/election.html.

Ling, Susie. "The Mountain Movers: Asian American Women's Movement in Los Angeles." *Amerasia Journal* 15, no. 1 (1989): 51–67.

Lipsitz, George. *The Possessive Investment in Whiteness: How White People Profit from Identity Politics*. Philadelphia: Temple University Press, 2006.

Liu, John, and Lucie Cheng. "A Dialogue on Race and Class: Asian American Studies and Marxism." In *Left Academy: Marxist Scholarship on American Campuses*, ed. B. Ollman and E. Vernoff, 139–63. New York: Praeger, 1986.

Lopez, David, and Yen Le Espiritu. "Panethnicity in the United States: A Theoretical Framework." *Ethnic and Racial Studies* 13, no. 2 (1990): 198–224.

Lopez, Elizabeth, and Eric Wahlgren. "The Latino Vote." *California Journal* 25 (November 1994): 29–31.

Lopez, Robert J. "California Elections: 7,000 Attend Protest Denouncing Proposition 187." *Los Angeles Times*, October 31, 1994, A16.

Lott, Juanita Tamayo. *Asian Americans: From Racial Categories to Multiple Identities*. Walnut Creek, Calif.: Altamira Press, 1998.

———. (chair of Government Social Statistics Programs of the American Statistical Association). Interview by author.

Louie, Miriam Ching. "Breaking the Cycle: Women Workers Confront Corporate Greed Locally." In *Dragon Ladies: Asian American Feminists Breathe Fire*, ed. Sonia Shah, 121–31. Boston: South End Press, 1997.

Lowe, Lisa. *Immigrant Acts: On Asian American Cultural Politics*. Durham: Duke University Press, 1996.

Lowi, Theodore J. *The End of Liberalism: The Second Republic of the United States*. New York: W. W. Norton, 1979.

———. "Toward a Responsible Three-Party System." In *The State of the Parties: The Changing Role of Contemporary American Parties*, ed. Daniel M. Shea and John C. Green, 45–60. Lanham, Md.: Rowman & Littlefield, 1999.

———. "Political Parties and the Future State of the Union." In *American Political Parties: Decline or Resurgence?* ed. Jeffrey E. Cohen, Richard Fleisher, and Paul Kantor. Washington, D.C.: Congressional Quarterly Press, 2001.

Lowi, Theodore J., and Benjamin Ginsberg. *American Government: Freedom and Power*. 5th ed. New York: W. W. Norton, 1998.

Lowry, Rich. "Selling Out? China Syndrome." *National Review*, March 10, 1997.

Lu, Lynn. "Critical Visions: The Representation and Resistance of Asian Women." In *Dragon Ladies: Asian American Feminists Breathe Fire*, ed. Sonia Shah, 17–28. Boston: South End Press, 1997.

Lupia, Arthur, and Mat McCubbins. *The Democratic Dilemma: Can Citizens Learn What They Really Need to Know?* Cambridge: Cambridge University Press, 1998.

MacIntyre, Alistair. *After Virtue: A Study in Moral Theory*. Notre Dame: University of Notre Dame Press, 1984.

Maisel, L. Sandy, ed. *The Parties Respond: Changes in American Parties and Campaigns*. Boulder: Westview Press, 2002.

Maitland, Anze. "Asian Leaders Accuse Democratic Party of Racism." *San Francisco Chronicle*, May 22, 1985.

Maki, Mitchell T., Harry H. L. Kitano, and S. Megan Berthold. *Achieving the Impossible Dream: How Japanese Americans Obtained Redress*. Urbana: University of Illinois Press, 1999.

Malkin, Michelle. "More Than Money Troubles at Harmony Palace." *Seattle Times*, August 5, 1997.

———. "Locke's Money Trail Leads to Buddhist Temple's Door." *Seattle Times*, September 23, 1997.

Marchetti, Gina. *Romance and the 'Yellow Peril': Race, Sex, and Discursive Strategies in Hollywood Fiction*. Berkeley and Los Angeles: University of California Press, 1994.

Massey, Thomas. "The Wrong Way to Court Ethnics." *Washington Monthly*, May 1986, 21–26.

Matsui, Robert T. "Statement of Honorable Robert T. Matsui, a Representative in Congress from the State of CA, Read by Mr. Fujioka, President Elect, Japanese American Bar Association." U.S. House, Committee on Post Office and Civil Service, *Role of Minority Communities in Decennial Censuses Hearing*, 100th Cong., 2d sess., May 20, 1988, 62–65.

Maurice, Arthur J., and Richard P. Nathan. "The Census Undercount Effects on Federal Aid to Cities." *Urban Affairs Quarterly* 17, no. 3 (1982): 251–84.

Mayeda, Greg (co-founder of the Happa Issues Forum). Interview by author.

Mayhew, David. *Congress: The Electoral Connection*. New Haven: Yale University Press, 1974.

McClain, Charles J. *In Search of Equality*. Berkeley and Los Angeles: University of California Press, 1994.

McConnell, Grant. *Private Power and American Democracy*. New York: Knopf, 1966.

McCubbins, Mat, and Thomas Schwartz. "Congressional Oversight Overlooked: Police Patrols Versus Fire Alarms." In *Congress: Structure and Policy*, ed. Mat McCubbins and Terry Sullivan, 409–25. Cambridge: Cambridge University Press, 1987.

McDonnell, Patrick J. "Clinton, Feinstein Declare Opposition to Prop. 187 Immigration." *Los Angeles Times*, October 22, 1994, A1.

McDonnell, Patrick J., and Chip Johnson. "70,000 March through L.A. against Prop. 187 Immigration." *Los Angeles Times*, October 17, 1994, A1.

McDonnell, Patrick J., and Robert J. Lopez. "Some See New Activism in Huge March Protest: Leaders of Sunday's Demonstration against Prop. 187 Predict Surge of Political Energy among Latinos." *Los Angeles Times*, October 18, 1994, B1.

Melendy, Brett. *Asians in America: Filipinos, Koreans, and East Indians*. Boston: Twayne, 1977.

Melnick, Daniel. "The 1980 Census: Recalculating the Federal Equation." *Publius: The Journal of Federalism* 2, nos. 3–4 (1981): 39–65.

Michels, Robert. *Political Parties*. Trans. Eden and Cedar Paul. New York: Free Press, 1959.

Milkis, Sidney M. *The President and the Parties: The Transformation of the American Party System since the New Deal*. New York: Oxford University Press, 1993.

———. *Political Parties and Constitutional Government: Remaking American Democracy*. Baltimore: Johns Hopkins University Press, 1999.

Mill, John Stuart. "Considerations on Representative Government." In John Stuart Mill, *On Liberty and Other Essays*. Ed. John M. Gray. Oxford: Oxford University Press, 1998.

Miller, Alan. "DNC Raises $19 Million But Is Still in Debt, Report Says." *Los Angeles Times*, August 1, 1997, A18.

Mineta, Norman Y. "The Scandal within the Scandal." *San Francisco Chronicle*, August 25, 1997.

Mitchell, Alison. "Gingrich Plans Panel on China and Clinton Tie.'" *New York Times*, May 20, 1998, A1.

Modell, John. *The Economics and Politics of Racial Accommodation: The Japanese in Los Angeles, 1900–1942*. Urbana: University of Illinois Press, 1977.

Moe, Terry. *The Organization of Interests*. Chicago: University of Chicago Press, 1980.

———. "The Politicized Presidency." In *New Directions in American Politics*, ed. John E. Chubb and Paul Peterson, 235–71. Washington, D.C.: Brookings Institution Press, 1985.

Montague, Ashley. *The Fallacy of Race: Man's Most Dangerous Myth.* 6th ed. Lanham, Md.: Altamira Press, 1997.

Moore, Joan, and Harry Pachon. *Hispanics in the United States.* Englewood Cliffs, N.J.: Prentice-Hall, 1985.

Morris, Aldon. *The Origins of the Civil Rights Movement.* New York: Free Press, 1984.

Mowry, George E. *The California Progressives.* Berkeley and Los Angeles: University of California Press, 1993.

Mulhall, Stephen, and Adam Swift. *Liberals and Communitarians.* Malden, Mass.: Blackwell, 1996.

Nagel, Joane. "The Political Mobilization of Native Americans." *Social Science Journal* 19 (1982): 37–45.

———. "The Political Construction of Ethnicity." In *Competitive Ethnic Relations,* ed. Susan Olzak and Joane Nagel, 93–112. San Diego: Academic Press, 1986.

Nakanishi, Don T. "Asian American Politics: An Agenda for Research." *Amerasia Journal* 12 (1986): 1–27.

———. *The UCLA Asian Pacific American Voter Registration Study.* Los Angeles: UCLA Asian American Studies Center, 1986.

———. "The Next Swing Vote? Asian Pacific Americans and California Politics." In *Racial and Ethnic Politics in California,* vol. 1, ed. Michael B. Preston Bruce E. Cain, and Sandra Bass, 25–54. Berkeley: Institute of Governmental Studies Press, 1991.

———. "When Numbers Do Not Add Up: Asian Pacific Americans and California Politics." In *Racial and Ethnic Politics in California,* vol. 2, ed. Michael B. Preston, Bruce E. Cain, and Sandra Bass, 3–43. Berkeley: Institute of Governmental Studies Press, 1999.

———. "Drive-by Victims of DNC Greed." In *1998–99 National Asian Pacific American Political Almanac,* ed. Don T. Nakanishi and James Lai. Los Angeles: UCLA Asian American Studies Center, 2000.

Nash, Philip Tajitsu. "Will the Census Go Multiracial?" *Amerasia Journal* 23, no. 1 (1997): 17–27.

National Asian Pacific American Legal Consortium. Annual reports of *Audits of Violence against Asian Pacific Americans,* 1993–1999.

Neal, Terry. "Asian American Voters Feel Stigmatized." *Washington Post,* September 8, 1997.

Neumann, Sigmund. *Modern Political Parties.* Chicago: University of Chicago Press, 1956.

Nguyen, Tram. *We Are All Suspects Now.* Boston: Beacon Press, 2005.

Ni, Perla. "Bill Lann Lee under Attack Again." *AsianWeek,* February 25, 1999, 10.

Nishi, Setsuko Matsunaga. "Asian Americans at the Intersection of International and Domestic Tensions." In *Across the Pacific: Asian Americans and Globalization,* ed. Evelyn Hu-DeHart, 152–90. Philadelphia: Temple University Press, 1999.

Niskanen, William A. *Bureaucracy and Representative Government.* Chicago: University of Chicago Press, 1971.

Nowrojee, Sia, and Jael Silliman. "Asian Women's Health: Organizing a Movement." In *Dragon Ladies: Asian American Feminists Breathe Fire,* ed. Sonia Shah, 73–89. Boston: South End Press, 1997.

O'Hare, William P., and Judy C. Felt. *Asian Americans: America's Fastest Growing Minority Group.* Washington, D.C.: Population Reference Bureau, 1991.

Ohnuma, Keiko. "Two of Five So. Cal Qualified Korean Americans Registered to Vote." *AsianWeek,* November 9, 1990.

Okihiro, Gary. *Margins and Mainstreams: Asians in American History and Culture.* Seattle: University of Washington Press, 1994.

Olson, Mancur. *The Logic of Collective Action.* Cambridge: Harvard University Press, 1965.

Omi, Michael. "Racial Identity and the State: Contesting the Federal Standards for Classification." In *Race, Ethnicity, and Nationality in the United States: Toward the Twenty-First Century*, ed. Paul Wong, 25–33. Boulder: Westview Press, 1997.

Omi, Michael, and Howard Winant. *Racial Formation in the United States from the 1960s to the 1990s*. New York: Routledge, 1994.

Ong, Paul. "The Affirmative Action Divide." In *The State of Asian Pacific America: Transforming Race Relations*, ed. Paul Ong, 313–62. Los Angeles: LEAP Asian Pacific American Public Policy Institute and UCLA Asian American Studies Center, 2000.

Ong, Paul, and Evelyn Blumenberg. "Scientists and Engineers." In *The State of Asian Pacific America: Economic Diversity, Issues, and Policies*, ed. Paul Ong, 165–92. Los Angeles: LEAP Asian Pacific American Public Policy Institute and UCLA Asian American Studies Center, 1994.

———. "Welfare and Work among Southeast Asians." In *The State of Asian Pacific America: Economic Diversity, Issues, and Policies*, ed. Paul Ong, 113–38. Los Angeles: LEAP Asian Pacific American Public Policy Institute and UCLA Asian American Studies Center, 1994.

Ong, Paul, and Suzanne J. Hee. "Economic Diversity." In *The State of Asian Pacific America: Economic Diversity, Issues, and Policies*, ed. Paul Ong, 31–56. Los Angeles: LEAP Asian Pacific American Public Policy Institute and UCLA Asian American Studies Center, 1994.

Ong, Paul, and Don T. Nakanishi. "Becoming Citizens, Becoming Voters: The Naturalization and Political Participation of Asian Pacific Americans." In *The State of Asian Pacific America: Reframing the Immigration Debate*, ed. Bill Ong Hing and Ronald Lee, 275–305. Los Angeles: LEAP Asian Pacific American Policy Institute and UCLA Asian American Studies Center, 1996.

Ono, Kent A., and John M. Sloop. *Shifting Borders: Rhetoric, Immigration, and California's Proposition 187*. Philadelphia: Temple University Press, 2002.

Organization of Chinese Americans. "National Asian American Groups File Unprecedented Civil Rights Petition Against Congress and Others for Scapegoating." Press release, September 11, 1997. http://www.ocanatl.org/pr91197.htm (accessed June 27, 1999).

———. "Red Peril and Chinese Laundry." http://www.ocanatl.org/aa61297.htm (accessed June 27, 1999).

———. "Asian Pacific American Groups Pleased with DNC Reversal of Immigrant Donations Policy." Press release, January 13, 1998.

———. "Asian American Outraged with US House of Reps' Overwhelming Disrespect for Legal Permanent Residents." Press release, March 31, 1998. http://www.ocanatl.org/pr33198.htm (accessed June 27, 1999).

Ostrogorski, Moshei. *Democracy and the Party System in the United States*. New York: Macmillan, 1910.

Ostrow, Ronald J., and William C. Rempel. "Hsia Indicted over Temple Fund-Raiser." *Los Angeles Times*, February 19, 1998, A1.

Packard, Le Anh Tu. "Asian American Economic Engagement: Vietnam Case Study." In *Across the Pacific: Asian Americans and Globalization*, ed. Evelyn Hu-DeHart, 79–108. Philadelphia: Temple University Press, 1999.

Parillo, Vincent. "Asian Americans in American Politics." In *America's Ethnic Politics*, ed. Joseph S. Roucek and Bernard Eisenberg, 89–112. Westport, Conn.: Greenwood Press, 1982.

Park, Edward J. W. "Competing Visions: Political Formation of Korean Americans in Los Angeles, 1992–1997." *Amerasia* 24, no. 1 (1998): 41–57.

Park, John S. *Elusive Citizenship: Immigration, Asian Americans, and the Paradox of Civil Rights*. New York: New York University Press, 2004.

Parry, Robert. "The GOP's Own Asian Connection: Reverend Moon." *Los Angeles Times,* November 16, 1997, M2.

Pegues, Juliana. "Strategies from the Field: Organizing the Asian American Feminist Movement." In *Dragon Ladies: Asian American Feminists Breathe Fire,* ed. Sonia Shah, 3–16. Boston: South End Press, 1997.

Peterson, Jonathan. "Clinton Defies GOP, Names Lee Rights Chief." *Los Angeles Times,* December 16, 1997, A1.

Peterson, William. "Politics and the Measurement of Ethnicity." In *The Politics of Numbers,* ed. William Alonso and Paul Starr, 187–233. New York: Russell Sage Foundation, 1983.

Pinderhughes, Dianne. "Political Choices: A Realignment in Partisanship among Black Voters?" In *The State of Black America,* ed. James D. Williams, 85–113. New York: National Urban League, 1984.

———. *Race and Ethnicity in Chicago Politics.* Urbana: University of Illinois Press, 1987.

Pitkin, Hanna F. *The Concept of Representation.* Berkeley and Los Angeles: University of California Press, 1967.

"Platform Prop. 187: 'Racist Initiative' or a 'Step in the Right Direction'?" Op-ed. *Los Angeles Times,* August 29, 1994, B4.

Plotkin, Manuel D. "Statement of Manuel D. Plotkin, U.S. Census Bureau, Accompanied by Leobardo F. Estrada, Special Assistant to Division Chief, Population Division; Nampeo D. R. McKenney, Chief Ethnic and Racial Statistics Staff, Population Division; and Daniel B. Levine, Associate Director for Demographic Fields." In U.S. Congress, House, Committee on Post Office and Civil Service, *1980 Census Hearing,* 95th Cong., 1st sess., 9-10, June 24, 1977, 156–73.

Pocock, J. G. A. *The Machiavellian Moment: Florentine Political Thought and the Atlantic Republican Tradition.* Princeton: Princeton University Press, 2003.

Polsby, Nelson. "The Institutionalization of the U.S. House of Representatives." *American Political Science Review* 62 (1968): 144–68.

———. *Consequences of Party Reform.* Oxford: Oxford University Press, 1983.

Pomper, Gerald, ed. *Party Renewal in America.* New York: Praeger, 1980.

Poole, Keith, and Howard Rosenthal. "Patterns in Congressional Voting." *American Journal of Political Science* 35 (February 1991): 228–78.

Portes, Alejandro, and Ruben G. Rumbaut. *Immigrant America: A Portrait.* Berkeley and Los Angeles: University of California Press, 1990.

Pringle, Paul. "Los Angeles Asians Seeking Political Clout." *Dallas Morning News,* June 11, 1987.

"Proposition 187 and the Law of Unintended Consequences: Anti-Immigrant Initiative Would Deny Medical Care, Roil Schools, and Make Snoops Out of Teachers." *Los Angeles Times,* October 2, 1994, M4.

Purkayastha, Bandana, Shyamala Raman, and Kshiteeja Bhide. "Empowering Women: SNEHA's Multifaceted Activism." In *Dragon Ladies: Asian American Feminists Breathe Fire,* ed. Sonia Shah, 100–107. Boston: South End Press, 1997.

Ranney, Austin. *Curing the Mischiefs of Faction: Party Reform in America.* Berkeley and Los Angeles: University of California Press, 1975.

Ranney, Austin, and Willmoore Kendall. *Democracy and the American Party System.* New York: Harcourt Brace, 1956.

Ratnesar, Romesh. "A Place at the Table: Led by California's Senate Hopeful Matt Fong, Asian American Politicians Come of Age." http://cnn.com/ALLPOLITICS/time/1998/10/06/asian.american.html (accessed August 13, 1999).

Reichley, A. James. "The Rise of National Parties." In *New Directions in American Politics,* ed. John E. Chubb and Paul Peterson. Washington, D.C.: Brookings Institution Press, 1985.

———. *The Life of the Parties: A History of American Political Parties.* Lanham, Md.: Rowman & Littlefield, 1992.

Rempel, William C. "Buddhist Temple May Be Indicted in Donor Probe." *Los Angeles Times,* January 30, 1998, A1.

"A Report of the Committee on Political Parties: Toward a More Responsible Two-Party System." *American Political Science Review* 44 (September 1950): 1–96.

"Resident Population Estimates of the United States by Sex, Race, and Hispanic Origin: April 1, 1990 to July 1, 1999, with Short-Term Projection to November 1, 2000." http://www.census.gov/population/estimates/nation/intfile3-1.txt (accessed August 12, 1999).

Reuters. "Limits to China Influence Peddling Probe Recognized." *Washington Post,* August 3, 1997.

"Riady Helped Kin Enter UC–Berkeley; Indonesian Magnate Wrote to Chancellor." *Washington Post,* December 14, 1996.

Rich, Spencer. "Census Listing: Approval Far from 'Global.'" *Washington Post,* May 11, 1988, A23.

Rimlinger, Gaston. *Welfare Policy and Industrialization in Europe, America, and Russia.* New York: Wiley, 1971.

Roediger, David. *Wages of Whiteness: Race and the Making of the American Working Class.* New York: Verso, 1999.

Rogers, David. "Battle over Immigration Bill Taught Washington's Ropes to Huang and Hsia." *Wall Street Journal,* May 15, 1997, A24.

Rogin, Michael. *The Intellectuals and McCarthy: The Radical Specter.* Cambridge: MIT Press, 1967.

———. *Ronald Reagan, the Movie, and Other Episodes in Political Demonology.* Berkeley and Los Angeles: University of California Press, 1993.

———. *Blackface, White Noise: Jewish Immigrants in the Hollywood Melting Pot.* Berkeley and Los Angeles: University of California Press, 1996.

Rohde, David. *Parties and Leaders in the Postreform House.* Chicago: University of Chicago Press, 1991.

Rosenbaum, David E. "Huang May Yet Testify to Senate Panel: As Hearings Open, Chairman Alleges a Chinese Plot." *New York Times,* July 9, 1997, A1.

———. "Smoke, But No Gun." *New York Times,* July 19, 1997, A1.

———. "Ex-G.O.P. Chairman Strongly Defends His Fund-Raising." *New York Times,* July 25, 1997, A1.

———. "A Day of Spin Follows a Month of Hearings." *New York Times,* July 31, 1997, A8.

Rosenfeld, Seth. "Tien Ties to Asia Money May Have Cost Him Job." *San Francisco Chronicle,* December 22, 1996.

Rosenstone, Steven J., and John Mark Hansen. *Mobilization, Participation, and Democracy in America.* New York: Macmillan, 1993.

Rosenzweig, David. "Rep. Kim, Wife to Plead Guilty to Misdemeanors." *Los Angeles Times,* August 1, 1997, A1.

Sabato, Larry J., and Bruce Larson. *The Party's Just Begun: Shaping Political Parties for America's Future.* New York: Pearson Education, 2001.

Saito, Leland. *Race and Politics: Asian Americans, Latinos, and Whites in a Los Angeles Suburb.* Urbana: University of Illinois Press, 1998.

Salisbury, Robert H. "An Exchange Theory of Interest Groups." *Midwest Journal of Political Science* 13 (1969): 1–32.

Sandalow, Marc. "State Treasurer in Election Probe: House Panel Wants to Ask Matt Fong about Donation." *San Francisco Chronicle,* March 6, 1998, A1.

Sandel, Michael. *Democracy's Discontent: America in Search of a Public Philosophy.* Cambridge, Mass.: Belknap Press, 1998.

———, ed. *Liberalism and Its Critics.* New York: New York University Press, 1984.

Sanger, David. "'Asian Money,' American Fears," *New York Times,* January 4, 1997, A1.

Sartori, Giovanni. *Parties and Party Systems.* Cambridge: Cambridge University Press, 1976.

Scharlin, Craig, and Lilia V. Villanueva. *Philip Vera Cruz.* Los Angeles: Institute of Industrial Relations Labor Center and UCLA Asian American Studies Center, 1992.

Schattschneider, E. E. *Party Government.* New York: Holt, Rinehart and Winston, 1942.

Schlesinger, Joseph A. *Political Parties and the Winning of Office.* Chicago: University of Chicago Press, 1991.

Schmitt, Eric. "Experts Clash over Need for Changing Census Data by Race." *New York Times,* April 24, 1997.

———. "Few Leads Found to Show Chinese Money in `96 Race." *New York Times,* July 9, 1997, B7.

———. "Parties Debate Joint Strategy for Hearings on China's Gifts." *New York Times,* July 15, 1997, A16.

———. "Kinetic Energy from a Senator's Words," *New York Times,* July 18, 1997, A16.

Schudson, Michael. *The Good Citizen: A History of American Civic Life.* Cambridge: Harvard University Press, 1999.

Schuman, Howard, Charlotte Steeh, and Lawrence Bobo. *Racial Attitudes in America.* Cambridge: Harvard University Press, 1985.

Schwartz, Herman. "The Constitutional Issue behind Proposition 187." *Los Angeles Times,* October 9, 1994, M1.

Sears, David O. "Symbolic Racism." In *Eliminating Racism,* ed. Phyllis A. Katz and Dalmas A. Taylor, 53–84. New York: Plenum Press, 1988.

Sears, David O., Carl P. Hensler, and Leslie K. Speer. "Whites' Opposition to 'Busing': Self-interest or Symbolic Politics?" *American Political Science Review* 73 (1979): 369–84.

Sethi, Rita Chaudry. "Smells Like Racism: A Plan for Mobilizing against Anti-Asian Bias." In *The State of Asian America: Activism and Resistance in the 1990s,* ed. Karin Aguilar-San Juan, 235–52. Boston: South End Press, 1994.

Shafer, Byron E. *Quiet Revolution: The Struggle for the Democratic Party and the Shaping of Post-Reform Politics.* New York: Russell Sage Foundation, 1983.

Shah, Purvi. "Redefining the Home: How Community Elites Silence Feminist Activism." In *Dragon Ladies: Asian American Feminists Breathe Fire,* ed. Sonia Shah, 46–56. Boston: South End Press, 1997.

Shah, Sonia. "Presenting the Blue Goddess: Toward a National, Pan-Asian Feminist Agenda." In *The State of Asian America: Activism and Resistance in the 1990s,* ed. Karin Aguilar-San Juan, 147–60. Boston: South End Press, 1994.

———. "Slaying the Dragon Lady: Toward an Asian American Feminism." In *Dragon Ladies: Asian American Feminists Breathe Fire,* ed. Sonia Shah, xii–xxi. Boston: South End Press, 1997.

Shefter, Martin. *Political Parties and the State: The American Historical Experience.* Princeton: Princeton University Press, 1994.

Shinagawa, Larry Hajime. "The Impact of Immigration on the Demography of Asian Pacific Americans." In *The State of Asian Pacific America: Reframing the Immigration Debate,* ed. Bill Ong Hing and Ronald Lee. Los Angeles: LEAP Asian Pacific American Public Policy Institute and UCLA Asian American Studies Center, 1996.

Siao, Grace. "Feinstein Meets with 40 LA Asian Leaders." *AsianWeek,* February 23, 1990.

Silbey, Joel H. *The Partisan Imperative: The Dynamics of American Politics before the Civil War.* New York: Oxford University Press, 1985.

Simpson, Glenn R., David Rogers, and Jeffrey Taylor. "Asian-American Institute Becomes Latest Victim of Controversy over Democratic Fund Raising." *Wall Street Journal*, March 5, 1997, A20.

Skelton, George. "Voters of Asian Heritage Slow to Claim Voice." *Los Angeles Times*, August 19, 1993, A3.

Skerry, Peter. *Counting on the Census? Race, Group Identity, and the Evasion of Politics.* Washington, D.C.: Brookings Institution Press, 2000.

Skrentny, John. *The Minority Rights Revolution.* Cambridge: Harvard University Press, 2004.

Smith, Robert C. "Recent Elections and Black Politics: The Maturation or Death of Black Politics." *PS, Political Science and Politics* 23, no. 2 (1990): 160–62.

Smith, Rogers. *Liberalism and American Constitutional Law.* Cambridge: Harvard University Press, 1985.

———. "Beyond Tocqueville, Myrdal, and Hartz: The Multiple Traditions in America." *American Political Science Review* 87 (1993): 549–66.

———. *Civic Ideals: Conflicting Visions of Citizenship in U.S. History.* New Haven: Yale University Press, 1999.

Sniderman, Paul M., Richard A. Brody, and Philip E. Tetlock. *Reasoning and Choice: Explorations in Political Psychology.* Cambridge: Cambridge University Press, 1991.

Sniderman, Paul M., and Thomas Piazza. *The Scar of Race.* Cambridge: Harvard University Press, 1994.

Sonenshein, Raphael. *Politics in Black and White: Race and Power in Los Angeles.* Princeton: Princeton University Press, 1995.

Sorauf, Frank J. *Political Parties in the American System.* Boston: Little, Brown, 1964.

———. *Money in American Elections.* Boston: Addison-Wesley Educational Publishers, 1988.

Sorauf, Frank J., and Scott A. Wilson. "Political Parties and Campaign Finance: Adaptation and Accommodation toward a Changing Role." In *The Parties Respond: Changes in American Parties and Campaigns,* ed. L. Sandy Maisel, 235–53. Boulder: Westview Press, 2002.

Stall, Bill, and Amy Wallace. "Brown Runs on Empty; Leader Wilson Coasts." *Los Angeles Times,* November 5, 1994.

Sterngold, James. "Political Tangle of Taiwan Immigrant." *New York Times,* June 9, 1997.

Stokes, Bruce. "Learning Game." *National Journal* 43 (October 22, 1988): 2649–54.

Sue, Stanley. "The Changing Asian American Population: Mental Health Policy." In *The State of Asian Pacific America: Policy Issues to the Year 2020,* 79–94. Los Angeles: LEAP Asian Pacific American Public Policy Institute and UCLA Asian American Studies Center, 1993.

Sun, Lena. "Asian Americans Seen as Foreign, Stopped." *Washington Post,* September 11, 1997.

Sun, Lena, and John Pomfret. "Some Sought Access to Clinton, Others' Motives Remain Murky." *Washington Post,* January 27, 1997, A1.

Suro, Robert. "Democratic Fund-Raiser Hsia Indicted: Temple Is Named Co-Conspirator." *Washington Post,* February 19, 1998.

———. "Gore's Ties to Hsia Cast Shadow on 2000 Race." *Washington Post,* February 23, 1998, A1.

Suro, Robert, and Peter Baker. "Clinton Aides Split over Next Step on Lee Nomination to Civil Rights Post." *Washington Post,* November 21, 1997, A13.

Swain, Carol. *Black Faces, Black Interests.* Cambridge: Harvard University Press, 1995.

Sze, Julie. "Expanding Environmental Justice: Asian American Feminists' Contribution." In *Dragon Ladies: Asian American Feminists Breathe Fire,* ed. Sonia Shah, 90–99. Boston: South End Press, 1997.

Tachibana, Judy. "California's Asians: Power from a Growing Population." *California Journal* 17 (1986): 534–43.

Takagi, Dana. *The Retreat from Race: Asian American Admissions and Racial Politics*. New Brunswick: Rutgers University Press, 1993.

Takahashi, Jere. "Changing Responses to Racial Subordination: An Exploratory Study of Japanese American Political Styles." Ph.D. diss., University of California, Berkeley, Department of Sociology, 1980.

Takaki, Ronald. *Strangers from a Different Shore*. Boston: Little, Brown, 1989.

Takami, David. "Can Asian Americans Influence the Election?" *AsiAm*, January 1988.

Takeda, Okiyoshi. "The Representation of Asian Americans in the U.S. Political System." In *Representation of Minorities in the American Political System: Implications for the 21st Century*, ed. Charles E. Menifield. Lanham, Md.: University Press of America, 2000.

Tam, Wendy. "Asians—A Monolithic Voting Bloc?" *Political Behavior* 17, no. 2 (1995): 223–49.

Tam-Cho, Wendy K. "Expanding the Logic behind Campaign Contributions: Lessons from Asian American Campaign Contributors." Paper presented at the annual meeting of the American Political Science Association, Atlanta, Georgia, 1999.

———. "Foreshadowing Asian American Pan-Ethnic Politics: Asian American Campaign Finance Activity in Varying Multicultural Contexts." *State Politics and Policy Quarterly* 1 (September 2001): 273–94.

———. "Tapping Motives and Dynamics behind Campaign Contributions: Insights from the Asian American Case." *American Politics Research* 30 (July 2002): 347–83.

———. "Contagion Effects and Ethnic Contribution Networks." *American Journal of Political Science* 47 (April 2003): 368–87.

Tamayo, William R. "Legal and Civil Rights Issues in 2020: Civil Rights Policy." In *The State of Asian Pacific America: Policy Issues to the Year 2020*, 153–66. Los Angeles: LEAP Asian Pacific American Public Policy Institute and UCLA Asian American Studies Center, 1993.

Tan, Cheng Imm. "Building Shelter: Asian Women and Domestic Violence." In *Dragon Ladies: Asian American Feminists Breathe Fire*, ed. Sonia Shah, 108–20. Boston: South End Press, 1997.

Tayabas, Ernestine. "Demo Drops Asian Caucus." *East/West*, May 22, 1985.

Tobar, Hector. "New Tide of Latino Activism Stung by Props. 187 and 209."*Los Angeles Times*, April 13, 1998, A1.

Tocqueville, Alexis de. *Democracy in America*. Ed. J. P. Mayer. Trans. George Lawrence. New York: Harper & Row, 1966.

Torok, John H. "Asians and the Reconstruction Era Constitutional Amendments and Civil Rights Laws." In *Asian Americans and Congress*, ed. Hyung-Chan Kim, 13–70. Westport, Conn.: Greenwood Press, 1996.

Truman, David. *The Governmental Process*. New York: Knopf, 1951.

Uhlaner, Carol, Bruce Cain, and Roderick Kiewiet. "Political Participation of Ethnic Minorities in the 1980s." *Political Behavior* 11 (September 1989): 195–231.

Underwood, Katherine. "Process and Politics: Multiracial Electoral Coalition Building and Representation in Los Angeles' Ninth District, 1949–1962." Ph.D. diss., University of California, San Diego, 1992.

Unemoto, Karen. "'On Strike!' San Francisco State College Strike, 1968–69: The Role of Asian American Students." *Amerasia Journal* 15, no. 1 (1989): 3–41.

United Way, Asian Pacific Research and Development Council. *Pacific Profiles: A Demographic Study of the Asian Pacific Population in Los Angeles County*. Los Angeles: United Way, 1985.

Unz, Ronald. "Why National Review Is Wrong: Value Added." *National Review*, November 7, 1994, 56–58.

U.S. Bureau of the Census. *1990 Census of the Population, Asians and Pacific Islanders in the United States.* Washington, D.C.: U.S. Government Printing Office, 1993.

———. "Findings on Questions on Race and Hispanic Origin Tested in the 1996 National Content Survey." Working Paper Series of the Staff of the Special Population Statistics Population Division. December 1996.

———. "Results of the 1996 Race and Ethnic Targeted Test." Population Division Working Paper No. 18. Washington, D.C.: Government Printing Office, 1997.

———. "Planning for Census 2000: Federal Legislative and Program Uses." March 1998.

———. "California Leads States and Los Angeles County, Calif., Tops Counties in Asian and Pacific Islander Population Increase." Census Bureau Reports, September 4, 1998. http://www.census.gov/Press-Release/cb98-161.html (accessed August 12, 1999).

———. "The Nation's Fifty-Something Population Projected to Grow by 50% during the Next Decade, Census Bureau Reports." http://www.census.gov/Press-Release/cb96-36.html (accessed August 12, 1999).

———. "National Population Projections." http://www.census.gov/population/www/projections/natsum-T5.html (accessed January 8, 2000).

———. Bureau of Labor Statistics. "A CPS Supplement for Testing Methods of Collecting Racial and Ethnic Information, May 1995." October 1995.

———. Census Advisory Committees on the African American, American Indian and Alaska Native, Asian and Pacific Islander, and Hispanic Populations. *Minutes and Report of Committee Recommendations.* May 22–23, 1997. Washington, D.C.: U.S. Government Printing Office, 1997.

———. Population Division. Population Estimates Program. "Resident Population Estimates of the United States by Sex, Race, and Hispanic Origin: April 1, 1990 to July 1, 1999, with Short-Term Projection to November 1, 2000." Washington, D.C., January 2, 2001.

U.S. Commission on Civil Rights. *To Know or Not to Know: Collection and Use of Racial and Ethnic Data in Federal Assistance Programs.* Washington, D.C.: U.S. Government Printing Office, 1973.

———. *Civil Rights Issues of Asian and Pacific Americans: Myths and Realities.* Washington, D.C.: U.S. Commission on Civil Rights, 1979.

U.S. Congress. House. *Content of 1990 Census Questionnaire: Race, Ethnicity, and Ancestry.* Serial no. 100-13, May 19, 1987.

———. Committee on Government Reform and Oversight. *Interim Report of the House Committee on Government Reform and Oversight: Campaign Finance Report and Related Matters.* Chap. IV, "Unprecedented Infusion of Foreign Money into the American Political System." http://www.house.gov/reform/reports/fundraising/4d_sioeng.htm (accessed June 6, 1999).

———. Subcommittee on Government Management, Information, and Technology. *Activities of the House Committee on Government Reform and Oversight: Subcommittee on Government Management, Information, and Technology.* 105th Cong., 1st sess. Washington, D.C.: Library of Congress, 1997.

———. *Federal Measures of Race and Ethnicity and the Implications for the 2000 Census.* Serial no. 105-57, April 23, May 22, and July 25, 1997.

U.S. Congress. House. Committee on Post Office and Civil Service, Subcommittee on Census and Population. *Hearings before the Subcommittee on Census and Population of the Committee on Post Office and Civil Service, Content of 1990 Census Questionnaire: Race, Ethnicity, and Ancestry.* Serial no. 100-13. May 19, 1987. Washington, D.C.: U.S. Government Printing Office, 1987.

———. *Review of Federal Measurements of Race and Ethnicity.* 103rd Cong., 1st sess. Serial no. 103-7, April 14, June 30, July 29, and November 3, 1993.

U.S. Congress. Senate. Committee on Governmental Affairs. *Hearings before the Committee on Governmental Affairs of the United States Senate on the Investigation of Illegal or Improper Activities in Connection with the 1996 Federal Election Campaign,* parts I–X, 105th Cong., 2d sess. Washington, D.C.: U.S. Government Printing Office, 1997.

———. *Final Report of the Committee on Governmental Affairs of the United States Senate on the Investigation of Illegal or Improper Activities in Connection with the 1996 Federal Election Campaign,* 105th Cong., 2d sess. Washington, D.C.: U.S. Government Printing Office, 1998.

U.S. General Accounting Office. *Census Reform: Early Outreach and Decisions Needed on Race and Ethnic Questions.* Report to the Chairman of the Subcommittee on Census, Statistics, and Postal Personnel, House of Representatives, Committee on Post Office and Civil Service, January 28, 1993.

U.S. Office of Management and Budget. "Directive No. 15, Race and Ethnic Standards for Federal Statistics and Administrative Reporting." *Federal Register* 43 (1978): 19260, 19269.

———. "Standards for the Classification of Federal Data on Race and Ethnicity." *Federal Register,* June 9, 1994.

———. "Standards for the Classification of Federal Data on Race and Ethnicity: Part VI." *Federal Register,* August 28, 1995.

———. "Recommendations from the Interagency Committee for the Review of the Racial and Ethnic Standards to the Office of Management and Budget Concerning Changes to the Standards for the Classification of Federal Data on Race and Ethnicity: Part II." *Federal Register,* July 9, 1997.

———. "Revisions to the Standards for the Classification of Federal Data on Race and Ethnicity: Part II," *Federal Register* 62, no. 210 (October 30, 1997): 59781–90. http://www.census. gov/population/www/socdemo/race/Ombdir15.html.

Uyematsu, A. "The Emergence of Yellow Power in America." In *Roots: An Asian American Reader,* ed. Amy Tachiki, Eddie Wong, Franklin Odo, and Buck Wong, 9–13. Los Angeles: Continental Graphics, 1971.

Van den Berghe, Pierre L. *The Ethnic Phenomenon.* New York: Elsevier, 1981.

Van Natta, Don, Jr. "President Is Linked to Urgent Enlisting of Top Fund-Raiser." *New York Times,* July 7, 1997, A1.

Van Natta, Don, Jr., and Christopher Drew. "Fundraisers' Moment of Triumph Seems Part of Pattern of Suspicious Gifts" *New York Times,* July 2, 1997, A16.

Van Slambrouck, Paul. "Asian Americans Forge Larger Political Role." *Christian Science Monitor,* February 24, 1998. http://www.csmonitor.com/1998/0224/022498.us.us.4.html.

Vobejda, Barbara. "Hill Reassured on Racial Checkoff Plan for Census." *Washington Post,* July 26, 1997, A4.

Volpp, Leti. "Obnoxious to Their Very Nature: Asian Americans and Constitutional Citizenship." *Citizenship Studies* 5, no. 1 (2001): 71–87.

———. "The Citizen and the Terrorist." *UCLA Law Review* 49 (2002): 1575–99.

Walker, Jack L., Jr. *Mobilizing Interest Groups in America: Patrons, Professions, and Social Movements.* Ann Arbor: University of Michigan Press, 1983.

Walters, Ronald. *Black Presidential Politics in America: A Strategic Approach.* Albany: State University of New York Press, 1988.

Wang, Ling-chi. "Trends in Admissions for Asian Americans in Colleges and Universities." In *The State of Asian Pacific America: Policy Issues to the Year 2020,* 49–60. Los Angeles: LEAP Asian Pacific American Public Policy Institute and UCLA Asian American Studies Center, 1993.

————. "Foreign Money Is No Friend of Ours." *AsianWeek*, November 8, 1996.

————. "Campaign Finance Scandal and Anti-Asian Exclusionism: Historical and Contemporary Perspectives." Statement before the U.S. Commission on Civil Rights. December 5, 1997.

————. "Race, Class, Citizenship, and Extraterritoriality: Asian Americans and the 1996 Campaign Finance Scandal." *Amerasia Journal* 24 (spring 1998): 1–21.

Wang, Theodore (policy director of Chinese for Affirmative Action). Interview by author, 1999.

"Washington Governor Received Money from China-Linked Donor: Report." *Agence France-Presse*, August 5, 1998.

Watanabe, Paul. "Asian American Activism and U.S. Foreign Policy." In *Across the Pacific: Asian Americans and Globalization*, ed. Evelyn Hu-DeHart, 109–28. Philadelphia: Temple University Press, 1999.

Watanabe, Paul, and C. Hardy-Fanta. "Conflict and Convergence: Race, Public Opinion, and Political Behavior in Massachusetts." Occasional Paper. Boston: University of Massachusetts, Institute for Asian American Studies, 1998.

Waters, Mary. *Ethnic Options: Choosing Identities in America*. Berkeley and Los Angeles: University of California Press, 1990.

Wattenberg, Benjamin. *The Decline of American Political Parties, 1952–1988*. Cambridge: Harvard University Press, 1990.

Wayne, Leslie. "G.O.P., for First Time, Admits It Accepted Foreign Donations." *New York Times*, May 9, 1997, A1.

————. "F.E.C. Fines German Citizen for U.S. Campaign Donations." *New York Times*, July 19, 1997, A8.

————. "Democrats Get to Scrutinize G.O.P. Ties to Asian Connection." *New York Times*, July 22, 1997, A13.

————. "Senate Committee Focuses on G.O.P.'s Ties to Foreign Money." *New York Times*, July 27, 1997, A18.

Wei, William. *The Asian American Movement*. Philadelphia: Temple University Press, 1993.

Weiner, Tim, and David E. Sanger. "Democrats Hoped to Raise $7 Million from Asians in U.S." *New York Times*, December 28, 1996, A1.

"What Does John Huang Have to Do with Me?" *Filipinas*, May 1997, 27–30.

Williams, Timothy. "Registration Efforts Are Paying Off in New Voters." *Los Angeles Times*, August 17, 1992, B1.

Wilson, Woodrow. *Congressional Government: A Study in American Society*. Baltimore: Johns Hopkins University Press, 1881.

Wolfinger, Raymond E. *The Politics of Progress*. Englewood Cliffs, N.J.: Prentice-Hall, 1974.

Wollenberg, Charles. "Race and Class in Rural California: The El Monte Berry Strike of 1933." *California Historical Quarterly* 51, no. 2 (1972): 155–64.

Wong, Diane Yen-Mei. "Will the Real Asian Pacific American Please Stand Up?" In *The State of Asian Pacific America: Policy Issues to the Year 2020*, 263–82. Los Angeles: LEAP Asian Pacific American Public Policy Institute and UCLA Asian American Studies Center, 1993.

Wong, Kent. "Building an Asian Pacific Labor Alliance: A New Chapter in Our History." In *The State of Asian America: Activism and Resistance in the 1990s*, ed. Karin Aguilar-San Juan, 335–50. Boston: South End Press, 1994.

Wong, William. "Asian Americans Shake Off Stereotypes, Increase Clout, as Political Activism Grows." Op-ed. *Los Angeles Times*, February 23, 1988.

Wood, Gordon. *The Radicalism of the American Revolution*. New York: Vintage, 1993.

Woodward, Bob. "FBI Had Overlooked Key Files in Probe of Chinese Influence." *Washington Post*, November 14, 1997.

Wu, Frank. "Clinton's 'Honorable Decision.'" *AsianWeek*, December 18, 1997, 11–12.

———. *Yellow: Race in America beyond Black and White*. New York: Basic Books, 2001.

Wu, Frank, and May Nicholson. "Have You No Decency? Racial Aspects of Media Coverage on the John Huang Matter." *Asian American Policy Review* 7 (spring 1997): 1–37.

Wu, Robin. "Profile: Joji Konoshima, Asian Americans in the Democratic National Committee." *Bridge* 6, no. 1 (1978): 61–63.

Yamada, Mitsuye. "Asian Pacific American Women and Feminism." In *This Bridge Called My Back*, ed. Cherrie Moraga and Gloria Anzaldua, 71–75 New York: Kitchen Table–Women of Color Press, 1983.

Yamamoto, J. K. "Democratic National Committee Chair Questions Need for Asian/Pacific Caucus." *Pacific Citizen*, March 8, 1985.

Yip, Alethea. "A Taste of Political Power: APAs Enjoy Increasing Political Clout." *AsianWeek*, August 9–15, 1996. http://www.asianweek.com/080996/PoliticalPower.html.

———. "Dueling Data." *AsianWeek*, November 15, 1996.

Yoshikawa, Yoko. "The Heat Is on *Miss Saigon* Coalition." In *The State of Asian America: Activism and Resistance in the 1990s*, ed. Karin Aguilar-San Juan, 275–94. Boston: South End Press, 1994.

Zane, Nolan, David Takeuchi, and Kathleen Young, eds. *Confronting Critical Health Issues of Asian and Pacific Islander Americans*. Thousand Oaks, Calif.: Sage Publications, 1994.

Zia, Helen. Presentation at the conference of Asian Americans for Campaign Finance Reform, San Francisco, November 4, 1997.

———. "Can Asian Americans Turn the Media Tide?" *The Nation*, December 22, 1997, 10.

———. *Asian American Dreams: The Emergence of an American People*. New York: Farrar, Straus and Giroux, 2000.

INDEX

Thomas P. Kim is Associate Professor of Politics & International Relations at Scripps College, and Core Faculty in the Intercollegiate Department of Asian American Studies at the Claremont Colleges.